Veronica,
you are more than a Conqueror!

Love Dorothy

Praise for ....
Whispers From God

"Whispers From God," is an exciting eye-opening experience into the heart. You will awaken to your depths of God given ability! As Dorothy proceeds to share her story, you will experience greater levels of wisdom, life and growth. If you are dealing with pain and rejection, are in a good relationship or are embarking upon a journey of love, you'll want to make sure you are God inspired and not entertaining self or a spirit of deception. "Whispers From God" helps you find the answers you're looking for to prevent and overcome disappointment and suffering, before it happens (again). Dr. Tolbert - School Administrator

I went to a meeting and saw a beautiful woman in the midst of many. Prophetically, I was sure that Dorothy was called to do something very special. I went over, introduced myself and knew that she was called to positively influence many. I wasn't sure when; but knew she was called to touch lives. I don't think I have ever met anyone who refuses to be anything but full of faith, no matter what she has gone through. Dorothy's story will bless and inspire you! She finds God's goodness in every situation and is humorous. The cry of Dorothy's heart is to prevent others from reaping the consequences of unnecessary pain and suffering.

There is great hope and insight for you to gain from Dorothy's wisdom, joy and betrayal. You will become immersed in her story and will know that you can survive the enemy's plan of evil, before deception. You will vicariously live through Dorothy's willingness to express the details of her heart and understand the weightiness of going your own way! Dixie McManigal - Director of nurses

"Whispers From God," helped me stop blaming myself. I realized that every relationship is not meant to come together in the first place. I will listen more carefully to God's voice and the intuition He gives me in the future and save myself from years of pain. Jan

"Whispers from God" will make a difference for you. As I travel, I meet lots of people who are weary from bad relationships; they need answers for their lives. I tell them to read "Whispers from God." This important book gives you answers from the Word of God, not from man! "Whispers from God," will inspire you in every area of life. You will learn how to stand at the gate doors of God and let nothing in, but that which God gives. There are real truths in this biographical teaching that uplift and build your life and discernment. I highly recommend "Whispers from God!" Angelina Jones - National Makeup Artist

"Whispers from God" is a must read. I found myself wanting to read more and more of the teaching. The book was life-changing for me and I will read it again for future success. No matter how down-cast and destroyed you feel right now, "Whispers From God" will make the difference for you! The scriptures and prayers will take you over and a long way. It blessed me to see how much God contends for us. I especially learned that God loves to defeat our enemies from within and externally. "Whispers From God" gives you your very own source of inside intelligence! Curti Nelson - College Student

Dorothy: I am on chapter 15 and just had to stop to say, "THANK YOU" FOR WRITING THIS BOOK!! THE INSIGHT, REVELATION and TRANSFORMATION has brought me PRICELESS HELP in just a short time. I realize that there are parts of me {co-dependency} that need to be healed and released. I need to let God take care of some core elements that at times make me feel unworthy. Thank you, Dorothy! Judy

"Whispers From God," helped me stop traveling down miserable paths of unworthiness. Paths that led me into more unneeded pain. Thank you! Mercy

Hi Dorothy, A great book. Excellent prayers to the Lord near the end that made me cry as I gave my emotional pain to the Lord. "Whispers From God" shows others how to have happier, more successful lives. Love you, Myra

I had let my loneliness push me into opening myself to the wrong people. "Whispers From God" showed me that we never need to yield to the words of the enemy by practicing a higher level of life and faith. I'm now enjoying God's presence and beauty, which pushed away the spirit of loneliness and desperation. Thank you for taking the time to write Whispers. Mike

"Whispers From God"

Creates joy and heals wounds

Removes all that hinders love and purpose

Helps you allow God to build strong lifetime relationships for you!

Transformation ...

Powerful teaching and workbook ...

Wisdom and Enlightenment

Liberating and Inspiring Stories

Find and Develop Lasting love

Identify Deceptive Presentations

Courage to Build Your Life

Empowerment for Your Relationships

Recovery that Impacts Your Life Decisions

Receive Strength and Ability

Life-Changing Teachings and Prayers

It is time to re-forge the sword!

Table of Content

1. WHAT'S WRONG WITH WANTING TO BE BLESSED?
2. BEYOND THE GATES
3. TIME AND TIDE
4. HAPPINESS ... A STRANGE FRUIT
5. THE HARVEST
6. THE DEVIL'S PROCESS
7. GLIMMERS OF LIGHT
8. CONVERSATIONS WITH ELIZA
9. CERTAINTY
10. SOBERING STORIES
11. WHY DO THEY COME?   *(Illegitimate relationships)*
12. ASSESSMENT
13. HEARTS DO HEAL
14. READY FOR LOVE
15. THE PATH OF THE RIGHTEOUS GROWS BRIGHTER
16. LOVE CONQUERS ALL

All scripture quotations, unless otherwise indicated, are taken from:

The king James Version by Thomas Nelson.
New King James Version
The new American Standard Bible
Holy, Bible
The Message Bible
New International Version

All right reserved. No part of this book may be reproduced or transmitted in any form or by any means, electronic or mechanically, including photocopying and recording, or by any information storage and retrieval system, without the permission in writing from the publisher.

Acknowledgment

To my God and King! I love you!

Deep gratitude to all who prayed for me and believed in this effort and mission of love. You have deeply impacted my life.

To my dear children: My rejuvenating gifts from heaven!
"James, Jamul and Jyndia"

To Mom and my brother's Craig, Robert and Richard. You are looking down from above saying, "Run on in faith and might!"

Thank You

Whispers From God

... Strengthen Your Life and Relationships!

A beautiful encounter or introduction can feel magical and wondrous. We can feel remarkable and electrified! Our feelings are phenomenal! – But, is the connection from God? Too often we deem an introduction as unimportant; we can flirt frivolously without question and turn off our spiritual hearing and intuition. We can overlook the magnitude and presentation of this one vital moment - a life changing moment ... when this is not an ordinary time. This very instance provides you powerful information and requires that you make an immediate decision. This moment has great insight and holds the ability to bless or curse your life. Your assessment can and will change your course of destiny.

If you want to find and develop lasting love, your essential times at the gate doors have to be judged correctly. You must know without a doubt; is this potential companion sent by God, and can they be allowed to enter your realm of life. At the introduction, you can hear God's voice precisely. What is He saying about this person appearing in your sphere of awareness? Are they sent from God or from the enemy of your soul?

"Prudent men foresee evil and hide themselves, but the simple pass on and are punished." (Proverbs 22:3)

The prudent and mature move past flattery and excitement and listen ... We quiet ourselves to hear God's protective and loving message. What is God is communicating to you? Is this your time to celebrate and linger a while, or to run for your life?

"Wisdom calls aloud. She raises her voice in the public squares, and calls out in the street corners. She delivers her message at the city gates. She cries in the chief place of concourse, in the opening of the gates. In the city she utters her words saying, "You simple (stupid) ones, how much longer will you cling to your simple ways? How much longer will mockers revel in their mocking and fools go on hating knowledge? Pay close attention to my warning. I God pour out my heart and tell you what I have to say at the city gates."
(Proverbs 1 v 20-21)

Without God's voice, we discover we are participants in our own demise, failure and aloneness. It is never God's desire that we experience "relationship disasters!" He designed you to live with glorious purpose! His voice, heart and spirit are there to help you choose well. The Light of the Resurrection is there to help you.

"The simple believe anything, but the prudent give thought to their steps."
(Proverbs 14:15)

Listening to God will change the fact that too many relationships capriciously begin and fail afterwards. But discernment (not impulsiveness) is a wonderful unseen force that can be felt and seen selectivity, with spiritual eyes.

Listening to God changes the fact that forty-five percent of Christian couple's head for divorce courts yearly. They have allowed the wrong mates to enter their life. Before long they want out; feeling sad or angry that they invested imprudently. Too many married couples want out; while eager, hasty singles want in! Unfortunately, our society fosters millions of unhappy and fragmented people in or out of damaging, configurations of relationships.

Without God's voice, we accept whatever comes out of the gate. We can even try to make square pegs fit into round circles. We can attempt to glue down wobbly, negated relationships; knowing they will never stabilize. We can act out of scarcity, because we feel inadequate, displaced or alone. We can learn to abandon ourselves by making other opinions greater than God's voice, presence, love and reward!

Are we gruelingly looking to acquire love and acceptance from others; instead of from God and ourselves? Are we choosing powerlessness and punishment, instead of joy and strength? Are we giving pain and disappointment permission to overwhelm our hearts? "Whispers From God," is an important read and tool that prevents the intrusion of "dastardly roads to nowhere." Roads that become thoroughfares to places you don't want to see; endure or experience.

I wrote this book because I am deeply concerned about the breakdown of family, ruined lives and unneeded pain. Too many of us share in the pain and demise of a relationship and in patterns of deception.

As a young Christian, I believed my commitment to God was enough to prevent the consequences of an impulsive decision; one that led to unnecessary suffering, confusion and divorce. I thought, "Well, I know how to pray; so, in no way will destruction come to my house." I thought that going to church and singing in the choir would make everything alright! I was astonished that the words I heard God speak during my initial meeting actually came to pass! Yes, God was showing me my future …. and those foreordained words, actually came to pass.

Within the gates you enjoy beauty, wealth, productivity, happiness and fruitfulness. You are privileged here to be the arbitrator of your own success. If you listen carefully, you will choose favorably. You will employ shrewdness and aptly distinguish between blessing and misfortune. You will recognize that an erroneous relationship will take years away from your identity, actuality and purpose.

Within the gates, Jesus delights in giving you His definition of preeminent love. He is your greatest admirer and knows what "Real love has to do with it!" Here, you will see His commitment to give you the desires of your heart. Here, God restores a "lost preciousness" that belongs to you. With trust, you will find that your loving creator knows more about happiness and good times than you knew! Your reliance on God's word will offer you an unimpaired defense.

"Whispers From God" is a dynamic read and study that helps you gain revelatory insight, light and vital truths from the Word of God. When we listen intuitively, we stop the negative effects of pain and deficit. But beyond the gates, Satan waits to sift us.

Your faithful Father cries out loud at the gate door, desiring to stop every bit of unnecessary suffering planned by the enemy. He knows that you will experience the cruelty of Satan's hatred, mockery and ruin. A decision to go your own way, by deciding on your own assessment; bequeaths years of agony, detour and sorrow; instead of the new possibilities offered by God.

God only wants to help you find authentic love and to navigate you into His safe waters of life and abundance. He offers you kindness, defense, love and acceptance and more than you imagine. Unnecessary suffering is not a part of Father's design for your purposeful and worthy life. Let us learn to trust our Father.

God does not oppress his people! Although He is Almighty and exalted in power. (Job 37:23)

Come to see the glorious exploits God has done. What marvelous miracles happen to His people! (Psalms 66:5)

Whispers From God" will help you heal every deep-seated, concealed wound through the Blood of Jesus and the Light of His Resurrection Power! There was a time when I was sure I'd never smile again! I thank God now that I now enjoy a beautiful life of joy and laughter, but I would not wish the path I walked on my worst enemy. God was kind to bring me through my many self-made calamities, but I could have been forever lost. I don't want that for you. Some never escape their choices, regrets and sorrows. This is why I care so much about your decisions, your singleness, divorce and marriage.

My story and others will show you that consequences are surely devastating. We will take you into some deep, dark and difficult places; places that could have been avoided before that started. Our journeys and successes would have been different, if we had not doubted the voice of God and His endowment of knowledge.

If you are married and you know that God ordained your togetherness, "Whispers From God" will help you claim what is yours and not let the devil steal it! If you are going through a divorce or hurting because of a broken relationship, this book will help you continually dwell in the Joy and Presence of the Lord. His grace and wisdom will deliver you. You will know that He will establish you again!

If you are hungry for more, this book is for you. If you know that you must strive to grow to be strong and you know you need to be in God's presence in every stage and age, this book will help you see more and do more for Jesus. You must fulfill your purpose and destiny!

Remember, you are a soldier who must daily prepare against a devil that will always try to draw you away. He will hide behind problems with family and friends and will work to get the wrong persons into your life again and again. He has to make you doubt the goodness of God.

"you must always listen and wait to hear from the one who loves you most! You have barely glimpsed of His vast affection and furious love for you! You can trust God. He and His Word are the only solid elements in the entire world. All else will change, but the power of God's Presence and Word will never change!

WHAT'S WRONG WITH WANTING TO BE BLESSED?   Chapter 1

Tia and I delight ourselves in another cup of tea. We thank God that we have come through some horrendous times. We share and grieve a little more about our joys and suffering; working out our feelings; having learned the significance of allowing wrong choices. It has not been easy to overcome the past, but we rejoice that God truly desires authentic love relationships for us – those that He creates in strength for a lifetime. And we did not have durable marriages at all.
At the time of our divorces, we had each adored our husbands; but God's divine will and the consequences of our actions did not give us many years of love and laughter. Tia reminisces about her good times in California, while I remember enjoying my husband's company in the cool of the evening; my favorite time of the day. At the time, I believed that God had come down to orchestrate and breathe on our own exquisite love. Luis was sent to be my big, wonderful blessing from heaven; especially after an exhausting first marriage.

Tia asks, "Do you ever think of Justin" (my first husband)? Her inquisitiveness opens my mind to our nearly twenty-year marriage. I coerce myself to think of him ... "Tia, you know what? I felt about as valuable as a broken doorknob to Justin. I stayed to please the Lord; otherwise I would have given up long before I got my walking papers." She is amused.

A mysterious call
Before Tia and I completed our commemorative discussion of memories gone by; my phone rings persistently ... Simultaneously, my nine-year-old daughter, Jyndia, signals for me to tuck her in bed. She'd been a little under the weather all day, but I feel compelled to answer the demanding sound of the call. Even with all the jostling of the evening, I intuitively knew I should answer. I motion for Jyndia to rest and Tia leaves the room.

Placing the phone to my ear, I hear a particular voice. Mystified and amazed ... I wondered why this person is calling. Why me of all people? Her voice is soft and kind. Her words remind me of my times with Luis. I am apprehensive of what she might say, but will learn that this call is an answer to my vicarious dreams and revelations. In the most unusual way, the unseen hand of God is uncovering Himself in my life. The one who is in control of cause and effect, and times and seasons is showing Himself nearby. He is awake and conscious of my frequent inquisitions. God is ready to bring light. Gradually, you will learn why and how this revelatory conversation is important and came to be, but for now I will tell you what I told Tia about Justin.

Justin
I had grown more than tired of being a "what not" on a shelf in Justin's world. Believing I was stuck, I waited for the right time to leave. I knew God hated divorce, so divorce in my mind was prohibited; and could not be a reprieve for Christians. Thankfully, years later the Holy Spirit would teach me about God's

true perception of marriage and divorce. I would learn that God not only hates divorce, but every kind of abuse, separation and pain that comes from disobedience. Seeing His children emotionally, mentally or physically dishonored is never His heart. His analysis of marriage was and is far more comprehensive than the few scriptures I knew. Knowing in part can indeed be dangerous.

At fifteen, Justin was introverted and often felt defeated. With a zest for the future, I thought I had the answers he needed. By sixteen, I was sure I could help him build his self-esteem. Ha-ha! I took on the vast humanitarian quest of trying to help him believe in himself. I thought I was making the world a better place by doing so, but I was extending unsanctified mercy to a relationship out of season. I don't ever remember asking God if He sent Justin, but I began to open my heart; thinking the choice was entirely up to me. By nineteen, I had grown to love him too. We married after a four-year courtship, but more out of our own self-defining codependency. Marriage seemed to be the right thing to do.

My sisters and I were more or less taught to get married and have lots of children. Mothers in our day felt that marriage itself was the pinnacle of life achievement. My mother's viewpoint was, "Honey, have lots of children, so you're never alone. Children will give you something to do and will make you happy." With that kind of programming, I did what I was expected to do. Justin and I awkwardly said our wedding vows and became two even more insecure and out of place people. What a recipe for disaster, as our wounds of rejection and fear intensified. We disliked each other more as the years passed by.

Justin's personal wounds kept him from committing to our marriage. He assumed guilt for losing his father at an early age. This added to his detachment issues. There seemed to be a secret code of silence; even about the most insignificant matters. My childhood neither provided much in self-assurance or positive direction. We each grew up in shame-based environments and lacked vision for the future.

I struggled to go on with Justin, but there was no strength to give now in a relationship that offered no cohesiveness. My attempts to help him grow became ineffective and unproductive. How could I help him when I needed to mature myself? Neither of us had anything extra to give. We ended up losing time, confidence and energy and needed intense spiritual guidance and support. Loving Justin was not working. Our personal frame of reference was not enough. We groped in darkness looking for the many answers we needed.

If we had known how to listen to God, we would have known our primary purpose for meeting was to pray for each other and to keep on walking. We had no clue that some destinies are not meant to intertwine. I wish I had known how to talk my feelings over with an older, wiser Christian before marriage. It would have been good to hear someone say, "Don't do this honey! You're not obligated." We were each disinclined to marry, but hoped we'd feel better about it later. I didn't know that unhappy, adverse feelings are God's way of telling you to change your course of direction, but until you see the light, you don't know you are making decisions in the dark.

We were as two silly youngsters, foolishly thinking that marriage would offer solace. Instead, we gave ourselves continual seasons of barrenness and futility. We needed a Holy Ghost mother, father and a strong "God identity." I was a miserable camper, while Justin grew reclusive and involved in his own world. He wanted to be a carefree college basketball boy and I wanted a loving husband.

A shocking premonition
On one Saturday morning things were different for me. The writing was on the wall. The information was against our marriage and stood stalwartly. I sat upstairs looking out of a bedroom window that day, some eighteen years later. I watched Justin go through his Saturday morning ritual. He drank whatever beer he had not finished on Friday night and left home to buy more. He returned home, sat under a big tree in his car and continually drank all afternoon. Later, he left to buy another case and he drank until he was miserable. Gradually he'd stagger into the house and the distress would start, or he'd leave for a club or to gamble.

On Sunday's, after church, while Justin slept, our oldest son James collected his beer cans and tossed them in the trash. It had been too many years of watching these events, but this day was simply the point of no return. My observation took me deeper than I had ever gone before. The vapors parted and the sea opened … I knew it was time to move on. I had no more power, human or divine to live like this. The straw had finally broken the camel's back. I was sinking and fading into obscurity. My heart had changed towards Justin, more than I was willing to admit. I had tried so hard, but trying had got me nothing.

It was peculiar for me that I had no more desire to stand, but living with an alcoholic had overwhelmed my young, naive life. I knew enough now to know that I couldn't fix Justin and it didn't matter who thought I should stay. I was ready to go! I didn't want to fight or believe anymore! The relationship was no longer my life line. My heart had concluded the matter for me. My love had run out. I had filed for a divorce twice before, but this time a new level of intervention and strength emerged.

Painstakingly, I learned, **"you can't change anyone but yourself!"** How stupid it was to think that I could change anyone. This is a humanly unattainable - preposterous deed. We simply can't make anyone else happy! The task is far above our pay grade. The possibility of changing anyone else is only in grasps of the Divine. If we need God for our own happiness, how can we generate it for someone else? I learned that producing happiness is never our job! If you are trying to do this, stop it! It won't work. You are wasting your time. You are an extension of your mate's happiness, but you are not the creator of it. And what do you do with a person who doesn't want to be happy with you, for a variety of ill-conceived reasons?

That day, I could see a future revelation unfold in my mind. As I watched Justin drink, I could see that staying in our marriage would only create more, prolonged and redundant pain. I would try to love him and make a life for my boys and me; alone. I knew we would continue to experience the same arduous relationship next week, next year and the year after. Ten, twenty or thirty years more would present the same drudgery and outcome.

He would still be drinking and ignoring our relationship; I would still be delving into a life of my own. His pattern of conduct would continue to define and confine us ... I would hurt, despise his ways and lose more time ... time I didn't have to give away. I had to accept that my fore-ordained future and destiny would never evolve with Justin. This revelation was certain and a sobering exposé of our lives.

Regardless, I had no power to endure or fix our illusive, mock marriage. I could no longer try to be his Savior. Our dysfunctional, dejavu' existence needed to terminate. Our marriage offered a community front, but with no real commitment. At heart, Justin was still the same unhappy teen I had met years before.

I wondered why I had spent so much time waiting for Justin to change. Why had I endured so many disappointments? I had waded through so many rivers and tried to please someone who knew so little about loving back. My protracted years of marriage revealed that Justin was God's responsibility, not mine. The truth registered deeply in my soul. Justin was God's business. He was Jesus' case. My assignment was that I needed to learn more about freedom and the truth that Jesus offered.

An angel's assignment
An intense confirming dream was God's way of transferring light to me. I sat on my basement steps crying my eyes out. An angel came from behind, on my right side and asked, "Why are you crying?" I said, "I am miserable, but I can't leave because God hates divorce." The angel, spiritually articulating on my level of understanding said, "God doesn't mean it that way." He inferred, "There are extenuating circumstances in these matters."

Now, considering his beauty, I was enamored with the angel's loveliness. With feelings of awe, I quickly forgot my problem. I emphatically asked! "You have seen Jesus, haven't you? Please tell me what He looks like!" The angel expressed, "Look into my eyes and you will understand." I gazed ... and saw the most breathtakingly, sky blue, crystal-clear eyes! They were beautiful, wonder filled celestial eyes, flowing divinely like rivers of blue! These magnificent eyes were full of infinity! What glory I beheld in that moment! I wish I could fully communicate the joy and understanding I received within the presence and conveyance of the angel. The knowledge he granted, was a convergence of spiritual wisdom, strength and understanding.

I knew the answer when I awoke; I was spiritually free to go on. In my case, according to God's complete understanding of marriage, I was personally dismissed from my toil. The dream was God's way of telling me, He knew I had suffered many years as I worked on our marriage alone. Justin's inability to commit to our marriage was completely known by God. He had given Justin every opportunity to change, but now, his time was up.

Time is a wonderful commodity, unless it is wasted
I had spent more than seven thousand and fifty days in a hurtful, unattainable relationship. What an enormous amount of time. So many sunrises and sunsets had passed on. My time investment would have allowed me to finish college four times, run a marathon, twenty times or travel the world fifty times. I could have gone to China, Africa, or Europe. At least, I could have invested more positively in God, my children and myself. But for me, no more, stinky beer cans under the tree! This part of my life was forever complete! Enough muddy water has been poured on me!

Yes, I needed a bigger vision and paradigm, but we know that it takes two to make a mess big enough to last almost twenty long years. I wondered, would Justin even care that I was leaving? He was never home. He already had as much freedom as he wanted. Would he even notice? He would now have the life he wanted, with no interference from me.

Without reservation, I believed God had given me my walking papers; I would not be remorseful. What did I have to miss anyhow? After all, unless God unites two people to walk together, how can a relationship endure? (Amos 3:3). How could we tolerate the night with no agreement in the day? I didn't have a partner, love or emotional support to miss. God was right to shed light on a new path for me.

I was far beyond tears. I had already worked out the pain of separation and divorce during our very trying marriage, therefore; I would not make moving on about him. Justin and I would always live in two different enormities. I was angry with myself that I allowed the marriage to continue and that Justin never appreciated my deep commitment to him. I learned an important lesson; it was never God holding me in the marriage or in a self-created hellhole of bondage with an insubordinate mate. That belief came from my own lack of knowledge and Satan took advantage of it. According to the Word, God calls us to live purposeful lives. We are never called to be doormats.

Separation
The ministry of the Holy Spirit made the answer clear; but I wanted to make sure. I prayed again ... "God, what did the angel mean when he said, 'You don't mean it that way?" ... (Unfortunately, we can know just enough scripture to be dangerous. We can distort and magnify only part of what God has said, instead of rightly dividing the Word).

Remember, a religious mindset can make us think we are obligated to keep on standing alone, but when we have done all we can do to maintain our marriage, there is a point in time in which God sets us free. He cares about us and is against a mate that continues to be abusive, neglectful or adulterous. God knows our eternity past, present and future. He knows if our mates will change or stay the same.

God is not pleased when vows are broken by a husband or wife who refuses atonement. It is not God who holds us to dwell with an unrepentant mate, without precise instructions. He also knows if a marriage is spiritually illegal or a covenant marriage in His sight. Listen carefully ... unless you have a sure Word from the Lord to stay when there is spiritual defilement; you are free to separate after seeking the face of God. Nevertheless, you must know that you know that God is speaking to you personally, with your emotions entirely shut down.

If God has joined you and your mate together, stand firm. Stand through reading the Word, prayers, and in obedience. You will see the glory of your God. He will not allow anyone or anything to destroy your marriage. Even if you are divorced or separated, stand strong if the Lord has said to. Your covenant marriage will once again be resurrected for the better. It will make a comeback! In the meanwhile, the peace and resurrection of God will prevail in your heart. You will know that it's God, because the circumstances will barely move you. Why? Because you will know from the inside-out that an affair doesn't matter. You know that you will see the exonerating hand of your God! But God does allow separation until repentance is accomplished.

Again, only with a sure personal Word from the Lord, through Biblical liberation and truth are you free to separate or divorce. God has not ordained every marriage and only protects that which He has established. His marriages are a full expression of His exuberant life and enduring love. His marriages can survive hell and high waters; but our self-endorsed marriages are put together from our desires and misunderstandings. When we choose without God's ordination or blessing, our relationships have an expiration date written on them. During these times, God is still good and extends His "precious mercy" to help us dissolve dishonest and disobedient relationships.

If God had been the author of Justin and my marriage, then Justin's continual rebellion and lack of repentance changed God's desired outcome for us. If the marriage had been right, we would have had strong personal confirmations within ourselves. Validations of righteousness, peace and joy through the Holy Spirit would have prevailed. We would have had waves of grace to help us stand against evil. Truthfully, we married on our own. We did what we thought was right in our own eyes. Consequently, our marriage was not equipped to stand the test of time.

The angelic, prophetic dream helped to make an absolute difference for me. The angel had come in response to my intense inner cry to God. God knew I wanted to please Him, and that I saw no way out of my dilemma. He knew about my very limited amount of knowledge and inadequate understanding of scripture. He divinely spoke to a religious minded lady who needed to increase her understanding. God used the dream as proof that He loved me. He loves to show His children the future. He is our womb of life!

> *"We know the truth through our eternal spirits in Christ Jesus.*
> *We have unction through the Holy One. We know all things."*
> (1 John 2:20–21)

Personal word

The dream was God's personal word to me. It is important to state that we should never apply another person's personal revelation to ourselves. If God has told you to hold on, then individually, you must continue to believe His Word for your marriage. When this is true, He will give you an absolute and distinctive Word or knowing that strategically quickens your ability to stand. Later, when the time is right He will bring every issue to pass.

Onward

Preparing for divorce, especially at Christmas was difficult. I felt depressed and shared my struggles with an old high school friend. Gina was savvy and now enjoyed a prestigious job in the aircraft industry. Materially, I had so much less to show for my life as a homemaker. I spent most of my time doing church work, raising my boys, taking college classes or working on developing seminars for youth and families. I loved my work and was proud that my program had gained some momentum in the community, but still I was far behind the "real achievers." My accomplishments felt diminutive in comparison to Gina's, but still, talking to her was refreshing. Her words were challenging and visionary and I needed someone to listen and care.

Gina asked me to go to a "hot-spot supper club," for professionals and teased me about never having fun. She said, "You're going through a divorce and you're stressed! Come on Girl, it's almost January! - This is a New Year! It will be good for you to get out of the house!" I felt she was right and how I wanted to get out of the house and out of my misery. Mostly, I needed to prove to myself that I was not a boring, home-based business, Christian-nerd. I was certainly not someone who never had fun. I knew how to enjoy life, but in different ways.

Gina appeared to be happily divorced. She stood strong, emotionally and financially. I wanted that too. Her input seemed important now. Perhaps her point of view would rub off on me. In school, without question, Gina had effortless confidence with no debate! We got us rides home because of her knockout figure and fabulous walk. It screamed, "Shut up!" Gina represented the fun I needed and hadn't had for a long-long time.

Uneasiness
I half-heartedly prepared to go out, but could not stop thinking about the difficulty of change. There was so much I didn't know. It's terrible not to know what you don't know. I worried, how will I support my sons? Would James be prepared to go to college? Everything was so expensive, and how much would the divorce affect my children? James' relationship with his Dad was detached and cool, but he still needed more than I could give him. James and I had seen the good, bad and the ugly, but how would he fair in life now, and what about Jamul? What about his security? Would he be undone in the move? He was only five and loved his Daddy very much. I wanted him to be a happy child. How would he feel having his Dad around even less? What would our outcome be? Would divorce or our miserable marriage make their lives better or worse?

My fears of the future were indeed paralyzing! Would I be able to get on my feet and achieve financial stability? Could I take my business and ministry to new heights or get a good paying job? Would I need to lower my expectations and settle for a low wage job? My primary career of trying to be a good wife, held no tenure. There was no such thing as, "a good wife degree." I fretted, but what was in the best interest of my sons? Their feelings were important and they needed a more engaged and responsive Dad. He was their only example of male orientation. But I set my face like a flint to go forth. I could not look back. I had had enough of the darkness; I knew what was behind me.

My self-respect and sanity depended upon my leaving. I had to try to dwell in the light now. I prayed, "Lord, help me trust you. I am afraid to walk forward. My faith is small. My soul is consumed with perplexity!" But, it was time to move forward. I had fought valiantly. I had to trust that God would take care of me. I had to try to fly as high as possible. This course of pain had to end!

My church friends symbolized more of the same old oppressive values. They would say, "Pray and wait for the Lord; someday Justin will change." But, they had not lived with Justin. They didn't know what I knew. And how could they ask me to stay in a plundered marriage, when I had to grace to do so.

Going out with Gina would be a deliberate step and struggle toward my personal freedom. It would provide the psychological green light I needed to build a new me. God had released me to go on; I would not look back. I would not be sorry. I now had permission to proceed. Gina picked me up and off we went for a little long overdue fun!

BEYOND THE GATES   Chapter 2

There are flesh (carnal) and spiritual people coming your way. You will need heavenly and keen discernment to identify the counterfeits. You must be able to recognize who they are before damage is done. The replica (sham) is coming to mess you up.

I could breathe! Getting out of the house felt great; I remembered that life could be amusing. Arriving, the club was filling quickly. The gaiety created lots of energy. I smiled and felt as though Gina and I were in high school again. We actually brightened the place a bit; with our laughter. I knew a few people; Gina knew a lot more. Later, I sat listening and making polite conversation, trying to act interested. After a while my heart was far away and the whole experience was a drag! The people seemed to look for something they didn't have. Only a few appeared to be sincere or truly happy. You know that people really know how to fake it.

The supper club experience was not getting it after all. I was not having fun. Maybe I was a home-based, Christian business dud, but I liked it far better than this. I thought about my love for Jesus and the purposes of God. I preferred being home with my boys, watching a television-minister or working on my business. I loved reading books. At one point I said, "Gina, I can't stand the way men look you over. I know the mating game is about someone wanting to buddy up with you, but this is not fun."

I might have been out of circulation, but I still didn't like the distasteful feeling. The exchanges were "primitive and obvious." The men looked women over like cows in a distribution ring. Both sexes were so superficial -- too worldly for my taste. I was hoping to have a good time, but I looked at myself and thought, "What am I doing in a supper club? Have you abandoned your senses woman?"

I wanted to ask Gina to take me home; until I noticed a good-looking man smiling at me from ear to ear. This went on for about forty minutes. I told Gina, "Why do men do that? They glare, gawk, ogle and smile." And this man's persistence was exasperating. He was a profiler, (and knew he was cute). I was flattered, "but what the heck was he looking to see?" Looking back awkwardly, was I supposed to smile too? Should I show him that I had good teeth too? Was this a smile contest?

Gina and I continued to visit, but I dared to look again. I wanted to see if he was still looking at me. I wasn't sure. Gina got most of the looks in high school, so maybe he was looking at her. I looked again, "Yes! Glory, it is me! You've got to be kidding, God. Someone is looking at me!" He was sending out an authentic mating call. His attention was indeed intriguing.

Was this attractive man, sent to delude an unsuspecting woman, like me? Or was he authentically a good guy? He came over to our table and asked, "Are you ladies meeting anyone?" Demurely, we said "No," but within my depleted soul I shouted, "Heck, NO! Have a seat! I've been waiting!" He asked if he could join us. We modestly said, "Yes." Inwardly, my emotions roared, "YES, you can have a seat right here beside me!" For a minute, I thought he might show himself friendly and then turn his attention to Gina, but no, he was there to talk to me! Jubilation filled my mind! I assured myself that I deserved a little adulation. Wow, I was amazed that someone wanted to talk to me! I pinched myself. I had been beaten down emotionally for years, but this man, unequivocally desired my company!

So, here I am, a good Christian girl, going through a divorce, dealing with uncertainties. I'm at a nightclub, with very little self-value. I'm vulnerable and suddenly a handsome man smiles at me and sits at my table! What do you do with all of that? Well, let me ask you this; what does the desert do with rain? What does rice do when it boils and mixes with water? Of course, they fully absorb it! And just like that; my lonely heart absorbed every bit of his attention. Life had finally come and I willingly soaked in its radiance. My little heart fluttered I was flattered and fascinated! I remembered the feeling of delight again. My cup ran over, smattered and renewed!

I was disjointed a bit, having male company, but still felt good enough to continue visiting with my new friend. Looking outwardly for soul restoration, I had not learned well that my worth and wealth lived within. It would never come from anyone else. But appearing sophisticated and aloof, in no way, would he know that I was excited to have his company. I was not about to let my guard down. I had heard plenty of bad stories about flattering men with big smiles!

Luis and I shared and laughed together easily. Our words flowed like destiny unfolding. Our eyes beamed into each other's soul and heart. I'm sure another dimension appeared as we flew into other worlds and cosmos. A wondrous stratosphere of awe opened to us, as the stars twinkled brightly in the heavens. I could literally taste colors, lights and ecstasy. We were the insignia of illumination. The earth trembled; I could hear the cherubim singing; "Dorothy you are blessed among women!" ☺ Several hours of pleasurable conversation evolved before we knew it.

I was suddenly cool, beautiful, and marvelous! The wind was at my back! I was Wonder Woman - free, black, and twenty-one! Luis felt like the good old shoe that fit Cinderella's foot perfectly ... My foot! ... Or, was he just too good to be true? Could he possibly be a wolf in sheep's clothing? Was he sent to mess me up? No, No, No! That would be impossible! Our meeting had to be divine and sincere, not a counterfeit or accident. Luis seemed to be the overflow I had heard about all my life! ... Was he the reason God gave me my freedom papers.

I forgot my problems and pains. Perhaps God was redeeming my time. I decided for a moment that it was safe to let the Joy bells ring! ... Wahoo! ... And then ... from somewhere in the deepest part of my spirit I heard these awful, disruptive and disturbing words! "Luis is a womanizer!" No, No, No! I pondered a moment ... "The devil must have found his way in here to sit at our table!" Not this wonderful God created man! That would be impossible!

Next ... I had the audacity to answer the intuition and voice of God by saying, "Well, perhaps he used to be a womanizer. People do change for the better Lord." (I wondered if God got His signals mixed up). I reasoned, "Luis is much too pleasant for that." Besides, this has to be Satan trying to make me doubt this blessing.

I had suffered a long time in my marriage, but the devil's days of miserable, manipulation would not affect my new God ordained season. I would not listen to him! The Red Sea had opened and it was time for me to walk across on dry land. I had met a wonderful man and I liked this Luis person! He was interesting and made me feel special. The night ended too soon as my expectancy overflowed. We happily exchanged phone numbers, so glad we had met! When Gina and I left, I staggered to the car on a new probability high. I had met an awesome man!

The next day Luis began to call. By now I had come to my senses and was trying hard to discern if I heard God correctly. Should I proceed with the strong attraction I felt or not? I didn't feel particularly peaceful about calling him back, so I waited ... He continued to call for several weeks. Finally, he left me a decisive message. He said, "I have called you for some time now. I really enjoyed our meeting, but if you don't call me back, I won't call you again." That was the clincher.

<u>Fear of loss</u> gripped my exasperated soul! How could I let this (seemingly) sincere, exciting and intelligent man get away? I foolishly pushed the womanizing message behind me and blamed the devil again. I nervously returned Luis' call. I wanted to know who he was. (Do you remember what happened in the story about the curious cat)?

Luis was happy and surprised to hear from me. I had euphoric feelings too, but minimal serenity about my decision. But cautiously I thought I could at least talk to him a bit. I had to know; was Luis from God or Satan? I didn't know it then, but the moment I disobediently returned Luis' call, is the moment I gave deception its right to move in against me. I had missed my God-ordained time to run ... before the entrapment began. The devil and his cohorts celebrated, "We've got her now!" Yes ... and I was on my way to seeing realms of darkness that I needed to know nothing about.

Challenging the voice of God was going to mess me up. I would learn the hard way that I was not missing out on anything. I already had everything that was special or good. But, when we don't realize that, Satan can easily work against us. Lord, help us learn to trust Your voice! That lack of trust allows the formation of erroneous relationships and hurtful situations. They ascend through fear and aloneness. But the voice of God is there for our benefit and well-being.

Fear of loss perverts our vision and hides God's truth from us.

New experiences and introductions create an easy time for Satan to deceive and pick us off. When emotions are engaged, spiritual truths can be undoubtedly overridden. Emotions are powerful elements that can work against us.

My lack of peace with Luis was my first indicator to turn back. I clearly knew the impression I received was from the voice of God. His sheep know His voice, but still, I allowed curiosity to overrule my intuition. I convinced myself that I could turn back at any time. I did not respect the power of emotions, especially when that are given to the proficiently of Satan himself!

"A prudent, far-sighted person foresees evil and hides himself; but the simple pass on and are punished." (Proverbs 22:3)

Captivation

The next eleven months would be fascinating. The song by Christopher Cross says: "When You Get Caught Between the Moon and New York City, There's Nothing You Can Do But Fall in Love!" … And we lived in the Villas of magical love. Yes, there was love and fun in the world after all -- so much fun. Our talks, dinners, laughter and planning were exciting and wonderful! - We enjoyed beautiful times! Becoming a restaurant connoisseur was fun with Luis! My hometown was as beautiful and exclusive as a night anywhere in the world. Luis was a gift giver, motivator and romanticist at heart. When he called me Angel, I flew on to glory! And he seemed to honor the life of Jesus too. I had it all - what else could a girl want? We were happy and feeling awesome, lighting up the room everywhere we went. Love had a new name for me! We were each other's missing factor! (Is this the way you originally felt about a potential mate)?

Our relationship shined radiantly! I knew Luis was not as strong a Christian as I, but he still had a heart to get into the Bible and God. During our courtship, he'd arrive at church before me. How nice! Yes, he was Interested in me, but his mind was on Jesus too. Luis had known God as a child, and that was good enough. Three months into our courtship, the man who told me, women get too serious too soon, proposed. He said, "I want you to be a permanent part of my life! You are everything I want!" Wow! I was floored, favored, and fabulous! Eleven months after our astounding courtship; I walked down the aisle into the arms of the man I adored! Our wedding ceremony was simple and beautiful. We said, "I do" with joy and positive expectation! What a happy day! Luis laughed jubilantly all evening. My sons looked so handsome, but were not so happy.

Nevertheless, Luis and I completed each other as one spirit and one life. Together, we'd be world changers! - The new Trumps! Kingdom shakers! We'd build an empire; and a legacy! We'd rock the universe with the power of love and glory! I had joy that surpassed my deep sorrows. People would say, "Luis is the coffee and Dorothy is the cream. You are two peas in a pod! Look what the Lord has done!" I thought; God just has to be in this. Certainly now, our marriage would erase my ambiguity ... But In the midst of all the celebration, joy and positive words; secretly, inner conflict racked my soul. I internally felt hesitant and afraid of the future.

The years passed quickly. We enjoyed dynamic occasions and each other. On weekends, Luis cooked dinner and helped me clean the house. That was new for me. He even washed clothes, ironed and folded laundry! How could life be any sweeter? His kindness and loving ways encouraged me to relax. It was special when our pastor used him to bring congregational messages. We also taught a weekly Bible study group in our home. Some in our church pronounced, "Luis and Dorothy have the most anointed Bible studies and prayer meetings." We could see God's hand on our lives. Our relationship stood tall in the community and so many prophesied over our lives and purpose together. We felt that God was positioning us for ministry and to win souls.

Like fine oiled machinery, we moved and walked together. We lived harmoniously; in sync and on the saddle. We talked about how to keep our relationship strong and pure. He'd laugh and say when admired by another woman, "Get your mind off me!" We had a plan to keep the door shut to other wanting eyes; deciding, "You can't help it if you look once, but you can stop yourself from looking twice."

I asked Luis why he and his first wife were not able to work out their differences. He prided himself on being a southern gent and said, he bent over backward to love Dixon, but she lacked maturity and was too jealous. Their problems were her fault. I questioned him at times, but forced myself to believe his unwavering commentary. Luis had to be right. Besides, how could he be with her, when he was supposed to be with me? I was the right person for him.

Our first five years of our marriage were enjoyable. I would testify to others, "Hold on and God will give you a pressed down, shaken together, and running over blessing! Know for yourself, God will give you a wonderful gift. He is faithful. God will exceed your expectations!" All the while I suppressed that harassing inner voice! Why wouldn't that nagging interference stop! I was agitated almost constantly. These negative assumptions were overwhelming. I often exclaimed, "Leave me alone devil!"

In our blissful seasons, before winter storms began to blow, our counterfeit marriage was quite beautiful. I did want to believe that we were peas and carrots too, put together by God! James (my first son,) never had good feelings about

Luis, but still, this had to work. Luis had to be my exemplary gift from God; my badge of honor. Surely this was God, but in the midst of the love, honor and acceptance, my anxiety continued to be pervasive.

Luis's big promotion
Luis finally received a job as a buyer. This would be a promotion for him; he had had a terrible time with the job market. We were grateful for the career break. I continued to work ambitiously with youth and families from home. Luis also worked part-time with military and for a Family Preservation Center. He was a group leader for boys. I appreciated his hard work and Christian stand. He often spoke of his commitment to family, saying he would be steadfast in good and bad times. He assured me, "I will give you a wonderful life." He told his father, "She is easy to live with." My family thought we were the perfect couple. Surely, God was smiling on us.

Our first important prophecy
During an exciting Sunday morning service, a traveling evangelistic-prophet said, "The hand of the Lord is on this couple for good. Luis and Dorothy, you will walk in power and ability to change lives. You will prosper and bless the Lord!" He said to me, "Lady you have a liberating ministry. You will set many free!" He prayed for us with passion and fire, in Jesus' Name! We received this prophet's words sincerely. They affected us deeply, right down into our spiritual bones.

Another evening at church, an African-speaking prophet asked, "Is anyone named Dorothy here?" He asked for Dorothy specifically! Whew! Astounding! I was the only Dorothy there. I went forward with an astonishing look on my face. The prophet asked my family to come too. He said, "Dorothy, God is thinking about you. You are special to Him. He will be with you always. God will help you." He prayed for my strength, asking God to help me stand. He asked the whole congregation to pray for me; letting them know I would fully need their prayers for future trials. When I returned to my seat, I thought, "Hum, stand for what? (This was not a good word). Stand for my children or business, hum ... but certainly not for my marriage!" That was the last area of concern entering my mind. We were too happy and "smoochie" for such worries. We had no problems that needed that kind of strength. I was sure the good prophet somehow missed it!

A faithful man
At a revival, Kim Clemmet, a nationally known prophet, said to me, "Woman! God has heard your cry and He will do it!" He told Jamul, "School will be easy for you! You will be a prophet of the Lord!" He turned to Luis and said, "And you shall be a faithful man!" ... "What? Could you run that by me again Lord?" My, My, My! Did my eyes open fast and wide? What did he mean? My husband would be a faithful man? ... On the way home I asked Luis, "Why would the prophet say such a thing? Are you being unfaithful to me?" Luis responded, "Why would you ask me that? Don't you trust me?" I considered a while and

questioned God; why would Kim say such a terrible thing about my wonderful husband? (I was not encouraged at all!)

Was God using these men to prepare me? Was He working ahead of schedule to get me spiritually, mentally and emotionally prepared for some serious times? Kim was actually trying to speak against Luis' developing agenda. (The words of a prophet when spoken in power and faith can change a matter, or create a desired result). The prophet was speaking against what he saw coming. He hoped the power of God would change Luis' decision to be unfaithful. God knew I was over in La-La Land, happy as a lark, believing what I wanted to believe. I was Clueless and not equipped for the storms developing ahead, thinking I dwelled in safety and soundness. I did not know my present sense of harmony was ticking away. Luis was already in his early stages of womanizing. He was collectively spinning his web and opening himself up to admirers.

Uncertainty
Even in the good times I felt uneasiness and uncertainty, which challenged my ability to go forward. But I kept fighting for my right to be happy, like other people. Why didn't I deserve some happiness? I was a good Christian! I had earned my stripes by surviving the long hard marriage with Justin. So, when I felt uneasy, I'd rebuke the unrelenting anxiety and devil on one hand, but quietly ask, "God, didn't you bring Luis to me? Do you want me to divorce him? What is it Lord? You did release me to move on with my life. Didn't the angelic dream confirm my freedom?"

Trying to encourage myself in the Lord, I knew the Bible clearly stated that wisdom speaks at the beginning of a matter, before disobedience incubates. In my heart, I knew I had gone past God's gate of protection; I had crossed over into my own desire, But, still I tried to believe that perhaps my apprehension was guilt coming from my unredeemed spirit. I talked to several pastor's wives about my feelings. They assured me that the devil was just trying to steal my joy. Therefore, I worked harder to press past every anxious and depressing feeling. I decided I had to overcome this evil foreboding and settle the matter permanently. This time I was going to get the fulfillment I deserved. Yes, surely, these feelings were just an unexplained fabrication of my imagination. Perhaps these were just old fears coming from my childhood neglects.

Unforeseen pressure
It was football season. Luis planned a party with his friends at our home. I helped him prepare the house and food. He noticed I was tired and I kept going to bed. I continued to drag around feeling ill all day. The smell of coffee made me sick. (I loved coffee). Luis kept asking me to get up and help. He was an irritating perfectionist that day. I scoffed! "I want to lie down. I'm so sleepy!" As an optimist, I usually felt upbeat and focused, but that day I needed to sleep. Before long, Luis recognized the problem. He sensed I was pregnant and he

was right! Amazed and surprised, we celebrated our pregnancy! We had not talked much about having a baby. We were too busy chasing the dream.

The day of my physical, a conventional sonogram would change our lives. I wondered, "What in the world is taking this doctor so long?" Disturbed and concerned … "Have, they forgotten I'm back here? My time is valuable! I need to go to work!" The doctor arrived to tell me I needed to talk to a specialist. Those words were suspect and disturbing, but I had faith in God. Later, I sat in the specialist's office being told that my two-month pregnancy was problematic. The specialist maliciously showed me pictures of grossly deformed babies. Next, he explained my child might look like one of them. How cruel! Later I learned those pictures had nothing to do with "Spina Bifida (S.B.)," a birth defect. S.B. affects the muscles and nerves in the lower body, but most children go on to live full and fruitful lives.

With the doctor's insensitivity, I knew what he thought I should do. The devil hoped to plant a seed in my mind to abort my baby. His words of death filled my mind for days. Disappointment and dismay, unsettled me. The doctors had inferred that the world did not need another disabled baby. I composed myself to believe and pray as I left his office. With the help of God, the doctor's words would be taken down.

Luis was away for weeks serving in Army Reserves during Desert Storm. Thank God, he would be home that coming weekend. When he arrived, I shared the doctor's grim report … together we vowed to fight for our baby. Saddened, but with brave hearts, hand in hand, we would defy the doctor's devilish prediction. Praise God, the Word of the Lord was indisputably stronger. The Word is always the higher calculative; If we can believe it.

Weeks later I proceeded to make an appointment to see my obstetrician. I could hardly believe it. I caught them off guard. They thought I had aborted my baby and was coming in for a post abortion physical. I was shaken with their conduct. The nurse and doctor acted nervously.

Worthy of life
My day of delivery came. Jyndia's birth would be a scheduled cesarean section. There were at least twenty people in the room. She was taken away quickly for surgery. They needed to close the opening in her back. She lay recovering for two weeks, needing a shunt to keep fluid from building up in her small head. So, small and helpless was our precious baby; her beautiful hair cut off. How devastating! She looked so frail. I was so sad and bereaved. I knew nothing about S.B. or a neonatal center, but had to make the adjustment to be there for this little person from heaven. I learned that there are special places in hospitals for very sick babies. I saw circumstances I never imagined. I had birthed two healthy boys, and went home in days, but S.B. presented lessons of deep pain

and fear for me. I learned that I had never truly been grateful enough to have had normal deliveries.

Jyndia's hospital stay was perplexing; so many doctors and nurses, in and out of the room. I was angry with God and all of them. How dare they be so pessimistic about my baby's future? Who did they think they were? They were all so very ugly. How could they say she would not walk! I hated their faithlessness! They had no spiritual vision at all for my child .... I would not allow them to speak over her life and not change their words in my heart. I didn't want anyone near us with negative thoughts or words. And who were the crazy scientist that took folic acid out of our foods? (S.B. is often caused by a deficiency of folic acid).

Released from the hospital, Jyndia had to return for more surgery. She needed another shunt. How could I ever trust God again? I huffed, "Lord, I have tried to live a good life for you. I don't understand. I thought, even loose-living men and women, doing every manner of evil, have healthy babies. Why not me? (Self-righteousness). What have I done to deserve such a trial? Why? Why? Why?" I argued, "God, You told me I was free to go on with my life, so is my marriage to Luis what this all about?!" (When testing hits, every manner of wonder fills our minds).

The magnitude of this trial inspired deep guilt and serious reflection. God fully had our attention. Was the birth defect, the result of our disobedient marriage? When I met Luis, and began to see him, I did have a word from God. I knew that I was free to go on with my life, but my divorce was not final. And according to the Bible, a legal divorce must take place before developing another relationship.

According to God's personal word to me, I was free to go on, but not necessarily with Luis, especially before the divorce was final. And Luis had no Bible-based reason to divorce his first wife. The facts of our disobedience were certainly there, in full view of God's eyes and Word. I knew that God was speaking to me, even though none of us <u>want to think that our sins are judged</u>. But this trial was bought on from our disobedience. Let's look at some of the scriptures that support what I know is true in some of the test we suffer.

Don't be fooled by those who try to excuse these sins, for the anger of God will fall on all who disobey him. (Ephesians 5:6)

Remember David's sin in 2nd Samuel
"Now therefore, the sword shall never depart from your house, because you have despised Me and have taken the wife of Uriah the Hittite to be your wife.' "Thus, says the LORD, 'Behold, I will raise up evil against you from your own household; I will even take your wives before your eyes and give *them* to your companion, and he will lie with your wives in broad daylight. 'Indeed, what

you did it secretly, I will do this thing before all Israel, and under the sun.'" Then David said to Nathan, "I have sinned against the LORD." and Nathan said to David, "The LORD also has taken away your sin; you shall not die. "However, because by this deed you have given occasion to the enemies of the LORD to blaspheme. The child also that is born to you shall surely die."

Loss of David's Child
Then the LORD struck the child that Uriah's widow bore to David, so that he was very sick. David therefore inquired of God for the child; and David fasted and went and lay all night on the ground. The elders of his household stood beside him to raise him up from the ground, but he was unwilling and would not eat food with them. Then it happened on the seventh day that the child died. (2nd Samuel 12:10-18)

David suffers great consequences - 2 Samuel 13
The natural consequences of David's sin begin to occur when his sons begin to imitate the things that dad had done. David doing lots of reaping for the consequences of his sin, both in his character and in the circumstances, he finds himself in. David's son Ammon rapes David's daughter Tamar, who was a half-sister to Ammon.

Next, David's son, Absalom, who is a full brother to Tamar and a half-brother to Ammon, keeps silent and feigns having forgiven Ammon for what he has done to Tamar, however all the while plotting to murder Ammon. Then, finally after two years Absalom murders his brother Ammon for what he had done to Tamar. Next, Absalom flees to a foreign territory and hide out from justice for the murder he committed. David paid a huge price for not inquiring of the Lord before he acts.

Reaping and sowing for past failures you have sown.
The apostle Paul wrote for us the following about reaping and sowing in Galatians 6:7-9, "⁷ Do not be deceived, God is not mocked; for whatever a man sows, this he will also reap. ⁸For the one who sows to his own flesh will from the flesh reap corruption, but the one who sows to the Spirit will from the Spirit reap eternal life. Let us not lose heart in doing good, for in due time we will reap if we do not grow weary." Note that there are reaping's to the flesh as well as reaping's to the Spirit, as well as an encouragement to continue doing good.

Sowing to the flesh is following the old sinful nature in disobedience to God's commandments. Sowing to the Spirit is following the leading and unction of the Holy Spirit, walking by faith and in obedience to the Lord.

It is important for us as Christians to realize that, "_Every single action we take is a seed that we sow. In time, each of those seeds will grow up and reap a certain consequence in our life, either good or bad_." As Christians, we must realize the importance of doing everything in our life in such a way that we will reap a harvest of righteousness, one which will bear fruit for the Lord.

The great English preacher of a century and a half ago, Spurgeon, once said, "What, man does is of itself, full of a power which will be to him what the harvest is to the soil; and whatever he sows he will be sure to reap one of these days, or in eternity, if not in time. If a man were to sow his field with garlic and expect to reap barley, he would be bitterly disappointed.

<u>When we sow tares, we might pray for a crop of wheat as long as is pleases us, but we will not get it. God never so changes his laws as to make tares come up wheat, and he never will. The sowing always is and always will be, the father of the reaping.</u>"

Can you deny that God has spoken clearly about sin?

My son, do not reject the discipline of the LORD or loathe His reproof, for whom the LORD loves He reproves, even as a father *corrects* the son in whom he delights. How blessed is the man who finds wisdom and the man who gains understanding (Proverbs 3:11-13)

Know then in your heart that, as a man disciplines his son, the LORD your God disciplines you. (Deuteronomy 8:5)

I will be his father, and he will be my son. When he does wrong, I will punish him with a rod wielded by men, with floggings inflicted by human hands.
(2 Samuel 7:14)

The LORD has chastened me severely, but he has not given me over to death. (Psalm 118:18)

I know, O LORD, that Your judgments are righteous, and that in faithfulness You have afflicted me. (Psalm 119:75)

As many as I might love, I rebuke and discipline; therefore, be zealous and repent. (Revelation 3:19)

For this reason, many among you are weak and sick, and a number sleep. But if we judged ourselves rightly, (own your sin) we would not be judged. But when we are judged, we are disciplined by the Lord so that we will not be condemned along with the world. (1 Corinthians 11:30-32)

The wrath of God is being revealed from heaven against all the godlessness and wickedness of people, who suppress the truth by their wickedness.
(Romans 1:18)

Put to death, therefore, the components of your earthly nature: sexual immorality, impurity, lust, evil desires, and greed, which is idolatry. Because of these the wrath of God is coming on the sons of disobedience. (Colossians 3:16)

While people are saying, "Peace and safety," destruction will come on them; suddenly, as labor pains on a pregnant woman, and they will not escape.
(1 Thessalonians 5:3)

Don't be fooled by those who try to excuse sin, for the anger of God will fall on all who disobey him. (Ephesians 5:6)

People will fight you to excuse their sins. They will quickly say that God doesn't allow various kinds of consequences for sins, but we must trust that the Word of God is solid and true. Like so many of you, I didn't want to believe that my very common sin of fornication and adultery would open the door to such a test, but I absolutely knew our sinful relationship was the reason for this awful season. My weary mind was inundated with every possible kind of discouragement. This was the evidence I feared? Could I dismiss my fearful introspection now?

Be convinced in your own heart that our God of grace and mercy, even in the New Testament, still judges sin. It is impossible to predict the price that will be extracted from your soul and spirit when you go past your Fathers voice.

I cried out for mercy and help
I had to stop the paralysis of analysis. I did know that I could ask for God's mercy, but I did not excuse my sins. I spent hours repenting. Still, I understood that this was not the time to stop believing that God would help me, whether or not; Luis and I were supposed to be together. I knew I had to fight a great fight of repentance and faith! I had to win this battle. I had to get victory for my baby girl! She needed me to be strong and sure now and to outlast the consequences of my test. This was not the time to think of what I should have done years before -- not the time to waver or permit Satan to shape my imagination. I knew I would not allow the devil to speak against my child or the goodness of God. God was still good and He would help us get back on the track of righteousness.

<u>God had no Spinal Bifida in Heaven to give me. It came from a door I had opened to sin.</u> I was angry enough to destroy the devil and his deception with

my bare hands now! I raged, "How dare you put this on my baby! We won't stand for this! God will snuff you out devil! We prophesy "VICTORY" over this - right in your defeated face! I declared; Jyndia's body is perfect right now!"

As the months passed, Jyndia's doctor's visits were frequent. They continually checked and rechecked her, but Luis and I agreed to stand for our baby girl. I was more than the shielding mother lion, absorbed and fixated on her triumph! She had to win. Her story would be a living testimony of God's healing power! She was my only focus. I declared she would not suffer in her innocence. Scriptures of healing and faith were spoken over her many times daily. We believed that our faith in God's Word and mercy would succeed.

During it all, I could feel His supernatural strength. Luis and I unfortunately kept our grief to ourselves and felt alone. He would try to do the "man thing" and act strong, but I knew he was worried and hurt too. We did well most days. I prayed that we might provide deeper comfort for each other.

At church, an evangelist said, "Someone here is fighting for their baby!" Luis and I gave a special offering that evening believing the evangelist could see Jyndia's situation in our spirits. We believed Jyndia's blessing would unfold. She would prevail, no matter what it looked like! God was with her and for her! Who could stand against her? No matter what our past had been, she deserved the best!

I got myself engrossed in the Word and up for the test! When your child's life is part of the equation, you soldier yourself and stand tall; until your miracle arrives! We are amazingly sturdy and strong during these times in the Lord. Yes, God would somehow stay the hand of the enemy! We would not relent! The devils plan for Jyndia would bow its knee to God's principles and good plan for her life. God would intervene, because He said He would help us, especially after sincere repentance with godly sorrow that leads to change.

For the kind of sorrow God wants us to experience leads us away from sin and results in salvation (godly change). There are no regrets for that kind of sorrow. But worldly sorrow, which lacks repentance, results in spiritual death.
(2 Corinthians 7:10)

View points
Luis loved Jyndia too, but could not feel the deep intensity a mother feels. He knew sitting around was not my style. I had assembled accounts and won bids that paid thousands of dollars for short projects, so why did this season have to be about money and success? We had had many financial victories before this. I loved working long, hard hours and had always helped, but this was not the time or place! Why was he being so faithless? God' would provide. He felt I should put Jyndia's surgeries and the S.B. on the back burner and help him carry our financial load. He thought I was making excuses.

Jyndia had changed my view of life. I needed to be there for her. I knew we had bills, but didn't care about maintaining a certain lifestyle. Stuff was just stuff now, and stuff was not as important as my Jyndia. I wanted Luis to understand. I could not put my baby in daycare. How could I trust strangers to treat my baby right? I would work and do my business another day, but not now! I did appreciate what we had, but could not be away from my daughter all day. Jyndia's well-being was the most important thing. I had to pour strength into her.

My lioness and motherly instincts seriously kicked in. I prayed, "Touch Luis Lord. Change him. Help him see what is most important, for now. Let me be the mother I need to be for Jyndia. Later, I promise to get back to work, when the time is right." God knew my heart. I simply had to watch, cuddle, and love my baby girl. No one else could care for Jyndia like I would. She needed my consistency and support. Her shunt and spinal surgeries were critical matters, engraved on my heart. Why couldn't Luis understand that? Yet he was unmovable. The undercurrents of disgruntlement grew between us.

God is wonderful and humorous
Our God is merciful, even in the trials of His children. We began to see victories take place in Jyndia's small body. Gradually, God allowed her to sit up and after physical therapy; she could stand and grew stronger. One night, while Luis was at work, Jamul and I watched the Eclipse. We noticed movement from the corner of our eyes ... Jyndia let go of the furniture and spurted across the floor! I screamed and worshiped God! Jamul picked her up and whirled her around and around! He was happy too! What an exhilarating moment! God has a sense of humor. She walked during the Solar Eclipse that occurred on November 3rd, 1994; at three and a half years old. Our Jyndia let go of a table and walked!!! Wow! Praise You God! Our baby girl walked! Our prayers had been answered! Jyndia darted across the floor, walking! God had pulverized the words of the doctors! I called Luis at work shouting with glee! Joy filled our souls! Yes, our Jyndia was blooming! We praised God, "Your great mercies are dynamic!"

Months later at a restaurant Jyndia held us captive. Sitting beside her father, the music started sounding really good to her. She pulled herself up and took hold of the back of the booth. First, she twisted slowly and then plunged herself into a full-fledged dramatic dance. Her little skirt flipped and twirled, all over the place! When we laughed, or when Luis said, "Now Jyndia, you are really showing off," she'd stop and sit for a minute and wait; but when we resumed talking she hilariously went for it again! Jyndia was funny, loved, and a wonderful blessing!

God alone saw her through! Gradually her legs were strong enough to stand, walk, and dance even more. A wonderful miracle had occurred! God did not forget us. My apprehensive feelings subsided a bit. Perhaps we had moved past the danger zone? With so much repentance, had God forgiven our disobedience now? After all, His mercies endure forever!

TIME AND TIDE — Chapter 3

"For God shall bring every work with every secret thing into judgment, whether good or evil." (Ecclesiastes 12:14)

With the help of a friend, a fortunate financial blessing finally came our way. I acquired a contract with Raytheon Corporation, now; I could peacefully work from home. "Thank you, God, for the wonderful contract!" Luis and I rejoiced! We felt we'd made it into the big league! We were going to go where the big boats float! How sweet it was! We had never made money like that! Perhaps God had put us together after all.

For a few years, finances were good, but layoffs caused the aircraft industry and our business to decline. Temporary workers were not going to be needed as much. The industry slowed down, but the supervisor promised business would improve if we held on a while longer. Luis thought we should quit, but in my Holy Ghost bones I knew things would turn around. Luis couldn't *see* it and feared we were getting too far behind on taxes. I exclaimed, "How is quitting going to help us catch up on our taxes?" His reasoning made no sense. Quitting the business would make our tax situation worse. I wondered, "Doesn't this man have any active faith at all? What is so hard about believing God? Why couldn't he see that our business would live again?"

Trying to reason with Luis, I argued that keeping the business would gradually help us get ahead again. The dispute went on for a year or more ... Finally, I gave in to establish peace in the house. I did what the Bible says, "Wives, submit yourselves to your husbands." (That means that you submit yourself to a righteous and wise husband's decisions. Or follow him as he follows Christ). Against my better judgment and deep spiritual knowing, I relinquished the business to restore agreement in our home. Nothing was worth separating our family. I wanted our love and friendship to exist again, but knew in my gut this was a bad decision. We signed the business over to my brother.

Luis wanted to give the business to one of his friends. (Oh Lord)! That was not going to happen! I said, "If this business is going to bless anyone, it's going to at least be a member of the family." A year later, as sure as you've been born, as the representative promised, my ex-awesome business was booming. I was happy for my brother but sorry for myself. My brother was sitting on easy street and Luis had given away our big bag of gold. I was angry because I knew better! I had been right all along.

I furiously, seethed and foamed to the Lord! "God my business is gone! It was my personal blessing from you! Why couldn't Luis see the truth? What kind of Christian leader is he?" I felt that Luis was faithless and superficial. I considered his blunder to be a part of his character weakness. He had no spiritual insight and had given away our big financial blessing. It was gone. Oh, how badly he messed up and missed it, but It was too late to go back after the fact! Instead of an open heaven, there was a heavy iron ceiling brooding over our marriage. Daily its oxidization increased in strength. Erosion was coming down all over us like a mighty mountain avalanche.

The price tag of our marriage was getting expensive and we still had the tax bill to pay. Our fun, passion and enchantment evaporated like steam on a hot summer's day. The loss of the Raytheon account set us up for other areas of contention. Losing faith in his wisdom, I would not give him permission to run us through again.

After losing our Raytheon business, Luis wanted me to get a job-job, right now. It was obvious that we should have kept our Raytheon business, but Luis was not about to admit he was wrong. Resentment grew in both our hearts, but he was the one who goofed up, not me.

Impact Seminars
I began working with youth and families again and deeply desired to build the program. Giving meaning and identity to others was part of my life calling. I was especially burdened with youth statistics. Low self-purpose; lack of vision and misplaced identity causes too many regrettable circumstances to occur. Too many youth and their families continually fall through the cracks of life. I wanted to help families gain functionality and the wisdom needed to prevent and overcome obstacles.

My purpose depended on helping families win, because destinies are at stake. The seminars helped us earn some additional income. There were times when "Impact" easily attracted new clients and revenue. I had taught and ministered to thousands of participants over the years and believed God for His best.

Now, with the Raytheon misstep, I believed I should hold on to my ministry calling. I was not about to give up another dream to a man who had no vision. It was disappointing enough that our blessing was completely gone!!! And Luis was the perpetrator of our lack. He should have known better. He was the reason our income suffered. I would not trust my providence to him again. I conveyed, "Luis, I trusted you when you gave away our business. We lost thousands of dollars so this time you are going to have to trust me."

I thought Luis should do more to develop his spirit and wisdom. He needed to know how to walk by faith. He would not decide for me again. How could I just stop doing my life's assignment? I had to obey God, not him. Years before, I had personally heard God speak to me, audibly. "Preach the Word!" I had to do this ministry and obey Him. I had to try to prosper minds, futures, and families. Luis had crossed the line asking me to let that go too. Chera, an old friend said to him, "How can you marry someone knowing who they are and ask them not to be who they are?" Right! My sentiments exactly! Impact Ministry was valuable to God, even if it was not producing lots of money. I was not giving up my calling, because of his blooper.

In my folly, Like Samson in the Bible, he knew not that his strength was gone when he who awoke to fight the Philistines. I thought, if I worked harder, a financial breakthrough would come, but failed to notice that I had no anointing to build. The harder I worked; the farther behind I got. Talking to God, I said: "Please come on, I'm your child, and I'm a hard worker. Help me! Your Word promises that You will financially prosper your children. What about me? We have to show Luis that You told me to do this."

What a wayward prayer huh? However, God was not about to reward me in this season of disobedience. No matter how hard I beat my very dead program, it would not live. With the growing disharmony in our lives, there was no atmosphere for building or blessings.

Mistakenly, I believed I needed a little more time to turn the business around! Another week or two would do it. Just one more push; but on tainted ground, I couldn't see that I was gambling on building a program void of grace. Success was nonnegotiable for me, but not God. This is when I should have listened to Luis. I was trying to do the ministry in my own might, without God's voice or guidance. But spiritual blindness inevitably comes with disobedient relationships.

I wanted to contribute more to my family's financial status, but even with all my hope and aspiration, eventually there was no more energy to continue. Impact Seminars sputtered and spit, but nothing came out … I was the one who had fallen through the cracks this time. Now I was the new blunder and couldn't see I was royally missing it.

My lack of financial contribution and business expense created more stress and reasons for Luis to agree with relationships outside our marriage. Nothing was good enough for him now. I was not helping him achieve the status quo he desired. Luis wanted to live the great American dream yesterday, but our illegal relationship, subdued the blessing.
"The foolishness of man subverts his way and ruins his affairs; then his heart is resentful and frets against the Lord." (Proverbs 19:3)

Test of fire
According to the Word of God, every marriage is tested by fire. The fire of God proves what is obedient or disobedient. Only that which remains after the fire can go into the future. But insubordination creates disharmony and touches every significant part of our thinking, motivation, feeling, behavior and self-evaluation.

Information surfaced during our sixth year of marriage that Luis was involved with a lady from his second job; the "Family Preservation Center." I walked into a Christmas party with him and noticed that one of his lady coworkers was not cordial. She was attractive and equally unfriendly, and she was really "hating on me!" One of his coworkers called me a few days later to say, "Susan is trying to get her hooks into Luis, and he is allowing it to happen. Be careful, because she has had venereal diseases." She also said, "Dorothy, you don't seem like the passive type. I hope you will inform Luis of her past."

I was becoming more concerned about Luis' depth of wisdom with women. He was always so eager to prove himself. He wanted others to know that he was a stimulating conversationalist. Luis loved the attention of attractive women and knew how and when to be delightful. I expressed my feelings, "Luis, you can't just go to lunch with the girls at work. If you do, it won't be long before an attachment grows. You're a married man, you can't be so friendly." He'd shun my words and say, "I'm not doing anything wrong - stop being insecure!" Luis didn't believe that when you walk on coals of fire (sensual arousal) you will get burned. Sooner or later, it's true; affections connect and emotions dominate our decisions.

I sensed that Luis might be charmed by Susan, but didn't feel too much uneasiness about it. When I asked him about her, he down-played the event and said nothing was going on and assured me of his devotion. I felt secure in his love and let the matter go. However, I did think about a discussion we had during courtship. Luis said, "Dorothy, I'm sincerely praying that I will always treat you right." He was really saying, "Lord; help me be faithful to my wife." Knowing himself, he knew what he was capable of doing again. During our season of bedazzlement those words were not important, but they were more important now.

Jamul
Nuisances and setbacks, continued to pile on from every direction. Jamul was outspoken, charismatic and loving. He was a young boy with great spiritual discernment and knew that Luis slighted him. They were seldom warm and fuzzy towards each other. Luis, as the adult was responsible for building an affirmative atmosphere, but he seldom tried. Jamul was not about to allow Luis to take his dad's place, especially because he slighted him and he felt left out at times. Jyndia absorbed most of our attention with her medical needs. He loved his little sister and respected her needs, but was just an adolescent himself. Like most children, he wanted his mom and dad back together.

Jamul always alleged that Luis was detached, flirtatious and too military. Luis' staunchness and strictness mostly agitated him. Jamul felt, "If you don't love me, I won't love you." He made his feelings known and mentally put Luis in the "You're not right" category. Sometimes the tension was so thick; it was enough to "fog up" the whole house. Their hostility made you squirm. They needed to see something more in each other, but psychologically, they muddied each other.

I'd tell Luis, "Be kinder to Jamul; he's just a boy. Didn't you play when you were a child? You can't make him become a military man overnight. He can't sit straight all day long and read books; he's a boy." But Luis seemed to expect him to grow up, right now. Jamul naturally wanted to follow in his dad's and brother's paths; they both played college basketball. I believed sports would help Jamul gain more confidence and focus too. Basketball would also contribute to good grades. I went with my instincts and allowed him to play. Otherwise, we'd see more rebellion coming from a disappointed teen. Jamul needed all the positive reinforcement he could get. (Divorce is devastating for our children). But Luis felt I took sides with Justin, who was the least of my concerns. What a mess!

Jamul grew angrier as the years progressed. By age thirteen, he knew our marriage was different too. When I was away, He noticed that Luis would have lengthy, sensual, phone conversations. Luis seldom invited Jamul to go to youth events with him at the youth center." He made excuses weekly. I said, "Luis, you work with a program that helps preserve boys and families; why won't you take Jamul with you? Aren't you mentoring young boys his age?" Of course, he was, but Luis didn't want Jamul to go and hear or see what he was doing. (Hey, weren't they supposed to be stabilizing families in there? But, Luis was busy preserving his own agenda).

James
My oldest son James lived in Kansas City. He was growing into a strong Christian man. Thankfully he was away from all our distresses. He had seen enough difficulty and struggle with his dad and me, but was still not sold on Luis. James always believed Luis had a hidden itinerary. He'd say, "Mom, I don't trust him no matter how hard I try. I just don't trust him." There I was with two sons, who robustly disliked my husband. Anxiety squeezed into every single crack it could find.

A senior citizen knew
Luis' dalliances never challenged me before, but he had authentically changed. Like a rock star, he had to have his adoring responses. He so badly needed the applause of women and women willingly gave him his emotional fixes! (It still amazes me that some women are so bold with married men). But they connected with an inner knowing that he was obtainable. My praise and admiration was commonplace by now. I could not compete with or suffice his growing lust-filled appetite. Luis sat dangerously close to wild fires. He moved past flirtation and took passion into his own realm of existence. An eighty-year-old saint told her daughter; "Dorothy's husband has a twinkle in his eye." What? If she could see that sparkle in his eyes, then what were the young ladies seeing? I was in big trouble! (How I wished I had listened to the voice of God at the gate, years before).

Insecurity
Security and peace are heartfelt, and love is a spiritual thing. When your mate is faithful, you know they are committed to you. You can sit down, cross your legs and rock away in the sun. All is good with the world! – But, when something is disconnected, you know that too! Nobody has to tell you that your mate is different. When they are playing around, everything changes - You begin to feel an exposure. It's as though the door is open. Your spiritual covering is gone or it feels like your dress is up in the back. You can feel a breeze blowing! You somehow feel a timidity and anxiety, like clouds gathering before the rain storm.

When infidelity is conceived, the break of security is spiritually known. Our internal alarms and sirens noisily rage within …God has put within us the heart status of our mates. The information is translated with accuracy. Spiritually, we know what we need to know, as we should. I'll put it this way, when you get the feeling, you're not the only one - you're not! You know without a doubt that another "person" is in your sacred, spiritual space. That other someone, is one, some-one, too many!

A demonic dream
Before, I tangibly knew about Luis' most obvious affair, God revealed his unfaithfulness in dreams. He kept me posted, even though I didn't want any part of the truth. I still wanted to be Luis' greatest cheerleader. One of those dreams portrayed Luis and I riding in a limousine. We enjoyed the evening together when suddenly, an evil demon jumped out of the dark, onto the back of the limousine! The hideous demon rode on the trunk for miles and beat gruelingly on the back window! Luis turned around and tried to hold the glass in place. But against the demon's great strength, the glass broke!

Luis fought valiantly trying to counter the demon. They fought for a long time, but the demon overpowered him -- pulling Luis out of the back window! The execution was vicious and bloodcurdling! Positioned on my knees, I glared out the back window, shocked out of my senses. I begged the driver to stop and help Luis! I cried and screamed, watching my husband roll over, repeatedly; fighting with a malicious demon. Again, I begged the chauffeur to stop and help … but he kept driving, as I watched my husband trundle to the side of the road.

Without expression, the chauffeur kept speeding down the road. He would not stop! He never looked back or seemed to care. I sat down in the seat shattered, sobbing and afraid. Confused, I held my head in my hands. When I opened my eyes, an older lady sat to my left, unmoved. Clothed in black funeral clothes, she looked straight ahead; however, I did feel a bit of comfort from her presence. I awoke abruptly! I longed to know what had happened to Luis. Was he dead or alive? And why hadn't that disinterested chauffeur stopped to help him? I was tormented!

The dream meant that Luis tried hard at first to resist the demon of self-desire, but finally lost his heated battle to the spirit of lust. He did not respect the enemy of lust and negated its vicious demanding power. Given permission, lust easily defeats us and wins every time it is given opportunity. It is a brutish fighter. Luis authorized its presence and the demon was given power to rear its ugly head.

Luis had already enabled the demon to pull him out of his marriage by opening himself to other women. The fight was spiritual, from within. In the end, he could not prevail over his own agreement with evil. Luis willingly gave Satan authority to rule and break the protective glass of our marriage, when he renounced his integrity. He did this long before he lay on the side of the road. There were two important reasons why Luis was overpowered. First, he needed *deliverance* from a spirit of lust long before we met, and he needed a pure heart before the Lord.

The demon in its appropriate ugly, grotesque form represented the obnoxiousness of the spirit and act of lust in God's eyes. God knows when empowered, lust swiftly devours and punishes. Therefore, He tells us to be on guard, by filling ourselves with His life and turning away quickly from flattery and gazing. With strong hearts full of God's Word, we are able to stop Satan's dark, terminating ability that wrathfully sentences us to death.

The older lady sitting beside me represented a mourner. She was showing me that our relationship was dead and over. The black limousine symbolized a funeral vehicle; it swiftly carried me away from the burial. (Cars often represent life movement in dreams). I was forced to move on, screaming and kicking regardless of what I thought or felt. Unwillingly, my heart, mind, and soul had to go on. The chauffeur represented the Holy Spirit; He is not moved by our emotions. He will not jeopardize His position with God, by allowing us to continually dwell in a wrong situation. He doesn't give us what we want, no matter how hard we cry and fall out, unless He has God's Signature on it.

The Holy Spirit is in the earth to do God's job. His mission in my situation was to eject disorder and to move me into obedience. He had to get me where I needed to go. He was not about to stop and help Luis get back into the car, (my life) against God's plan for me. That was that! It didn't matter that my (seemingly) precious gift from God was dead on the side of the road, rolling and tumbling with a demon. The Holy Spirit had a job to do and He did it! He moved me away from my waywardness, knowing I could not do it myself. I had to be driven out of an unfounded relationship. My pain was good pain, as far as Holy Spirit was concerned. Luis was put out, because we could not defy God's will and desire in His universe. No discussion!

Sad awakening
The dream filled my soul with waves of terror. Waking up, I felt doomed. I wanted to go back to sleep to try to change what I saw. I'm sure the Lord was

saying, "Can you hear me now?" I could hear Him loud and clear, but unfortunately, I wondered if the devil might be trying to confuse me. (Oh yes, you know we know how to rationalize). After a while, I denied and resisted the magnitude of the dream. I didn't want it to be true. I wanted to blame the devil and a spirit of fear and believe I should fight for our marriage. That had to be the true heart of God. I could not bring myself to tell Luis about the dream. It would have to be my secret for now. If I told him, I would be admitting that it was true or that our marriage was doomed. Regardless of my denial, the collapse of our marriage was still in motion.

A woman between us
I continued to deal with disturbing dreams. After establishing a personal relationship with Jesus, I had become quite the prophetic dreamer. The dreams were vivid and hurtful; God used them to speak to my inner wisdom.

… As my husband and I rode down the street in our car, a woman sat boldly between us. Looking at her, I wondered, Lord, why is this lady sitting between me and my husband, in our car! "God I'm so tired of these awful dreams and why is Amy riding between my husband and me?" I sweltered, fumed, and was traumatized; still not wanting to face the truth. I also noticed that Luis comfortably allowed her to be there without criticism or discomfort.

The dream was so real and I knew who she was. She was someone I didn't like very much. She was uppity and oh, so fake! She was known to be cool and self-centered and had a high scale position in city government. She clearly went for what she wanted. I talked a friend into going with me to spy on her house. I needed to see if Luis showed up there; he was certainly showing up somewhere. We waited several hours and nothing happened. He never came! Hum, if it wasn't Amy, then who was it? He was leaving home to see somebody! (I couldn't believe myself. "Oh, God, I am spying on my husband. I have turned into a very desperate Christian housewife!)"

I asked Luis if Amy was the woman he was seeing. He said, "I'm not seeing anyone. You have problems. I'm not doing anything, stop being insecure!" Other times he'd mockingly say, "Since you're so spiritual, you should know if there is someone else." Jeering contemptuously and smiling – he'd say, "Why don't you tell me who it is? Don't you know? Hasn't God told you?" Other times, he acted insulted and offended. What an actor! This was not the man I knew. His responses were no longer comforting or sincere.

The woman in the dream was not the actual person Luis was seeing. It is vital to remember that dreams are most often types, shadows and figures. They don't necessarily represent the actual person or place. This woman represented the type of person Luis was seeing. She was very much like the figurative person in the dream. That part was true. She was truly brazened enough to ride between a man and his wife.

(If God had not helped me apply the data correctly and if I had accused Amy or shown up at her house, I might have been locked away from that day, till now. "Whew! - Thank you Lord! She was not home and for keeping me from acting on feelings and limited knowledge)."

Whatever is in you, comes out
My husband's true colors had emerged with claws unveiled. He really was a womanizer and a remarkable con artist after all! He continued to redirect my concerns with, "You're the one creating all the anxiety. I leave because you are stressing me out." Whatever manual Luis read from had taught him well, or had he gotten his skills through a great deal of education and practice. Yes, he had every reason to be defensive. I was a hurting, angry, betrayed woman; watching his every move. He worked to cover his tracks. I tried to uncover them, as if I needed to!

I guarantee you this; you can write this down. When your mate is betraying you; your insecurity will grow like weeds. My feeling of anxiety and fear increased daily. Simultaneously, I was trying to keep the marriage together. I exclaimed, "Oh my God, I can't hold my peace any longer. This is too insulting. Who is this man? He is pretending that dust in the house is the reason he's leaving to lay with his woman!"

Luis found every excuse in the world to leave. (Craziness - Insanity)! He performed the white glove tests on glass shelves or found small spider webs to keep the blame and light on me. He had to validate his behavior somehow. Sleeping with someone else mandated that he had to keep his wife off balanced, as much as possible! Luis had gone as far as saying he needed to jog or wash the car at midnight, all dressed up! How disrespectful!

Of course, nothing was right. He'd bring up past issues and matters we had settled and released long before. He looked hard for faults, told countless lies and constantly picked fights. How could he imply that I didn't appreciate him? He knew I did. I was committed, but Luis willingly bent low to put his indiscretion on my back. I had heard about how ruthless a mate can be when they are involved with someone else, but I couldn't believe my eyes.

Praying and trying to save our marriage, I did the typical things. I tried to remind him of how we believed God had put us together. I reminded him that we were proud ministers of the Gospel. I made the changes that bothered him. I stopped the program and kept Jyndia and Jamul quiet and happy. I set the dinner table beautifully, lost weight, firmed up and cleaned house. It was the shiniest one on the block. Nothing was out of place - all the spider webs gone.

The breaking of a marriage covenant is spiritually dynamic. It happens long before words are spoken. According to the Bible, when lust or sin is fully-grown, it brings forth death, devastation and regret. That described our marriage perfectly. Luis' season of enticement with other women bloomed. His affair was full-blown in stages of high level passion; while our marriage daily disintegrated. We had acted independent of God's will and rebelliously tried to meet our own needs.

During our happier times, Luis would laugh and say, Dad told me and my brothers, "Sons don't lose your head over a little piece of tail!" … hum … Luis had not followed his Dad's good advice. He had certainly lost his head over a little piece of tail!

Lust has taken down kings and urchins alike. Egotistical, haughty and naive people seldom escape its tentacles, because we refuse to protect our souls. We cannot see or believe the devastating wreckage behind the thrills of lust, until it is too late. Only trust in the Blood of Jesus is strong enough to help us run quickly enough to break its reprehensible pull. Protective living is learning how to guard our eyes and hearts through fearing the consequences of going our own way. God arduously tries to speak before the tentacles and claws of lust and desire ripen.

> "Many waters cannot quench (lust) love; neither can the floods drown it. If a man would give all the substance of his house for love, it would utterly be despised." (Song of Solomon 8:6-7)

The seven-year scratch
By our seventh year of marriage, I hardly knew this cold-hearted, devilish man. I wondered how I could have believed he was a blessing from God. He was gone all hours of the night; his common impertinent rule and chosen pattern. At night, my imagined gift from God would brush his teeth, wash quietly and leave. My immoral husband was smitten, bitten and obsessed. He happily rolled with the demon in the dust, on the side of the road.

> "A prudent man foresees the evil and hides himself, but the simple pass on and are punished." (Proverbs 27:12 and 22)

> "Whoever strays from the path of the prudence will rest in the assembly of shadows." (Proverbs 21:16)

> "Insolent and haughty, the name is detractor. Overwhelming pride marks such behavior." (Proverbs 21:24)

HAPPINESS A STRANGE FRUIT — Chapter 4

Relationships appearing dynamic are often not from God...

"Wisdom calls aloud in the streets. She raises her voice in the public squares. She calls out at the street corner. She delivers her messages at the city gates. You simple people, how much longer will you cling to your simple ways? How much longer will mockers revel in their mocking and fools go on hating knowledge? Pay attention to my warning. If you listen, I will pour out my heart and tell you what I have to say." Proverbs 1:20-23)

There is a generation of people that are pure in their own eyes. Yet not washed from their filthiness. There is a generation, oh, how lofty are their eyes! Their eyelids are lifted. (Proverbs 30: 12-13)

What a terrible decision I made allowing Luis in my life. After months of denial and worrying, it was obvious that our failure to hear God's voice mounted an indomitable tower against us. I knew my husband and our future was slipping away. Our relationship might have looked like oceanfront scenery on the outside, but underneath we lived in sinking, murky sand. Our lives unraveled like an old pair of shoestrings. I paled beneath his betrayal. I asked God, "Where are the strong and principled Christians when you need them?" I hoped that someone might talk some sense into Luis. However, his Christian friends were imprudent, unethical and passive. Satan had strategically situated the "right cast" to carry out his plan for destruction. These caustic, churlish individuals were in place to do his bidding.

Job's comforters
Was there anyone who would help us stand for the sanctity of marriage? Luis' friends pretty much agreed that he should do what he felt like doing. They had little interest in helping us turn our sinking ship around. I wondered if anyone sincerely tried to influence him to stay committed to his family. Did anyone tell him what God said about marriage?

Lyle was an incongruent evangelist, full of irreligious poison. He was certainly one of the devil's advocates, assigned to help in the chiseling away of our relationship. The waves were boisterous and high Lyle came to visit me. (I understood how Job of the Bible felt when his associates arrived). Lyle and Luis were as thick as thieves. He said, "Luis is a woman magnet. He can't help it that women desire him." I answered, "We can't stop admirers, but allowing your magnetism to be a sexual tool can be stopped! Being attractive was not Luis' problem, but making himself available was." Lyle continued, "You have to give your man the same amount of time to get out of this affair, as it took him to get into it."

We needed a righteous counselor, someone who would boldly confront Luis' sin. Lyle was not the one! (Glad he wrote no books on marriage restoration). He had lived his life as a womanizer too and spoke according to what he knew. He said, "Dorothy, you don't throw your man out, just because he lies with another woman. All men will take their "pencil" out of their pocket sometime! Remember, you're going to have to give him all the time he needs!" He went on to tell me that another woman tried to entice Luis. She left a key for him at his job. He showed up at her hotel room, but left before anything happened. Lyle said I should be patient and proud that Luis left the hotel without sexual involvement. I was speechless! Had the man lost his mind?

In the middle of my crisis and misery, when my world was falling apart, he came with a double-edge blade. Sadly, this evangelist could have done so many mighty things for God. He was an anointed preacher, but allowed a spirit of deceit, lust and jealousy to fallaciously use him. He could have helped Luis choose to be a holy man, but he heartened and esteemed infidelity. For years, he told Luis about pastors who were involved with other women. "Lord, tell me; do you have a place to put shameful, forked tongue evangelists, at least until they repent? Please close the door tight, so no one else is released!"

Once our marriage was over, Lyle was long gone. He and his wife divorced too. He was trying to maintain two households; one with his wife of five years and one with someone in another city. Years later, Lyle told me he regretted leading Luis astray. He wished he had encouraged him to be strong in the Lord. I responded, "Lyle, it's too late now to apologize. Some things can never be reversed. Some doors can never be opened again, once they are closed. When you had the opportunity to make a difference, you filled Luis' head with trash and added to his weakness."

Mark
The devil's bad boys were all in place. Mark, one of Luis' best friends was another player with a leading role in our demise. He was conveniently a great promoter of the devil's dirty work. He knew exactly what to do for his architect.
When Mark called for Luis, he'd sheepishly say with humor, "Can Luis come out to play?" I wasn't sure what to think of a grown man, saying such a foolish thing. However, his sinister words were full of truth. They did go out to play.

Mark was experienced and street- wise; he masterfully helped men have their secret affairs. He (the devil) liked the drama of seeing marriages fall apart. I could literally see horns sticking from both sides of his head! Luis allowed himself to foolishly connect with a man like Mark. His terrible reputation went before him. For years, he had covered for other married men too and their mistresses. Mark stood in the shadows hiding and smirking as usual as a friend's husbands got himself involved with another man's girlfriend. A fight ensued which took her boyfriend's life. Sadly, her executive husband ended up in court and jail. Thousands of dollars were spent from their life savings.

Mark blocked and covered for Luis too. He would come to our home pretending to pick him up to listen to jazz. I always questioned their friendship saying, "Luis, we are Christians, we are in ministry, why are you going to jazz clubs with Mark, a single man? Mark has no dedication to Jesus Christ." Luis would seldom answer. It was painful to see my husband go back to his party lifestyle, thinking he was committed to the Lord. But ... well; didn't I meet him in a club? Luis had simply reverted back to type. Mark and Luis were not that different? The truth was their souls matched perfectly! God tried to tell me that when I met Luis.

"See a man wise in his own conceit and philosophies? There is more hope for a fool than for him." (Proverbs 26:12)

The people we allow in our inner circles are always a reflection of who we really are. If you want to know who your mate is, look at their closest friendships. Show me their confidants and I'll show you their character. We simply attract people, just like we are on the inside; "good or bad. Luis was also a slick figure of a deceived man. Luis and Mark needed a real relationship with a personal Savior. Mark quickly faded from the scene of our lives when his assignment was over.

Family reunion
One of the last things Luis and I did together was travel to his family reunion in Mississippi. I worked hard to talk him into going. I hoped our drive together might help him remember our (seemingly) great love. Perhaps the romantic fires would blow again. If he'd just bring a little butane, we might be on our way to reconciliation. Perhaps, he'd remember how much I meant to him at one time

While driving late into the night, Luis was very sleepy. I awoke, with a loud scream, just in time. "Luis, there's a car on our side of the road!" Luis swerved, and maneuvered our screeching car and barely missed the coming automobile! In a moment, without notice, we might have all been dead! How terrifying! We panicked and held our breath! "Thank you, God, for keeping our car on the road." I urged Luis and Jamul to praise the Lord for saving us as Jyndia cried uncontrollably. Luis remained uncommunicative and curt, even after all of that! He did nothing to comfort his family.

I could hardly believe he allowed his new attraction to isolate him to that degree. I felt as if our lives were just as bad, as a devastating head-on car wreck! The carnage is oh, so devastating. I could see the power of his deception. Adultery rips the stationary partner's heart out, one vein at a time; just like a head on car collision. Perhaps, this was another foreshadowing and forewarning of our defeated, shattered, marriage. I still did not want to believe what God told me the night I met Luis.

Luis couldn't tell his family why we were estranged, but would disappear for long periods to talk to Lacy, his present girlfriend. I had no power to keep him away from her, not even a thousand miles away. I thought about how our trips used to be talkative, fun and full of life, but this one was dull, long and so very boring. Luis offered no love, life or energy. He was aloof, detached, and oh, so hateful. It was difficult pretending, so I asked his family to pray for us and wished we had not gone. I could hardly believe I knew and loved this man.

When we returned from our miserable pretend vacation, I took a job trying to do all I could to save our marriage. I was willing to do it his way. No one wants a divorce! Nothing mattered; Luis' and Lacy's connection continued to burn like California wild fires. But I would stand my ground! Lacy and Satan were not going to take our marriage. Marriage in general is worth fighting for! I'd rest in the Lord at times and bolster myself in Him. I'd say, "Have faith in God, Dorothy - Don't give up yet!" However, I couldn't come to grips with the fact that I was fighting for what God was not fighting for!

Luis' Mother
Luis and I fought more and more about his affair. I confronted and cried; he lied and denied. One day, to my amazement, in the middle of my growing depression, his mother called. Her urgency surprised me. She seemed hurt about a dream. She asked, "What is going on down there? I feel turbulence!" In her dream, she saw Luis walking away from God! How insightful! I was so happy that God spoke to her. I could finally let it all out! I could share my pain with someone. I spilled out tears faster than a newborn baby. "Oh God, somebody knows and understands!" God was showing her what Luis was doing. My husband's ungodly affair was on His "hit list." He was finally exposed.

I hoped God would use her words to turn things around. Was this the breakthrough I was praying for? Surely, Luis would see the magnitude of his sins now! She said, "I knew something was wrong, because in my dream he was walking away from God." That night she called Luis to express her concern. He assured her, "all was well." He was just leaving home each night, because he was stressed. He denied his true agenda and told her, "He had no problem with God." It was so disrespectful to put God in a "no problem" category. I thought, "You have no problem with a Holy God in the middle of your lust fest!? But much is lost with the cost of disobedience.

The conversations with his mother went on for a few months. She tried to counsel us, but Luis kept lying, engineering and bearing false witness against me. He vented, "I am not having an affair; my wife is just imagining things or has fallen off the deep end! She is just being insecure!" Why couldn't he just tell the truth! Finally, she disregarded the dream and took Luis' side. He was convincing and an excellent detractor and obstructer of truth. Losing her friendship was amid my saddest of moments. I loved and missed her. I was hurt that she believed his lies. I encouraged her to counsel her son righteously. As Christians, we were responsible to speak the truth, son or not.

The most difficult and astonishing element for me was how Luis could lie to her and others the way he did, about me! Why would he need to make me look like a bad, deranged person? How could he twist his tongue this way to lie about someone he once loved and someone who loved him …? Why couldn't he just admit he let his guard down or was choosing to get out of his marriage? I couldn't believe that Luis would lie about me, that way!!! This was incomprehensible! His lies were as bad as the offence of adultery he committed. I questioned this again and again ... How could he, paint me with such a lying, degrading brush, in the worst light possible! His mistakes had been far worse than mine! He had given away our business, his integrity, his faithfulness and our marriage. I was the one standing for it! What could be shoddier than that? Didn't he fear God at all?

The duffel bag
Luis was coming home from a two-week army reserve trip. I prayed that he had missed us. Perhaps God had touched his heart by now. By autumn, of our seventh year of marriage, fasting and praying, I dared to believe that we might have a wonderful family evening. But, mysteriously, he came home walking down the street, dressed in regular clothing. Something wasn't right and why wasn't a male friend dropping him off like before?

Luis seemed happy about something, but it wasn't me. He was not interested in hugging or talking. I quickly felt his derision. He was evasive and ambiguous. I was happy to see him and tried to show it, but before long he made his usual excuses to leave. He remained elusive all weekend. I knew what had happened, but was too weary to confront him again. After all, who walks home after two-weeks of military duty? Who does that? I chose not to fight or react.

When I took Luis to work that Monday, I noticed, he kept clutching an army duffel bag, not letting it out of his sight. Rushing to get to work he forgot to stop by the cleaners. When he arrived, he reacted strongly to forgetting. I asked, "Do you want me to take your clothes to the cleaners?" He answered stalwartly, "No! I will do it myself!" He was uneasy and angry. His response significantly heightened my suspicion. I was now enormously aware of the mysterious duffel bag. When he got out of the car I planned to look, but was distracted by heavy traffic. My heart was so oppressed and wayward in this season of falling leaves that I focused on driving and forgot to look. I was lost in my pain as usual. My marriage was dissolving before my eyes.

When alone, I'd think, declare marriage scriptures and pray. I needed lots of emotional strength for survival. My mind was double-minded and full of fear and hope for reconciliation. My husband's infidelity and disrespect was more than I could grasp. I never expected Luis to act like this. Our lives seemed to belong to someone else now. Picking Luis up, he got in the car and abruptly wanted to know, "Where is my duffel bag!" I said, "It's still in the back seat." Now, with absolute silence in the car, he was waiting to see if I looked. He seemed relieved with my silence. I kicked myself, "Why did you forget to look in that bag?"

Luis stopped by the cleaners without delay. He held the duffel bag tightly going through the door. Luis took me home, dry and removed and proceeded to his second job, preserving families. By now, all my suspicions were back! I had to know, what was in that bag? How did I forget to look? I had that bag all day long! But it was time to muster up courage. I had to know; I needed proof to confront Luis.

The cleaner was only ten minutes from our home, so despite my fears I began to walk. By the time I entered, I had come up with a reason to ask to see his clothes! I told the attendant, my husband just dropped off clothing. I need to check to make sure a credit card was not left in a pocket. (So sorry God, I desperately lied)! When the attendant handed me his shirts, I thought I would collapse in the middle of the floor. The hair stood up on the back of my neck. My God! The fronts of Luis shirts were covered with brown make up. I was absolutely shocked! I stood there with my mouth open! I was sure I would faint or die.

I walked home shaking, trembling and comatose. I didn't think I'd live another minute! I would crumble in the street. It had to be the Lord that helped me walk home that day; in wobbling and quivering steps. Perhaps He transported me ... Possibly, the angels carried me home! I was devastated and distraught. I was a walking dead woman. My world and hope had grown completely dark and destitute in minutes. The evidence was boldly there in my face. I could no longer repudiate the truth.

The love of my life was truly having a full-fledged, rotten affair! God was right! He was undeniably committing adultery! He was not a good man, but was a liar. He was not special, but a regular dog! Luis had not been serving our country at all! He was serving Lacy and his own flesh. He had smiled and charmed his way into another woman's heart and bed. "Yes Lord, you were right, he is a womanizer!" The sun deflated, renouncing the end of our marriage. But what was I to do? I was not prepared for this. My hopes destroyed. Everything in me furiously yelled! *"My husband is sleeping with another woman!!!"*

Arriving home, I sat down and cried, dying a million times over. "Not my husband, Lord, please, not my marriage!" I decided to call him at work to say, we needed to talk. I asked him to honk when he got home and I would come out. We decided to go to a local park to talk. I told him I knew about the shirts and makeup and asked why he was destroying his marriage. Never in a million years did I predict his retort ... (Hold onto your hat) ... This answer came from the heart of a true professional, womanizing demon, a fully armed terrorist! Luis was an expert! In the middle of my betrayal and grief, he said, "I don't know what you're talking about, maybe the makeup is yours!" ... WHAT! ... WHAT? ...

WHAT? ... I could hear the sound of many "AFRICAN DRUMS AND SHRIEKS in my head!" (People have been taken out for less)!

I looked at him in amazement ... I had met the master of deceit, in person. Within the corridors of my psyche, deep fear, pain and emotion emerged! I could see Luis was entirely worldly, smooth and well-skilled. I was out of my league. I had seen movies of men scheming to drive their wife's crazy, but how could he play me this raggedy? This was sheer evilness! Were we on the Jerry Springer Show? Was this moment real? I was dumbfounded and speechless! "My makeup!!!" How callous! How barbaric! Even a person with severe psychological problems would remember the scenario that took place with those shirts! I was beyond life and humiliation! Silently, we started home. Who was this very wicked man (demonic spirit) sitting beside me? I knew him not.

Enormous fear, is no way to live
I tried to gain my composure. To top this off, he dared to argue to delude and protect himself. In the face of makeup all over several shirts, He said, "How could you accuse me of such a thing? You have disrespected my manhood (What an ego this lying demon had)!" I shockingly zoned out, but could not believe my ears! I expected him to repent and change his direction. Luis proceeded to say, "If you are going to accuse me and be suspicious, then I am going to leave. I'm not going to put up with your allegations. I am not going to jump through hoops."

There was no repentance but ruthlessness! I was not prepared for his response and shroud of lies. Finding proof was supposed to bring clarity, but I was being told, (non-verbally) to shut up and put up with this woman or Luis would leave the family. God knew I knew nothing about deception on this level!

The substantiated truth failed to help our marriage. Our conversation turned from the verification of makeup, to me being put under the microscope. His pretense of ill-deserved incrimination was of course a game that the guilty play and Luis was proficiently established. (How much practice did he have)? His discourse was better than Johnny Cochran defending O.J. In dismay I thought, "This could not be the same man that swept me off my feet and promised to give me a wonderful life!"

Again, I thought he might cry, repent and promise to break it off. His words, "I will leave, if you don't stop accusing me," threatened my very existence. I shook and shuddered in the dark. Terror of the unknown caused enormous fear to enter my mind. I was not prepared to make it on my own; neither did I want a divorce. I didn't want the truth to be true either. I wanted peace and reconciliation.

I made a life-changing, life-degrading mistake. (Listen, no matter how afraid you are, never, never, never do this! Never give away your self-respect or leverage, not even if you must live on a park bench for a minute. I emphatically tell you, you must trust in your God and He will make a way out of no way for you!) I said, "Why are you talking about leaving? We can work this out. We have had a good marriage and good life together. We can do it again. We are supposed to be together Luis." These were the words he counted on to seal his ungodly plans. He already knew I did not want a divorce or I would have put him out long before the shirt incident evolved. But, I would love to relive the sequence of events from that evening all over again, and especially that moment. (I can't, but at least I can try to help you react differently).

Because we don't know God, we are often too afraid of the unfamiliar and afraid to exercise tough love. Yes, it takes a lot of knowing and trusting God to venture out into the abyss, when it looks like a chasm in the earth is going to swallow you up. When we are afraid and don't know what to do, or where to go we too often submit ourselves to absolute disrespect and contempt, instead of jumping into God's arms. This is always wrong. <u>Once the respect is gone from a relationship, everything is gone!</u>

Even though, I wasn't ready to see my family split up, I certainly should not have shown Luis that I was willing to stay with an unrepentant man. My state of fear helped him pursue the pleasures of his flesh more easily, even while keeping his marriage intact. Luis was saying, "Be deaf and dumb. Leave me alone while I pursue my fantasy. Perhaps in a year or two when I am finished, we'll have a chance to put the pieces back together. Grow up Dorothy, men play around! Put on your big girl panties, this is how the world is today. I need to have a little fun with Lacy now. She's good for my ego. She relieves my stress. Stop being a drag, this won't hurt that much!"

I prayed, "Lord, this fight is bigger than me. I am not prepared to be on my own. What am I supposed to do? I didn't know people lied like this. Why won't he repent?" I had grown apart from Justin gradually, within the course of our long marriage, but this departure was disruptive and heartless! Luis inflicted pitiless, cold-blooded "surgery," without anesthesia. In a short time, we had gone from compatibility and kindness, to harshness, disrespect and dishonor. I kept looking for the old Luis to come back home, the one I knew. I simply could not comprehend this life and where had my husband gone?

Double-minded me
I wanted to see Luis as someone who loved his family. He said he would spend a lifetime with us. I wanted to believe that could still happen. Perhaps God would work all of it out for our good. Vacillating; could this be a part of a victorious testimony someday, or are we over? In sadness and quietness, I tried to detach from the belief that Luis was my gift from God.

"God, where are you? Can't we work this out?" Collections of thoughts filled my mind. I daily considered our wonderful past, but combined it with our horrible present. If he would just repent, this episode could be over. We could start again, but Luis was worse than a brazen hussy who skillfully built his own justifiable interlay. He convinced himself that sneaking around to see Lacy was alright. He played blissfully in the sun, no matter who he hurt. Now a harsh new reality filled our once buoyant home. Luis was blasting our love and marriage a part moment by moment, but saying he was not going to leave. My anger and melancholy increased as he'd come and go to see Lacy.

When Luis was home, I fluctuated between, "I love you Luis, let's work this out," to "Get out of my house you wretched man!" At times, I tried to lay low, be quiet, and hope. Most days I couldn't do it. No matter how hard I tried, I could not ... I had to let him know, I knew what he was doing, and I knew who he was. I'd say softly and forcefully, "You're not slick! Now go and do what you want to do Judas! But remember, your mess is not concealed from God's eyes! You may fool everyone else, but God and I see you, lecherous man!" Sometimes, I'd reprove him unmercifully; other times, I'd try to reason with him in the spirit of love.

His level of deviousness created anguish and upheaval that daily filled my soul. Our arguments escalated. At times, I stood for my right to be respected, at other times; I'd wait up till he got home to talk. I'd say, "Luis, don't throw your marriage away. From the beginning of time, men have regretted losing their power and blessings to women. Think of Samson and the price David paid in the Bible. Do you want a legacy like that? On and on, I'd try to reason with him. Other times I just disappeared feeling so ashamed and rejected. My husband, my protector had become my crucifier!

I desperately tried to hear from God. I needed guidance, but wrought with indecision; I read marriage books, studied tons of scriptures and prayed with a few true friends. My emotions were off the chart; my spiritual hearing blocked most of the time. I couldn't get centered long enough to wait on God or to rest in His word. I wanted results, but God was trying to prepare me that Luis was going to leave. I would not allow myself to hear or receive these words! I was a woman of faith! I tried to push my will on God's will. "Can't our marriage be saved? Help him let Lacy go!" I twisted God's arm with scriptures and promises that vowed to save marriages. "God, You can bring this to pass for us."

The fence
You don't have to be very smart to figure out something is wrong when you have to sneak around to do it. Luis underestimated the depth of his lust. He thought he was shrewd enough to keep his girlfriend under the radar. Our marriage had deteriorated past the point of no return; so, he was bolder than before. So much that he tried to have Lacy pick him up down the street, without being detected. One night I pretended to leave in our car. I drove around the block and parked by the fence. Seeing the light, he thought I was Lacy and came out of the house. (She'd circle around the block to pick him up. He pretended to be jogging). I saw

him creep out of the house and peek around the side of the fence, hoping to bounce into her car. When he saw me, he panicked and headed full speed back into the house! He looked clueless and confused, like a deer glaring into headlights! I sarcastically asked, "Were you looking for me?" He continued to deny that anything was going on. (You see God knew all of this would happen)!

Luis' decision to connect with Lacy, took our marriage downhill quickly. I walked on eggshells and he ran harder. I had not learned; if someone wants to leave, encourage the sidewinder to go! ... Their leaving is really a gain for us, not a loss. Put them in God's hands and trust Him to take care of you. Oh, if I could have done that quickly, I could have returned to happiness much sooner. But in the fog of war, I could not grasp that I had missed God so badly.

"For a whore (man or woman) is a deep ditch and a narrow pit. He or she lies in wait as for a prey and increases transgressions among men and women." (Proverbs 23:26-27)

"The mouth of an adulterous woman (or man) is a deep pit - Into it falls the man whom Yahweh rebukes." (Proverbs 22:14)

"Lust not after her (his) beauty in your heart, neither let her capture you with her eyelids. A harlot brings a man (woman) to a piece of bread. The adulteress stalks and snares (as with a hook) the precious life of a man. Can a man take fire in his bosom and his clothes not be burned? Can one go upon hot coals and his feet not be burned?" (Proverbs 6:25-28)

"But whoever commits adultery with a woman (man) lacks heart and understanding. He who does it is destroying his own life." (Proverbs 6:32)

Still trying
Luis distanced himself, but remained in our home. He was not ready to leave. What happened to our love story? Unfortunately, my best friend was no more. Our sweet home had become a massive war zone. Our sanctuary gone! We were living separate lives and nothing could stop the fire that burned between Luis and Lacy. I prayed in the spirit, groaned, travailed and fasted; nevertheless, nothing would halt the hand of the devourer! Our seventh year of marriage was only full of finishes. It seemed that a controlling hand from hell had come to claim all its assets!

"So, he (she) who co-habits with his neighbor's wife (adultery and fornication) will be tortured with evil consequences and just retribution. He who touches her shall not be innocent.

Do you see why you must develop the ability to discern correctly and immediately? Selectivity must happen long before emotions, compromise and illusions take hold. You have to know, before proceeding; what God is speaking to you about a potential mate? God knows them. you don't. Later you will become astonished when you see the authentic Machiavellian. The gate of "introduction" is critical. It is a solemn time for spiritual evaluation. This is not the time to enjoy flattery and high expectation.

THE HARVEST   **Chapter 5**

"In the end, he (she) is as bitter as wormwood, sharp as a two-edged sword. His feet go down to hell. Death is the goal of his steps. He is far from the path of life. His ways are movable. <u>You cannot know them</u>. Hear me children. Depart not from the words that I speak. Remove yourself far away from him. Do not come near his door. If you do, you will give your strength and honor to the years of the cruel. Strangers will get your wealth and labors. When your body and flesh are consumed, you will groan and exclaim, alas! I hated discipline and instruction. My heart spurned correction! How I wish I had listened to my teachers and the voice of the Lord!" (Proverbs 5:4-12)

Quiet yourself, if you find yourself in the crucible of fire. Obey, wait on, and have faith in your Lord. He is present. He will give you instruction. When your marriage or relationship is dying, step aside and trust God. He knows and His plans are good for you. Only God knows for sure, but if your relationship needs to die – let it die and if it is the will of the Lord He will resurrect it.

I tried hard to make the scriptures work for my erroneous marriage. My personal faith was not easily obstructed. I knew that God could end the destruction, with a wee stroke of His pen. He could give us a miracle and stop the darkness. - (This represents the confusion of disobedience.) How did our days come down to such evil times? And what is it about that blasted seventh year of marriage that determines if the wheels will fall off some marriages?

Wasn't the remembrance of our purpose somewhere in Luis' heart? No! - Because he perpetually lied to our friends and associates. He told them that I was the problem and pretended to be committed to our marriage. Some sought to counsel me on how to have enough confidence to keep my man. Others were saddened to see what was happening. Most believed what he said. How sad it is not to be believed.

I was long past the gates of peace and conformity and too ashamed to open to others about how terrible Luis was. How do you tell people, "My husband is happily involved in a "grand-slam-affair! - In my face!" My microscopic existence consisted of worry, stress, hope and confusion. My entire focus was for reconciliation.

As much as Luis wanted to bring Lacy out of the shadows, he had to keep her under wraps a while longer. He wasn't ready to physically leave, but had long departed spiritually and emotionally. I waited to hear a new word from the Lord. I wanted to know; should I stand or prepare for another divorce. Wavering back and forth, feeling like my brain would pop; I'd rebuke the devil and command him to go or try to pray. If I felt God was saying, be still and let me do this. I'd complain, "God, I can't do this! This has to stop today!" How could I wait to let insanity take its course? There was no grace to rest in the Lord.

I was a prayer warrior and loved to declare God's Word. I believed, I knew how to make the devil "let go" of my property! I thought I could just grab hold of the horns of the Altar and get my desired result. I'd wait, until God showed up. He'd have to move on my behalf. He had to honor His own Word and marriage. I would just stay in His face and wrestle till morning came. After that, surely, God would change my name, (the situation) and bless me with the inheritance of a strong marriage. I convinced myself; that's exactly what has to happen! But vacillating, "Lord can I trust You to fix us, if I say nothing? Should I totally give up?" (Yes, there is utter confusion in disobedience, because you have given your honor and strength to a cruel demon!)

I'd fight boldly one day, and the next, doubt would descend upon me. I'd ask God; "Won't this affair stop? Please tell me that it will! We, can't let this wickedness win over Your Great Word!" I continued to go the extra mile fasting and praying. I had to keep the pressure on God. I used scriptures like this one: *"Thus says the Lord, refrain your eyes from weeping and tears. Your works will be rewarded. They will come again from the land of the enemy. There is hope for your marriage." (Jeremiah 31:16)*

In my own determination, I'd say. "Now God, You have to get us reconciled according to Your Word. You should reward me and destroy Luis' path of sin." I wanted results! It didn't matter that Luis made no effort to resolve our marriage; I would not accept his coldness as truth. I believed he still had to care. He just didn't know it. The true Luis had to still be in there, somewhere. I could not be 'just nothing' to Luis anymore. I tried to assure myself that God would use this damage to bring a great testimony. We would get a hundred-fold more for all the trouble! We would arise with an earthshaking verification of our purpose together! All I had to do was agree with the Word, and walk by faith a little while longer. *Unfortunately, I would not acknowledge the scriptures only work according to God's preordained will.*

I claimed many other scriptures, trying to twist God's Arm. *"In the same way husbands ought to love their wives as their own bodies. He who loves his wife - loves himself." (Ephesians 5:28)* I set my eyes upon the Lord's goodness and tried to look up. Something had to happen to turn this ship around. The Red Sea would open; even at the last moment! Like Lazarus, something more miraculous would arise. The ashes from our hard times would bring the anointing our marriage needed. Besides, God loves the odds and raising up dead situations. I had seen many relationships reconcile for the better and the devil was not going to win! His plan for devastation would somehow be stopped!

An unbelievable prophecy

Alone, at Church one evening, prophet Ratliff called me out and declared, "You and your husband will come forth in a ministry anointing. You will make a difference for marriages!" On and on he went for twenty minutes in elaborate and visionary tones. I could see a prosperous future come alive again. He declared God would use Luis and me together! Hum? His words gave me hope; until considering Luis' constant refusal to work on our marriage. I wondered, "Is the prophecy true or is this dear man just trying to encourage my very downcast spirit?" I didn't feel the words come alive in my soul; neither did I have a quickening from God.

I so wanted to believe he was right. I tried to rev up my faith, but had no power to do so. I knew that all prophecy should be a confirmation of what God has spoken to you, and God had not said to me that our marriage would be restored. You see, if a prophet says a storm is brewing, you should see the rain clouds forming for yourself. I shared the prophecy with Luis; it fell on anesthetized, aloof ears.

God speaks

God understood my deep sincerity. One night I tossed and turned in bed, continuing to pursue God. I travailed, prayed, declared scriptures and cast out darkness. (Whew, spiritual warfare is lots of work!) But, Luis had to change. Our marriage had to improve. When I quieted myself, I could hear God clearly speak. Finally, being so worn out, I allowed myself to receive his voice and directive, but these were not the words I cared to hear. "My child you have planted a seed of adultery. Your disobedience has created this harvest. No matter how hard you pray, you will have to walk through this field, (Simultaneously, God showed me a vision of a wheat field), all the way to the end. But I will be with you every moment, all the way to the other side."

I was bewildered. His words were intense, but kind. Soberly, I roused myself and knew I had to take responsibility for my own miserable life situation. But, I didn't want to hear that kind of talk! This was not good news. I wanted Him to say, "Hold on my daughter. I will fix Luis' heart in three days!"

God tried to tell me that Luis was planning to leave, but I had not allowed myself to receive the message. Now, I heard God gently and personally tell me to prepare for more change. I responded, "What do you mean? Are you saying you can't reverse the circumstances?" I quarreled, "God, I have repented for moving ahead with Luis. I know I am forgiven! Won't Your forgiveness, change our dilemma?" I debated with Him all evening, wanting to change His convicting words. Surely, God would not hold a few months of dating against us. After all, I hadn't done anything worse than anyone else, and we got married! Why would dating before a divorce was final, be so important?

I had asked God to forgive me. I did regret neglecting His voice and letting Him down. I had grieved and felt guilt for my sins, many times over. Wouldn't God just let that be enough and let us have a good life together now? Wasn't the sin canceled by now? How long can an old sin stick around and do damage anyhow? Wouldn't God bend His righteous laws of seedtime and harvest just a little bit, for me? Dear God! We got married! That should count for something. Didn't marriage purify our adultery? Was I supposed to leave after we took our vows? Wasn't I obligated to work on our marriage now? Weren't we free to go on with our lives?

Repentance in God's eyes means that we must completely turn around, and go the other way, no matter how difficult the situation.

Yes, I had agreed with the world's viewpoint to some degree, but pastors and other spiritual leaders did the same things. It seemed to me, that they got away with their indiscretions, why couldn't I? They repented later and they did just fine. So, what was the difference? I was sure I could do the same thing. After all, didn't God want me to be happy? When I met Luis, I loosened up a bit, like other Christians. I was just trying to be normal! I was released from my first marriage and had peace and a valid spiritual reason for divorcing Justin. Luis and his first wife, Dixon had divorced long before we met. So, what was so bad about what we did?

In pride and ignorance, I spoke to the Lord again. "God, I have conducted myself far better than the average Christian. I have seen Christians that sing and shout in Church doing every manner of evil and they are just fine. I was just following suit. Everybody sins -- but you promised to forgive us. Lord, there are so many pastors that say you understand; so, go ahead and enjoy life. We are only human."

Well, God was not buying my justification for disobedience. God is Holy, and He gives us empowerment to be holy. His forgiveness sets us free but does not cancel a harvest we sowed for. There was no case that I could build, capable of helping me substantiate a good case before God. I had broken his commandment. "You shall not commit adultery!" ... God was not about to lower His high standards for me. I had gone past the gates of obedience and activated the power of sin and death. I could almost hear the bloodhounds of hell arrive for full payment. I was in spiritual trouble and felt a sinking sensation from my head to my toes.

The fear of Yahweh is the beginning of knowledge. Fools spurn wisdom, discipline, regulations, order, and forming good habits. Fools spurn restraints, obedience, harmony, authority, self-control, instructions and training.
(Proverbs 1:7)

The God of the universe had now spoken to me personally! I had sinned against His will, but perhaps in His mercy and grace, He would count my present misery (time served) as full payment. The last year and a half with Luis had certainly been horrible enough. Perchance, the wheat field would only last a day or two more. Other people seemed to get fast turnarounds after trials of faith. In the movie, "Diary of a Mad Black Woman," Kimberly's husband was dealt with quickly and her problem resolved. She came out on top in no time. I hoped for that kind of solution, even if it was just a movie. I wanted nothing to do with that dreadful-looking wheat field. Surely, God would apply all my good works and prayers toward a tranquil deliverance or would the wheat field be do-able? Would our marriage be renewed afterwards?

I hoped I misunderstood His words. And, what would a walk through this unfamiliar wheat field entail? What would the day of my evil harvest feel like? It had surely arrived. I was warned and told to prepare. This season would be more than I comprehended. I was entering a more tumultuous time than I ever expected. The devil wanted compensation for every moment of enjoyment he gave. I had taken his package and endorsed his presence, *but his gifts are not free*. We never see his tentacles of pain wrapped within a disobedient relationship. They are hidden well, amid the joy and excitement.

God spoke something else: "Dorothy, when the devil is the originator of your situation; you can't rebuke him and make him leave. Your marriage was established outside my will, and never should have happened." This illumination helped me understand why the enemy never had to back off. Deviously inspired relationships have no power to cast away darkness. <u>They are the darkness</u>. No matter how wonderful they feel initially; they cannot go into your next season. They are fallacious and have not been endorsed by God.

We can think that breaking God's law is a small thing, but we have no idea that we are not prepared for the way our fruit will return. I would now understand the seriousness of sin. Feeling afraid, I meagerly trusted that I could still depend on God. He had promised that He would not utterly leave me alone. However, He seemed removed and far away. I hoped against hope that the process would not be that bad. Crying out, "Father, please don't make me drink this bitter cup! Release me from this dreadful time!"

Nevertheless, I had no choice. I could feel the lowering of the boom. It was time to stretch out as a living sacrifice on the Altar of God and trust Him alone for resurrection. It was time for deep repentance, humility and total submission. I would need supernatural power to endure the surgical separation of ego and spirit. My purification time was at hand. I meekly conceded to wait for God's grace and mercy.

Our last drive
It was Friday; Luis had been out all night. He came home early in the morning, in time for work. He acted proud of his covert operation. By now, he loved to punish and torture; because narcissist love to be in control. My commitment to him reminded him of his sin, but he just didn't care anymore. I told him, "It's time for you to move. You need to pack your things and get out." He said, "I'm not going anywhere." He justified his disrespectful actions as usual. We argued as I drove him to work. He yelled, "I'm not going anywhere!" The arguing was so ugly! I was enraged enough with his lying tactics, and shouted, "You will need to catch a ride home today. I won't be picking you up! This is one Friday night you won't take the car and vanish!" It was time that he got a little taste of his own malicious medicine. I would do the disappearing this time and stay with a friend for a day or two. I needed a serious change of scenery.

I finally stopped talking and decided to do something. Luis needed to consider his ways. I packed a few things for Jyndia and me. Jamul would stay at his Dad's and was more than happy to escape. It was tough being away, but I hoped the confrontation might open Luis' eyes. Perchance, it would matter that he was losing his loving family. A crisis might be the formula he needed to change his mind and our circumstances. This deceived man needed to snap back to reality! How long could male menopause last? Didn't he fear God and the results of his actions? Was Lacy worth going to hell for? Didn't he have enough of her by now?

I returned home on Sunday; Luis had not come home all weekend. I was heartbroken. My plan had not worked. Finally, He arrived about three, long enough to change clothes. He had purchased new sweaters. It appeared he had been to church and had a rented car. When he came into the room he was cavalier and arctic. His bitterness amazed me. How could he be that way? He stopped and loved on Jyndia a minute and began to leave. I said, "Luis if you don't want to work on our marriage, take your clothes with you!" He staunchly passed me. He boldly flaunted his sin in my face. Without a word, in arrogance and defiance, he left!

Even in the disarray of our fragmentation, an unstoppable, prevailing rage and defiance stood up within; for my righteousness! I deserved respect, dignity and honor! Perhaps it was a God-survival command, but I was glad I told him to get out and should have done it years before! Putting a demand on Luis was the right thing to do. The brain is hardwired to stay alive after all. Self-dignity is a great gift from God. The truth could no longer be sanitized. (Subliminal messages, even feelings of love cannot easily override self-actuality).

Thank God, His commandments are written on our hearts and help us reject injustice. This "holy indignation" rose to say, "No, Dorothy, you will not disrespect yourself or Me anymore, by putting up with this insolent, unworthy, disobedient man!" "The Spirit of the Lord said, "This is why I've given you My

Word, dreams and righteous prophets." That day I was strong in the Lord and in the power of His might. I had clarity and it felt good to trust God! It was time to go all the way, ready or not! I heatedly packed his clothes, placing them neatly in hanging bags. I put them on the floor in the living room. With confidence, but in deep pain and remorse I continued to work, cry and pray. I was at my deepest level of crisis.

The impossible had to happen now, or it was over ... As I packed, I remembered Luis' mother's dream. Was this the ripeness of what she saw? Was Luis walking away from God's best? I prayed, "Lord, can you use all of this to help us talk it out, or is it over? Let the clothes on the floor bring him to his senses ...and, please destroy Luis' corrupt allegiance to Lacy!" If it were possible, I just wanted my husband, marriage, and family back in place.

Tina and Carl
Luis returned about ten p.m. To my surprise two of his friends, Tina and Carl walked in the door with him. I had waited all day for a personal encounter, but now it would be in front of his cronies. Tina began to scold me. "Luis is not playing on you. You are stressing him out. You should have picked him up from work! He said you are insecure. You are the one causing the trouble! Why are his clothes on the floor?" She defended Luis, as Carl (her husband) helped him take his clothes to the car. Luis had already planned to leave like God said. Life left my puny body as the three of them brashly accused me.

Tina continued to rail on Luis' behalf. Finally, she said, "If you're big enough to put your husband's clothes on the floor, you're big enough to be by yourself!" I said, "Tina you don't know what goes on in my house, but it will come to the light. You will regret your words! One day you will know the truth!" She rolled her eyes contemptuously. Luis acted wounded, his acting skills impeccable. The scene was beyond words. Jyndia, cried fiercely with her arms up for her Daddy. Jamul was stunned, but this was not a TV show, it was a living drama with real hurting people. My children and I witnessed a horrific dishonor. We were dismayed, disorientated and defeated. Luis left without mercy. He walked out the door and persecuted his own family. He and his entourage of deceived admirers were gone!

Our last day together was a trajectory of insanity! Tina and Carl had no idea that they inadvertently, involved themselves unjustly. They aligned themselves with Luis' darkness. Tina couldn't wait to get on the phone. She told everyone she knew about my personal catastrophe. Tina was a colossal witch - a revolting creature – bold and totally out of place! She belittled me in my own house -- in front of my children! Luis was no better. How could he shame his wife or any human being that way? Luis had accompanied demons from the darkest fractures of hell. There are no earthly words or way to tell you how disgraced I felt. I am surprised I could stand at all. My soul fainted in disbelief ... Lastly, our marriage was destroyed. A mighty breaker had taken it to the bottom of the sea. There was no human consolation to be found.

Rumors
The enemy of my soul poured out a horrific cup of grief and pain to consume me. Why did I deserve such degradation and ruin? The next day, Tina called to tell me how wrong I was again. She blasted me with more lying rumors. A mutual acquaintance had joined in with the lies and laughter. Tina told me she said, I had hassled Luis when, "He was such a wonderful husband to you. You should have been more thoughtful of him!" She then abruptly broadcasted; "I've got to go. My "HUSBAND" is calling me!" She cruelly emphasized the word "husband," not knowing a semblance of the truth. Listening to Luis she acted as though she could see through walls, but knew nothing about our private lives.

(We would stay out of other people's relationships, if we only knew how little truth we know - when listening to only one side of the story. We should be afraid to torture and judge others because we don't know. Remember, there are always two sides to every story, and then God's story. He alone knows the truth).

Couldn't Tina see, I had not, woke up, gone crazy, and put my husband's clothes on the floor! ... And, why would anyone deliberately lie about their husband having an affair, if he were not? No woman in her right mind would haphazardly whisper such a shameful thing. The shirts full of makeup were real. The many nights Luis was gone were real -- His coldness and disrespect was genuine. The doctor's report of a new bacterium in my body was infallible evidence of his unfaithfulness! His indiscretion was real, but who cared about really knowing the truth?

Dimensions of pain
All I hoped for had vanished. Putting his clothes on the floor had only worked in his favor. I helped him get the empathy he needed from others and set him up perfectly. I helped Luis become the poor victim and played into his hands. Luis and Lacy had to be jubilant! They had the excuse they wanted now. I began to understand the message of the wheat field and giving my strength and honor to the years of the cruel.

An unimaginable realm of pain is released when someone says, "I don't want you anymore." There is nothing on earth that can stop your feelings of treason, betrayal, and rape. I was abandoned and publicly dragged through the streets; naked, and ashamed. There was no protection, or safety and nowhere to hide. Without remedy, the assassin, the slaughterer, the evil one had come for our marriage ... and he got it; it was his to take. *How I wish I had listened to my teachers and the voice of the Lord!" (Proverbs 5:4-12)* A stranger had taken my wealth and labors, leaving my body and flesh consumed. I groaned and exclaimed, alas! I hated discipline and instruction.

I never imagined I would see my husband pack a rented car and leave his family. All my praying and warring against adultery had done nothing - nothing at all. My husband was gone - like nothing at all. Despite my many prayers, I found only desolation and swallowing burrows of pain and confusion. "In the end, he was as bitter as wormwood, sharp as a two-edged sword. His ways were unknowable to me and movable, far from the path of life. No, I didn't know him but God did and he tried to keep me from going forward with calling him back. He was just what Father said he was.

October
I tried to comfort my children and attempted to rest my mind. Our existence was so very miserable and daunting. I stood alone, crying out to God, "Please stop this disaster!" I expected to be treated better as a Christian! I reminded God that I had served Him from my youth! "Didn't I deserve better than this? Please deliver me from this pit!" I was a mixture of pain, injury and uncertainty. Appalling memories persisted, with no joy to be found. I was betrayed, deserted, and very much alone! My siblings and I were not close, and true friends were hard to find, so I kept my despair from most. One of my sisters had just lost her husband and she needed the family most. A few personal friends tried to encourage me, but my burden was great. All because I refused to take heed to the voice of God.

As far as I was concerned, October thirty-first, was the most horrific day God ever made. November would have been our eight-year anniversary, our new beginning, but just days before Luis walked away. He cared nothing about our precious milestone! He left us on a Sunday, just before the Christmas season … and I knew the reason he couldn't stay. <u>He left, because he had to go. He left because disorder can never stand before the face of God</u>. God's justice equilibrium and perfection always expels iniquity darkness, just as Luis was expelled from the limousine; and the driver, (Holy Ghost) hurried on without him. Ultimately, Luis left because he and I embraced a despicable area of disobedience and the balancing day had come. It had to come.

Tormenting spirits
The breaking of a soul tie is severe. It creates a sorrowful convergence of separation: spiritually, emotionally, physically, socially and mentally. Intellectually, I understood why Luis was gone, but emotionally my penalty and journey through the wheat field was entirely a different matter. Parting can emotionally consume us, because disconnection hurts. Anxiety attacks arose within and depression opened realms of satanic attack and life-sucking dejection. The dimness of my life was laced with poisonous sounds of melancholy. I listened to Satan blame me and agreed with his words. I accepted my enemy's accusations. Without God's help, we have no hope. We can literally endorse disaster from a spirit of dire grief and self-punishment.

"It is evil to rebel against God; therefore, a stern and pitiless messenger will be sent against you." (Proverbs 17:11)

Disobedience creates walls

I was sure God had hidden Himself from me. His presence was elusive. I was a good wife and faithful to Luis, but was still painted as the problematic partner. Others supported Luis and believed him; therefore, I had to be a terrible person. This must be my fault, factually or not the inspiration of hell was strong. How else could Luis be such an atrocious, trifling man and get away with being respected for it? My disobedience had created a hazy, murky wall between God and me. I was afraid; it seemed, my world changed overnight!

I wished I had never gone out that Saturday night with Gina. What an expensive price to pay. And why had I called Luis back instead of following the impressions of Holy Spirit? I knew better. God had warned me fair and square. Yes, I heard Him correctly, I knew His voice, but allowed the relationship to galvanize anyhow. I did it, even after I had no peace to call him back or to go forward with the marriage. I chose to please myself and a man and now the consequences that I thought would not apply to me, I was living out. The true source of my problem was simple, yet devastating; I moved beyond the protection of God. My disobedience had purchased this test of fire; a hardship God tried to prevent. He could see the coming entrapment and reimbursement required. He knew all that I was inviting to happen.

My compliance empowered the destroyer. My actions called him out of his pit and put him on the throne. The words I heard in my spirit were plain now, *"Luis is a womanizer!"* God was right. I should have respected my Father's voice. Why did I reason with His Words? How could I answer life and wisdom with, "Well maybe Luis used to be a womanizer?" How stupid! I changed God's words at the gate, the place of decision. I put myself on the enemy's ground and was paying a hefty price for doing so. It was never God's will for me (or you) to open such a door -- one that unleashes satanic oppression.

"You will have to eat the fruit of your own way of life and choke on your own scheming. The errors of the simple lead to death. The complacency of fools works to their own ruin" (Proverbs 1)

Now, it was time to stop blaming Luis, Lacy and the other women. My actions had been no better than theirs. How could I justify myself and throw stones at them? I was no poor sacrificial lamb or a paragon of virtue either. Who was I to judge their foul lifestyle and not my own? We had all sinned and fallen short of the glory of God. No matter how difficult my first marriage was, I had no right to disobey God in the manner of my leaving. Justin's standard of living gave me no right to break God's rules. His sins would not excuse my sins. I was released from Justin, to trust God and to live for Jesus, not to connect with a perpetrator like Luis. I had committed adultery! My sins were filthy too. We were all in need of forgiveness and restoration.

Will you shut the door?
Sharing my story and this book are worth it all, if you can see that you will not escape the consequences amassed from going your own way. If I can help you shut a door to sin and suffering, then my part in your life is vital and important. For this reason, I ask you to pray honesty about your life and relationships. Examine for yourself what God has or has not said to you. If needed, you must stop an unconfirmed relationship before you activate the same spirit of destruction that I did. You already know what God has said about the relationship you're in. Don't parley with His words. You already know the truth. What is the truth?

If God has not ordained your togetherness, you have an immediate decision to make. Will you change course, shut the door and stop an absolute onslaught of darkness from occurring in your future? Or will you walk on pompously like an animal to the slaughter? Do you really want the pain and emotional upheaval I and the Bible are describing? Will you endorse the presence of the "savage hater?" If you choose your own way and defy God's direction, you will indisputably experience the same feelings of torture and loss, or worse.

If you sow in Satan's field, you will enable him to defeat you. You cannot change spiritual laws, but you can choose today not to allow your enemy to cut off your reasoning, value and purpose. He is no respecter of persons; and will attempt to destroy you at your lowest point of existence. He hates your Jesus and accuses Him daily. If he can hurt you, he can hurt God too. Satan's imps will work hard to make you believe that God is the hater and taker, when in fact, he, the devil, is.

Death to self
I will continue to share with you what disobedience reaps. It acquires a place called true repentance and death to self. When the fullness of sin is completed it brings forth death. I would learn that the scriptures do not lie. I was not going to dinner; I was going to be the dinner. I would be dissected, grinded, digested and purified! I was the oblivious seed going into the deep dark ground. God's purification process was part of my restoration and could not be stopped! There was nowhere to run or dissolve before the King of the universe!

The Holy Spirit reminded me that God was with me. He would walk with me all the way to the end of the wheat field. I exhaled! "Thank you for that Lord. You are all I have now. I am naked before You and wish I had known and trusted you before, but help me trust You now." I felt as vulnerable as a child in the dark, but the balancing of my deeds had to occur. It would be as though I'd need to walk backward, away from my sins, fully returning to obedience. I grasped for air, courage and faith. I had not feared or honored God's Precious Voice enough.

Sadness as intended by God produces a repentance that leads to salvation, leaving no regret, but worldly sadness brings about death. 2 (Corinthians 7:10)

Don't be misled--you cannot mock the justice of God. You will always harvest what you plant. (Galatians 6:7)

"*The Lord your God travels along with your camp to save you and to hand your enemies over to you, but your camp must be holy. If God does not find holiness and sees indecency among you, he will turn away from you.*"
(Deuteronomy 23:14)

It is true, we do reap, what we sow. God gives us His grace and power to do what He says, not to feed our flesh. Grace and power are not extended to give disobedience strength; neither does His grace exclude us from a difficult harvest. If we belong to Him, He simply helps us walk through His processes of purification.

Choose not to go, where the voice of <u>God's love</u> is not

THE DEVIL'S PROCESS　　　　　　　　　　　　　　　　　　Chapter 6

Places you won't like...

"They have hated knowledge and choose not to honor and respect Yahweh. They did not take notice of my advice. They spurned all my warnings, but whoever listens to me will live secure and enjoy a good and quiet life, fearing no mischief. (Proverbs 1)

The first holiday season without Luis was excruciating. He was gone at the very worst time of the year. I grieved that we never got our eight-year wedding anniversary. It was supposed to be our new beginning, not the break-down and break-up of our marriage. Emotionally I hoped that God might use our anniversary or Christmas to reconcile us, but no, and my gifts were containers filled with sorrow, rejection and pain. There was no warmth to find in the season. I asked God a million times, "How can a Christian man get involved with another person, harden his heart and literally walk away from his family? How can he just be gone?"

I was on my own for the first time in my adult life, living in an arena of incurable uncertainty. I didn't want this wretched state of existence. Why hadn't I followed my first impressions about Luis? How bitter my life was from just one decision. My depression and desolation increased. What had I done to deserve such evil public spurning?

The devil whispered in my ear, "It's Christmas, the happiest time of the year, but God has betrayed you! Everyone is laughing at you. No one believes you! You are a disgrace in this town." Day after day, his seducing voice charmed and enticed me to agree with his method of healing and relief. I progressively feared life and separated more from others. It seemed that no one really understood my depressing pain. Everything was wrong in prehistoric proportions -- disappointment was my constant companion!

Throughout the holidays, I continued to experience panic attacks. I knew nothing about panic attacks, but could hear Satan's hideous whispers, "Don't you want real peace Dorothy? No one deserves all the pain you have faced. God has been unfair to you. He is against you. You are a Christian. You have served God with all your heart. You don't deserve this betrayal and shame! God treats others better than this. You deserve peace and tranquility. I can help you overcome this tiredness. I know you want rest from this toil."

Satan shrewdly released his evil seducing comfort. Blow after blow, day after day, he bombarded my faithless mind, mocking God convincingly. At times, 'I'd quickly reach for my list of names and ask someone to pray for me, but I had to act swiftly. The panic attacks grew and intimidated me. They were a terrifying new encounter, each long wearing day.

Jyndia's and Jamul's pain
Jyndia was tremendously broken. Like a little emaciated - withered dishrag, she'd fall into my arms. At four years old, she sorrowed, wanting her Daddy to come home! Seeing my child suffer doubled my pain. It was more than I could endure. I bitterly realized there was no such thing as magical love. There is no temporary pleasure in this world worth this kind of agony. Nothing Luis and I experienced was equivalent to seeing my child's heartbreak. She knew; when Daddy's leave their families and little girls behind; something is very much out of order.

I helped Jyndia grieve and get through each difficult day. Not only did she have physical challenges to overcome, but now would be raised without her Dad. I prayed for Jyndia continually. My time to lament would come late at night when my responsibilities were over. Watching her reminded me that my Dad left me too when I was about five years old. The same generational curse had visited again.

Jamul had his own growth and pain going on, but was less affected by Luis leaving. He could feel our grief, but spent most of his time at school, with friends or involved in sports. Spending time with his Dad was a positive conduit for him. Jamul never liked Luis much anyway. He was relieved that he was gone. Jamul knew Luis was playing his mama and didn't like it. He wanted him exposed! Jamul showed empathy for me at times by saying something heartwarming like, "Mom, he didn't deserve you anyway!" He told his older brother, "Mom is getting too skinny, you need to come down here and talk to her." I had lost a great deal of weight fasting for strength and trying to process my trauma. Going past the voice of God was much more serious than I presumed.

Hurtful information
The obliteration of a covenant is grueling. It was impossible to face a new day. Getting out of bed was a monumental task. What kind of man had I given my heart to? What realm of evil and deception did I activate? In my incongruity, I asked God the same questions endlessly. "Is it possible that you would give us a new day Lord? How can we just throw away our marriage? How can Luis justify his blatant sin? How can a man walk away from his family? Would you change his heart and take away his ruthlessness?"

Satan, the author of suffering and unbridled agony was determined to snuff me out. Hurtful information flooded in from every side. Just weeks after Luis left, I learned more than I wanted to know. Jyndia spent the night with her dad and reported, "Mom, I woke up and saw dad on the floor with Lacy; they were kissing." This is how I learned her name. Jyndia was stunned and upset. My soul melted with her words. How could he do this disrespectful thing and in front of his own child? My heart burst into a million pieces. He had just left us weeks before and we were still very married! Would the pain ever subside? Jyndia shared, "Mom, Lacy has two sets of twins. Two of them stay with their dad and I don't like her!" I was surprised that Luis involved himself with a woman with so many children. Perhaps, Lacy would incalculably change him.

I was embarrassed when Lacy's cousin apologized to me one day. He said, "I am sorry about this Dorothy, but you know what? He will leave her too!" He had introduced them at a community music project. Another time at our local laundry, the attendant said, "I saw your husband and your daughters washing clothes!" Slam! Lacy was years younger than Luis and I were. I heard he was running around with a very young crowd, doing the proverbial, younger woman, male menopause thing! He even cut his hair off. My departed husband was bald headed after all these years, going through his own identity crisis!

Bragging publicly
Luis was gone for a month and Lacy was bragging about their wonderful relationship. She flippantly broadcasted her new love to friends and foes, long before our divorce was discussed. What an outrageous, deceived woman! They deserved each other! Didn't she have just a little bit of shame? She told a mutual acquaintance, Luis was an awesome man. She was thrilled that she received exciting gifts and flowers. He was the love of her life!

Lacy told others she was justified to be with him, because I put Luis out! Oh, that made me angry! Did she really believe that in her heart? She knew why I put his clothes on the floor and it wasn't because I wanted too. Luis was out there because they had planned it for months. She bet on them pushing me to that end result. They had decided this long before I accelerated things for them. Luis was coming home that night to pack up and leave anyway! But none of the real facts mattered to Luis or Lacy. They had joined the ranks of the "lying, diluted and deceived!"

"The mouth of the adulterous woman (man) is a deep pit. The man or woman Yahweh God rebukes will fall into it." They wipe their mouths and say all is well.
(Proverbs 22:14)

Ignoring flares
I wondered if it ever dawned on Lacy that she was dating a married man. Did it bother her that he had a devoted wife and children at home that loved him – a praying wife who stood night and day for reconciliation? Lacy was a churchgoer. Didn't she think about her evil deeds in the sight of God? Didn't she think of what her future repercussions might be? She and Luis were inflicting pain on one of God's children, regardless. When I heard of Lacy's comments, I ironically remembered something that seemed insignificant years before. During courtship, when I first went by to visit Luis' apartment, a young lady knocked on

his door a long time - about an hour. She begged him not to break it off with her. (God continually gives us signs).

Luis finally went outside to see her, hoping she would not do something suicidal. When he returned, I broke it off with him and went home. I was appalled! Luis called again and again, going on about how unstable she was. (This was the same words he used against me and his first wife). He swore he had just taken this lady to dinner one time. She just misinterpreted the friendship. He had done nothing to make her feel that way. Over a period of time, I allowed him to convince me that she might have read more into the relationship and chose to believe him.

A friend also argued in his defense; "Dorothy, women do expect more sometimes. Give him another chance." I chose to let him influence me with his famous well-structured soliloquies, avoiding the warning in my heart. A major flare in the sky was ignored, because I wanted to believe in love. We often select blindness, when there is a chance for romance. We settle for delusion and like it better than the truth. Of course, I foolishly believed that Luis would be different with me and now I was the problem!

> *"That the righteousness of the law might be fulfilled in us, who walk not after flesh, lust or self, but after God's Spirit. To be carnally (worldly) minded is death, but to be spiritually minded is life and peace. The carnal mind works against God. It is not subject to obey God; neither does it have the ability to do so."*
> *(Romans 8:4-6)*

Hard places
Some had strong allegiances with Luis. One of his work associates, once my mutual friend, called to say they thought I was a fool for putting my husband out, because of my insecurities. She said, "Luis is very happy now." Only a demon of persecution would make a person deliver such a vindictive message. People didn't seem to have an ounce of sensitivity when they didn't know the facts. How spiteful, to say a thing like that to a woman barely able to lift her head! How the lions devoured me!

I saw Luis walking downtown one sunny day, smiling and stepping high. He was visibly enjoying life. I was happy to see him, but he looked at me and turned his head. What a letdown! (I was the unpleasant reminder of his sin and need for righteousness). My hopeful smile turned into a big sad frown. The stabs kept coming from many directions. While driving with Jyndia, she said, "Mom!" (Pointing to a group of mailboxes), "That's where my daddy picks up his mail." More pain! He even had his own sleazy mailbox! My husband had a secret mailbox! What else was there to know? Who was this man? How did the devil plant this tare in my life? Oh yes; when I listened to him and lingered moments past the gate!

I got myself together enough to do a fashion show for a salon in town. The owner was an acquaintance from a prayer group. She knew of my pain and struggle. I had confided in her and asked her to pray for us, but the devil is all about pain. He used her in an impish way in front of everyone. She loudly proclaimed, "Dorothy, I heard Luis is getting married!" That statement cut like a knife! She stood there to see if I would die. How malicious! Somehow, I felt God's strength and compassion, enough to give an offhand remark ... "Well ... life goes on." I forced a stressed smile on my face and made it out the door, bowed over in pain. Why did she do that to me? Her words were like fiery darts. I trembled to my car and hurried home to hide behind my protective walls of pain.

Help
Shortly after Luis left, I called the pastor of his church to ask for help again. I had also called before our separation. I believed he might make a difference for us. Luis continued to go to this Church and Lacy was a member there. The secretary told me the pastor would not talk to me. I would have to share my request with a deacon. Several weeks and several talks later, the deacon told me the pastor had visited with Luis. His answer, Luis didn't want to talk about it. "What? What do you mean he doesn't want to talk about it? Isn't a pastor supposed to make a member talk about affairs and leaving his family? Couldn't he see that Luis was involved in a loose relationship with a member in his church? Didn't he know He was singing in the choir with his girlfriend! What kind of songs were they singing in there anyhow?

How could the pastor accept that a man just didn't want to talk about his failing marriage? Aren't pastors supposed to fight for marriages? I could not believe my ears. I wanted to say, "What kind of pastor are you? Are you afraid to confront sin? Why don't you talk to this man about doing the right thing? You should be standing for marriages!" (As you can see, I was trying to go on and trying to reconcile at the same time. What a muddle).

But, Luis mastered in great impressions and deceived impeccably. He and the pastor became best friends. *"I don't get it God?"* A friend told me the same pastor would neither get involved with the breakup of her marriage. What a sad indictment for a pastor. He will have to answer to God for this. Another load of depression and grief was dumped on my front porch to dig from underneath. Not even the man of God would take a stand and believe me.

Luis needed to be met head-on! Somebody needed to "man up" with him. "Please God; you've got to rattle the heavens now! His lies must be bombarded! This has gone too far! I know you're not going to let the devil get away with this. Luis and his Church are totally tolerating open adultery. Lord, take this down!" But the meltdown continued! *(Years later, this pastor was harshly dealt with for compromising with sin and lost his license to preach. May God bless and deliver him. God often gives years of grace before he deals with sin. He is very patient).*

Luis' continual tale about me was told this way... "Dorothy has issues. She is insecure. She woke up one day, went crazy and put me out! What is wrong with that woman?" And people believed him! I kept hoping and praying that someone would address his sinful state, but most were besot with his charming ways. But why couldn't spiritual people get past his fabricated stories? Where were the powerful Christians with discernment? Someone should have been able to see through his persuasiveness. Luis' mom, friends, and pastors all went along with the fraudster.

Too much information
I hoped I would be spared more new information. I became paranoid about what I might learn next. I was going through an evil harvest while Luis' promotions escalated. "How could this be right God?" Why wasn't he being dealt with? He had the best job of his life, traveled, had his girlfriend, (girlfriends) and stayed visible. Luis was well respected and ministered at the biggest church in town. I heard he preached good sermons too. How could any of this be right? Why wouldn't God deal with him for his sins? I became angrier with God by the minute. How could a man have multiple affairs, leave his family and be blessed? This question plagued me. It was the most penetrating of all my queries. "Lord, are the unrighteous blessed more than the righteous?"

My pain turned to fury and righteous indignation! A woman scorned indeed! I constantly reminded the Lord of His Word. "You said You would deal with those who commit adultery - not bless them for doing it! Hello! Father, are you there? Luis, not only destroyed his family, but he is prospering! I'm the forsaken one here! How could Luis and Lacy sing in the choir, have a forbidden sex life and still be blessed? For heaven's sake! This is too wrong God!" The truth was, I was not the problem, neither was his first wife, or the girl knocking at his door.

I ran into Luis one day and told him, "There is nothing worse than a church whore! Why not take your mess back to your nightclubs!" For me, "No more nice girl!" I asked, "How can you lay with Lacy on Saturday night, take communion and preach a sermon on Sunday?" That was shocking blasphemy and wretchedness! "Lord, where is Your retribution and vengeance for me? When will you chastise him for this? You said You chastise those who are Yours. You said if we are not chastised, we are illegitimate (bastard) children! My question is: Is he yours Lord or the devils?

This is how we know who the children of God are and who the children of the devil are: Anyone who does not do what is right is not God's child, nor is anyone who does not love their brother and sister. (1John 3:10)

"My son, do not make light of the Lord's discipline. Do not lose heart when He rebukes you. The Lord disciplines those He loves and chastens everyone He accepts as His child. Endure hardship as discipline; God is treating us as His children. For what Children are not disciplined by their Father? If you are not disciplined, you are not legitimate children at all, but bastards. If we have earthly parents who discipline us and we respected them for it, how much more should we submit to the Father of Spirits and live!" God's discipline cleanses us for our good (Hebrew 12:4-10)

Questions

I now traveled the road that the disobedient shifted upon. The proverbs rang true; in the end, he was as bitter as wormwood, sharp as a two-edged sword. I wished I had trusted my own mind and never called Luis back and had chosen not to be persuaded by Gina to go out? Why did I compromise to prove anything to anyone about myself? I continued to feel like a forgotten flop, put away in the undergrounds of nowhere. I felt like a leper. No one cared about my downward spiral of pain. The world stood by to bless a man that persecuted me unfairly.

"I am with you and I will not make a full end of you. I will correct you in measure, but will not leave you altogether unpunished. For thus says your Lord, your bruise is incurable and your wounds are grievous. There is none to plead your cause. You are bound up and have no healing medicines. All your lovers have forgotten you. They seek you not, for I have wounded you with the wounds of an enemy and with the chastisement of a cruel one, because of the multitude of your iniquity. Your sins were increased against me, so why cry in your affliction? Your sorrow is incurable for the multitude of your iniquity. I have done these things to you." (Jeremiah 30:11-15)

I wanted to see the veracity of God within my dungeon of chains. Was I that bad of a person? Was I that far out of balance? What was in me that needed such hard chastisement? I felt like Tamar of the Bible, in 2nd Samuel 13:15. Initially, Luis was lovesick (lust-sick) for me. He expressed deep and profound love for my presence, but after fulfilling his passions, his feelings turned to hate. The same measure of lust/love he expressed conveyed itself in excessive hate.

Continual anxiety

The evenings were intolerable as tormenting spirits came to mock and pierce me through. How much sadness and grief could I stand? It would have been easier to die as a family on our last trip, than to live through these ungodly, vicious, unrelenting anxiety attacks. I felt as though I would electrically jump out of my skin. How could I prepare myself for such degrees of harassment? Fear consumed my soul. Physically, my nerves were shot. Spiritually, the attacks felt like a demonic army devouring every cell of my mind, body and soul.

I would meltdown when I felt one coming. I wanted to crawl into a fetal position and just go back to Heaven. Anxiety attacks are enormously brutal! It would have been easier to run down the road a hundred miles an hour, or drive into a bridge or jump in front of a two-ton semi-truck! I believe there is a demonic realm that provokes "suicidal car crashes!" I have spoken to others who experienced mystical inclinations to crash their cars during harsh anxiety attacks. The overshadowing of this evil spirit comes in many ways to kill, steal, and destroy. Demons have many names and assignments. Therefore, we can never judge anyone that takes bleak actions to deal with darkness and gloom. Nevertheless, submitting to God is the right thing to do. He can take down every wall of mental and emotional destruction.

Dysfunction
The only good thing about Luis leaving in the winter was the nights came early. I could hide myself away easier in the dark of night and sneak to the store when no one could see me. I lived for the nights. Still in shock and shame, I began to tell a few people that Luis was having an affair and had left us. Each stage of separation was so difficult. One day, it was this and the next day, that. Insanity is the best definition. One day you want them back and next you can't stand the thought of it! Some days you're sure about your direction and the next minute you're not.

Mostly, I emotionally felt that God betrayed me. How could I go on, when God Himself had thrown me into the lion's den? There were a few good days when I'd stop weeping and declare; the creep and liar just isn't worth it. "Lord, please help me look forward!" On those days, the statement and feeling was good enough - He really didn't deserve me. I knew I would do just fine without him. I was glad that our sinful relationship was over. How could it stand the test of time? It had to abort, but at other times, especially at night I'd think of Luis. I was Like Forest Gump with his undying love for Jenny. At night, he'd think of Jenny and I'd think of Luis. I'd watch the cars pass by, hoping he'd come home. "Why Lord, why? Will the sun ever shine again? How long will this last?" My singleness was a thought I could not bear!

Would morning ever come? – And if it did, what would it look like? Would I even be able to recognize the light? It had been midnight so long. How could life go on as usual? Where would I go and what would I do? How would my soul survive this? How could my love for my husband just stop existing? Where do the brokenhearted go when their souls are distraught? Where do feelings and emotions die? You awake to find yourself in an indistinguishable space just to feel unending unhappiness. You are somewhere or nowhere at all, seldom sensing the presence of God. You think … and think … wonder … and waver, reliving every incident again. You die a thousand times more. You obsess, hate, love, process, and hope for a miracle. You cry, gnash your teeth and pray that you will wake up from your dreadful truth.

The seduction of suicide
I felt so small and insignificant. Each moment, Satan's penetrating and enticing words seemed to bring relief to my mind. Although I fought not to listen, and to change his words, but his arrows savaged my mind and overwhelmed me in my isolation. My state of depression grew. Satan was ready now for the big attack. He had worked hard with his counterfeit words to get me to this point of defeat. It was time to destroy his prey!

One lonely Friday night, just before Christmas, he spoke more overwhelmingly than usual. "You know that God has betrayed you. I'm the one that understands what you need. You are emotionally exhausted and frail. It's not fair. You have been a good Church going Christian. This should not be. I know you want peace, don't you? You deserve to be far away from all of this. (Exaggerating, accentuating and double-dealing)! God doesn't care that you are the laughing stock of town. You've been treated poorly. God doesn't care that your husband is gone. He could have prevented this. Look how pitifully the Lord has blessed you for serving him!"

On and on his seducing voice rang vigorously in my ears ... until I felt completely enthralled in the attractiveness of his skillful and articulate offer. His sweet relief had to be my answer to anxiety. I felt compelled and seduced to agree and to do exactly what he said. He spoke again, "Just look under the kitchen sink, get the liquid plumber out and pour some into your drinks. In just moments; your disgrace will be over. You then will have the rest and renewal you deserve. You will have peace in a far better place! Your pain will be over. Let me help and deliver you. Let this disgrace be over tonight." Persistently, his false compassion showed me a way out. His soothing and comforting words resounded and filled my weary mind.

He was right. I didn't want to live with this rejection, shame or pain any longer. God had abandoned me! I walked downstairs to look at my Jyndia. I sat on the steps despondent, hopeless and dejected. My baby looked so beautiful. She did not deserve this life either. She had no idea just how alone I felt. The house was physically and spiritually empty now. Laughter, hope and expectation were gone. Why should she or I live in an evil world like this one? A world where people believe the perpetrator? ... She looked at me and smiled. She was watching a Christmas show on television. She trusted me and had no awareness that our lives were in deep devious jeopardy. Her mom was disheartened and depressed, far away from light and truth.

Holy Spirit Help!
Suppressed and detached, I could hear the Holy Spirit praying for us and helped me say: "Lord, help me! I don't want to hurt my baby or myself! God, help me now or I will do this! I need your intervention!" I rushed in terror to the phone and called a prayer partner. The Duels were aware of the "satanic attacks." Thank God, they answered the phone and were quick to pray and rebuke the voice of

my enemy! I needed help on that horrific night of broken bows and shattered shields. Praise God, they prayed with power and conviction for me! To the devils chagrin the oppression lifted and he had to go! Only God - Only God could have shut the mouth of the slanderer, the father of lies that discolored midnight! Jesus Christ, with might and power rebuked the persistent voice of the murderer. That night, someone prayed for me and held back the hand of the devourer.

These extracting demonic attacks were extremely intimidating. I felt even more afraid and powerless now. How far had I fallen? I was somewhere between clinical depression and death. I had never known such warfare! This dimension of hell and treachery was beyond my ability. The hater of my soul; almost convinced me to accept his brand of relief. I was so grateful that God was watching over me. He knew how to intervene to strengthen my malnourished mind. To imagine that I might have taken our lives, this is never the right thing to do. Do you have a friend nearby that knows how to pray? If not get one!

Zandra
Weeks later, Zandra, a good friend, felt a strong impression to come by and pray for me. When she arrived she immediately took authority over the spirit of darkness. She prayed with authority, rebuked devils, travailed, cried, and spoke the Word of God in faith! She entered my pain and stayed there until it was broken. God showed her a vision of me "walking on hot coals of fire barefoot!" He showed her that my agony was excruciating. She was devastated to see me in such a place of torture. Zandra's obedience was a tremendous seed planted to help me stand a little stronger than before. I will always appreciate her honor to God and sensitivity to follow His voice. As a mature Christian, she knew how to enter in and make darkness bow its vulgar knee. When she left, I could feel the shadows pushed back. I could almost take a deep breath of relief! (Purification is serious business).

Wobbly world
A year after Luis left, I was not looking forward to being alone on a beautiful fall evening. Jyndia was with her dad and I drove Jamul to a skating rink. When he got out of the car, fear of an anxiety attack leached within my soul. The attacks would most likely come when I was alone. I began to tear up, "God please help me. The devil is going to harass me again. I can't handle this anymore! Lord, if you don't stop these demonic attacks, you'll have to take me home. I can't stand feeling like this!" Strained and afraid I sorrowed, waiting for the hit. I cringed and panicked. Would I be able to get home in time to call someone for prayer? I felt myself sinking down in my car seat. I would not be responsible for what I did next.

I braced myself ... I waited, but in the middle of my most fearful expectation, I could feel and hear the resonance of Holy Spirit ..."Shhhh ... IT'S OVER... NO MORE TORMENT!" I could hardly believe my ears. God occupied my mind with holy quietness. I sat back and relaxed. I could hardly believe I felt peace and security. I had been harassed and attacked for a year! I listened, waited and cried; wanting to be sure the peace of God was still there. I was so happy to have heard the Lord's voice! These attacks were more than I could tolerate. I began to worship God in amazement! For the first time in a long time, I was not afraid. God delivered me from satanic tormentors! Just like the attacks came, they left. They were gone! The door was shut! From that day to this one, I have never experienced any unnatural anxiety attacks like those, even during very stressful times! God, showed up for me, bringing a pageantry of peacefulness and love. I dared to believe this encounter meant that I was coming out of the wheat field and evil harvest.

When Prayer Does Not Work
The shame and rejection persisted. I couldn't seem to get it; prayer does not work if it is against God's will! I tried hard to learn the lessons God was trying to teach me, but my relationship with God had degraded to confusion and offence most days. I'd repent for my ambivalence, but emotionally fluctuate back and forth like a pendulum. I loved God, but still blamed him for my misery. He could have prevented this. Why wouldn't He understand and give us a simple miracle? I had repented!!! I balked at times, "God, I thought prayers changed things! Now I must survive on my own as a single mother. I am not equipped for 'Singledom.' Aren't you the God of a second chance?"

My mother had occasionally teased me about a play in grade school. She said I was extremely passionate about my one and only line. It was, "Oh No! - A thought I cannot bear!" When I thought about it, I must have foreseen these terrible times. The separation of soul and ego from desire, created thoughts I could not bear! Even my worst enemies did not deserve this sentence. I was losing so much in time, energy and focus. Disobedience to God never got me the love and permanency I thought I would get!

Distant Shadows
I was indeed broken, but still longed to see the word of God answer my prayers for reconciliation. Marriage was my only familiar lifestyle. It is difficult to change old habits. A few good friends came over to pray for my strength. This meant a lot to me; I was so glad they really cared. They asked God to give me back my laughter. Nancy would sit on the arm of my chair, hug me and sing a song of the Lord to encourage my heart. Myra, Deb, or Darlene would give me a word of encouragement, but my life felt like a terrible nightmare. Almost everything and everyone seemed to be a distant shadow. I was just a seed, deeply planted in the deep dark ground waiting for resurrection. I was there alone.

I moved into an apartment to escape the expenses of our town home. Everything continued to spin. I tried to maneuver my life in a new arena of existence, one arduous moment at a time. Singleness was a path of mystery; I had never walked this way before. I had been married since nineteen years old, but was now living in a splintered room called "singleness." I wish I could tell you

I was just fine, strong in the Lord and the power of His might, but I was not. I still hoped for a miracle. Marriage was my only reality. Slowly and gently I tried to move ahead, but everything perpetually reminded me of my Life with Luis. Seconds, minutes, and hours passed along… Days and nights… nights and days, moved on reluctantly. Weeks and months … summers, falls, winters, and springs, unbearably shifted on. Birthdays passed … Thanksgivings … Christmases … Valentines days, and Easters lapsed out of time and space.

Two years later, my spirit was stronger, but soul ties are egregious and almost impossible to break. They can hang on for long periods of times. They have to be renounced repetitively through deliverance, until they are gone. In spite of what I knew, my deep emotional landscape needed a better paradigm. (Bible deliverance provides a threefold cord that is not easily broken. Find a church or group that understands inner healing, emotional freedom and deliverance).

Lyle's words
When you are going through divorce, social and soul-separation, be prepared to think about the same things obsessively, until you don't need to think about them anymore. I thought again about my conversations with Lyle. There were times I wished I had been like the women of old. They hushed themselves and prayed for their rotten husband's. They waited till the storms passed and their husbands changed. (Some waited thirty years till he put his pencil back in his pocket.) Those women remained true until the fire of lust went out between their whorish husbands and girlfriends. They knew that lust turned their husband's brains to puddin! Fortunately, I had no grace or substance to do that. How could that be the will of God? How did they stand for an elusive man quietly, no matter how much they needed financial covering? (God bless their hearts!)

If I had continued to allow Luis to have his affairs, I would have lost more self-dignity and purpose, and never learned that God was available to help me. It was the mercy of God that helped me stop sowing more deadly seeds into a disobedient relationship. Living through the aftermath of dwelling in sin longer, would have required even more spiritual or physical death and purification. I was already living through far more than I wanted to work through. I knew I had to move on with the limousine or experience more losses.

The Royal Gorge
My challenge and fight with depression was much better. There were days when I felt good and laughed! Healing was beginning in diminutive steps and stages. Glimmers of light and hope shined through. I had had some new experiences and believed I was going to be all right, but the devil is not an easy loser. He would try for our lives again. He wanted back the price of the temporary pleasures he gave me with Luis. I was invited to visit the Royal Gorge in Colorado with a church group. I went because I thought a change of environment would expedite my healing. I wanted to be cheerful again and the

drive out of town would be what Jyndia and I needed. It felt so good to be going somewhere special again.

When we arrived, the mountains were breathtaking. Everyone took to their cabins to rest, to get ready for some exhilarating fun. The group was new for me, except for the lady that invited me. I wasn't feeling connected with the group, they didn't seem friendly or was it my own state of mind? It didn't help that some of the couples reminded me of Luis and I. this showed me that I wasn't as healed at I thought. I didn't feel like socializing. The beauty and scenery made me wish we could share the experience with Luis; like the old times.

The experience made me think of my perceived losses again and how I should have been better rewarded for my commitment to Luis. I had planned to have a good time, but the emotion of this extravagant beauty activated my will to entertain thoughts of my immoral marriage. Before long, I felt depressed and tearful, which is part of a spirit of darkness. The next day the scenery was even more magnificent. The group prepared to go to lunch, crossing over on a rope-swinging bridge. The canyons were a panorama of intoxicating wonder and beauty. Everything was spectacular and captivating. How awesome are the Creations of our Lord! How we enjoyed the splendor and elation, but a sense of melancholy remained. Eventually, I pulled back and allowed myself to grieve about my pitiful marriage and feelings of betrayal. Would I ever have closure?

Jyndia and I walked slowly as the group walked ahead. This was our time to slow down and enjoy the exquisiteness of God. We looked out at all His presented depths of perfections and delicacies. What stunning revelation! How awe-inspiring is our God! What gorgeous and marvelous canyons. Moving toward the center of the bridge, hundreds of feet from the ground, every emotion in my being felt alive and connected. How beckoning and overwhelming was every sensation …. On and on, we united and fellowshipped with God … But then out of nowhere, a forceful penetrating voice began to invade my thoughts. "Dorothy, isn't this all so beautiful? Look at the peace and the beauty here. Isn't this marvelous? Just look at God's creation. I know how much you love this serenity.

The force appealed to my grief … Wouldn't it be wonderful to be a part of this peace, love and beauty? You have been through so much … God has withheld from you… Just look at the peace here. Dorothy, this is where you belong. This place will complete all that you seek. God has forsaken you. He didn't heal your marriage when He had the power to do so. You are barely getting by when you have been a good Christian… You have worked so hard for God… You know people are laughing at you. No one cares about the truth or your story. No one even believes you! God had treated you poorly. Look! … Look! … Rest now and be a part of this peace and beauty today. You don't have to go back. All that waits for you is pain and persecution. Wouldn't it be wonderful to stay here? ...Here with all the glory of this mountain?"

His words continued in constant sounds of beauty and relief. In reverberating echoes, I could feel a strange tranquility infiltrate my being. I listened ... I liked the idea of being free from pain, stress, confusion and depression. I agreed with the aberration and said, "Yes, I have gone through enough ... Way too much. God and my own husband have betrayed me. I gave them everything!" Satan reengaged... "He treats you like dirt! He laughs at you. He knows he has succeeded in destroying your name to exalt himself. He promised to love and honor you, but continues to lie and put you down. God agrees with him! He is blessed and free while you are rejected. Just look at the beauty here! Doesn't this feel wonderful? This is what you deserve. This is astonishing! Feel the joy and the wind ... become a part of this beauty with me. This breath-taking beauty and renewal is part of you. Jyndia does not have a father that cares either, but I am here for you."

"Weary one, pick Jyndia up and fall gently into my arms of peace and beauty. Lean into my splendor. Pick her up now! I will hold you up. Come and be with this peace and serenity!" I surrendered to the allure and charisma of this voice and place. A surge of empowerment and belonging completed my soul. I loved feeling connected there.

I wanted to belong and wanted the replenishment the mountain offered. I could belong to the beauty and this aristocratic canyon. Its life and glory filled my senses with substance and joy! There was no reason to go back home. Go back to what? The mountain was the more excellent place for me. It felt so good. The glory and total acceptance of this place had to be the answer. My undying complexities had to change! I considered the chance to be free. I wanted to belong and collapse into the vigorous life and voice of the canyon.

But Jesus
In the midst of this enticing invitation, the spirit of the Lord arose within me to take His stand. God's own injection of nourishment and presence now invaded my inner being. He was there. He was with me! He was there to claim His own against the will of depression's darkness. Jesus came for me. The Holy Spirit urged me, ever so faintly, "Ask the Lord to help you now. I am here to protect you. You won't do this!" I resisted momentarily ... but, I knew this voice better .... "Lord, help me. I don't want to think like this. I don't want to fall over this rope with my child, but the provocation and proposal is great. I am sad and afraid. There is no reason to go on. I have nothing to go home for. Help me Lord! Help me believe!"

Immediately ... I felt a swarm of angels surround us on the bridge. A subterfuge of protection defended us without delay. God's dynamic warring angels burst through the stratosphere majestically with power and might. They were full of vibrancy like a scene from a panoramic movie! I felt God's strong guard of holiness, as the angels arranged themselves around us. God miraculously lifted a veil of life over us to stop Satan's scheme of death and evil. His powerful, shielding wings dispelled the seducing voice of the enemy ... Holy Spirit said, "Don't look down, look straight ahead and walk ... Just walk. I am with you!" God's voice was pure, persuasive and convincing. I obeyed. I picked Jyndia up, looked straight ahead and briskly walked to the other side!

Deliver me not over to the will of my enemies. Lord, for false witnesses have risen up against me. They breathe out cruelty. (Psalms 27:12)

Vulnerable times

During times of depression, loneliness and grief, the devil's voice is enticing. For a moment, his offer of peace and comfort seems beautiful and offers the solutions we need. When we are betrayed, death can feel like the answer to our weary, disillusioned heart. A heart that believes it has nothing to look forward to. The persecution and mockery at home was severe, as Luis finagled in the background. I wanted to be as far away from those terrible, deceived people as I could. They waited to rip me apart even more; like a pack of dogs they conspired against me. They were happy about my misfortune. I could feel their hate and rejection. What had I done to them to be treated like a leprous throwaway? Luis had told so many lies and so many people believed them. Satan had aligned those people to destroy me; he needed them to twist his screws.

In my grief Satan twisted my admiration of the beautiful canyon. He worked my depression, fear and loneliness to his advantage. Distortion is his best game, especially at vulnerable times. This time he was more cunning in his ability to seduce and conquer <u>through peace and beauty</u>. How compelling. I felt powerless, just as I had the first Christmas after our separation. Without God's intervention, the devil can and will take us out. We must live our lives in the "life of the Jesus or his welcoming false ideologies will work. But, if our lives are hidden in God, through the Blood of Jesus, he can never overtake us.

God loves to fight for us and can effortlessly stop the robbers plans when we adjust and obey, even if we have to suffer to do so. For Jesus, Satan is just a prissy-pissy-sissy, that intimidates depressed men, women and children. Even when our essence is small and full of momentary darkness, God is still continually great! He is always at the zenith of His Power! The lying spirits that are sent for our jugular veins can feel too horrendous to deal with for us, but they run fervently from the presence of God. It is good for us to know that we are powerless without God. Yes, the influence of his evil seduction (the dark side) is overwhelming without God.

Many lessons are learned living in the life of Christ. Though all the pain and adjustments, we are growing and being purified, planted and moved on into a higher plane of actuality. We are also learning to fear disobedience. None of it feels good, but it can't; not when we are coming out of dwelling in darkness.

Especially during times of depression and stress, make sure you are savvy and taking care of yourself physically with good vitamins and minerals, or your body and brain will drain energy quickly and perceive incorrectly.

Home to Love
Yes, the cleansing of God feels like torturous persecution; but you remember; it is only bringing us back home to love. Jyndia and I made it to the other side that day because Jesus is the power and principality that rules over darkness! He cannot be trifled with. Satan waited for another opportunity to destroy us, but he was stopped again in his tracks, by the author of true love and beauty. "Thank You Jesus, for your wonderful presence and intervention!" My Beloved showed up for me. "Lord, you brought me through that awful wheat field and over the Royal Gorge!" You did it!" I worship and praise God to this day that He stopped the lying mouth of the devourer. Jesus saved us! Mercy said "No!"

When the enemy came in like a flood, the Spirit of the Lord raised a higher standard against him! He was not allowed to overtake me in my grief and disappointment. (Hope deferred makes the heart sick). God is still love, kindness and mercy, even when we are angry with Him. Our deliverer lives and is able! The One who has the highest authority in the world said, "No devil, you can't have her! – Back off you liar!"

"God, delivered us from the power of darkness, and translated us into the Kingdom of his dear Son. We have redemption through His blood, even the forgiveness of sins." (Colossians 1:13-14)

God's intervention is just one of the many magnificent benefits of being in personal relationship with him. He makes the difference! Our safety is in the Lord. His presence and power will always get us through. On our own there is not enough strength to make it to the other side of the mountain or canyon, or to overcome a broken heart. We need the Lord more than we know and must untie His hands through obedience! I would have fallen into an unthinkable realm of afterlife, without God! Our answer to the spirit of suicide is this: <u>"Give your life to the cause of God in trust."</u> We belong to Jesus and to life, not to death, destruction or ourselves.

"For as many as received the Lord and believed on His Name, to them He gave power to be sons of God!" (St. John 2:12)

Develop strong godly friendships
When you are hurting and are wounded, stay in touch with your feelings and stay around highly developed, "Jesus" people. Never feel ashamed of your soul state. Let go of your pride. Healing takes time. It's all right to be in the process of healing slowly. I was pushing myself to be stronger than I was; and was out of touch with the deepness of my emotional pain. I needed massive doses of inner

healing and godly love that had more to do with feelings that stemmed from childhood mistruths and unworthiness. Luis' words and schemes hurt more because I lacked faith in myself. I allowed his disbelief to make me distrust myself.

<u>Never abandon yourself</u> and don't hinder your course of grieving and healing. We all need help to get to the other side of our life situation. We are where we are and who we are, because what is-is. It can only be over, when it's over. Don't let anyone tell you when they think it should be over for you; but hear the voice of Jesus for yourself!

"For you are bought with a price, therefore glorify God in your body and in your spirit, which belong to God." (1 Corinthians 6; 18)

A bruised reed he will not break, and a smoldering wick he will not snuff out. In faithfulness, he will bring forth justice. (Isaiah 42:3)

He has sent Me (Jesus) to heal the brokenhearted, to proclaim liberty to the captives and heal those who are brokenhearted, to announce that captives will be set free and .... he had a mission and commission from his Father; he came not of himself, (Isaiah 61:1)

Pray for separating spirits
We have no power in ourselves to overcome oppressive, unseen forces, but Jesus can. The Greater One will always intervene if we let Him. If you are going through your own panorama of trouble, ask God to stay close to you. Just say, "Lord, help me. I don't know the way, but fight for me!" God will gladly do it. Even if you were wrong or have put yourself in the snake pit, God will show up and joyfully help you through the process; but first, you must do all you can to bring your life into obedience.

God will help you and is your very source of life. He delights in being there for you, if you ask Him to be. Even if you don't feel His presence, ask anyhow; but give up and surrender; stop fighting against life itself. Let JESUS get you back home to joy, purpose and life. He knows why and where you made the wrong turn. He knows where the juncture was and is.

Your Father loves to get you to the other side of the mountain and canyon! We must diligently pray for those going through divorces and breakups, even if we think they are wrong or terrible people. Accept that you don't know all the facts.

Prayers
"Lord, help _____ be strong and get them through all of their processes of pain! Lord give _____ joy, empowerment and peace right now! Help them align with your will!"

Pray for them as though they are you. Pray for them every day. There are many precious souls who do commit suicide in their plight between light and darkness. We don't know what happens during their last minutes of decision, or why the devil is able to overpower and captivate them. Pray for everyone involved. Every person in your realm of influence needs your help to cross over and through their difficult rivers and valleys. And please take time to listen to their side of the story.

Let us fear disobedience and disharmony with God. Let us fear the consequences of sin. Evil harvests are only released through going our own way. "But among you there shall not be even a hint of sexual immorality or any kind, or impurity, or greed. These are improper for God's Holy people." (Ephesians 5:3)

"There is a way that seems right to a man, but in the end, leads to death." (Proverbs 14:12)

"The fear of the LORD tends to life: he that has it shall abide satisfied. He shall not be visited with evil." (Proverbs 19:23)

"Lord, I pray: Strengthen the person reading this book. Help them acquire an ear to hear and obey the sound of Your voice. Help them vigorously respect your instruction and wonderful Presence. Help them obey, especially during times of introductions. Help them realize the seriousness of these moments. Help them see the present beauty and purpose of their life. I pray and believe that they will not give desire and emotion an opportunity to manifest. Help them stop and prevent, dastardly roads, times and seasons! Amen."

GLIMMERS OF LIGHT   Chapter 7

Light and Wisdom for the journey...

The Lord is on our side and the devil always loses when we call on the Name of Jesus. The voice of the Lord is mighty and strong; - Sharper than any two-edged sword! The Holy Spirit reminded me, "Remember, Dorothy, fear not. God told you He would walk with you all the way to the other side of the wheat field. Just trust your Father."

My eyes turned unhurriedly from a marriage I once believed in. Healing was revealing itself; oh, so slowly. The chauffeur drove on. He had no plans to turn around. Luis was gone and defeated on the side of the road. Almost three long years of struggling had passed. God had been trying to show me another side of life. I wasn't bouncing back marvelously, but dared to believe I could look forward. I was not the strong, self-assured, career woman I once was; nor could I leap tall buildings with a single bounce, but I did notice an undercurrent of godly strength. I ventured to think about life without marriage. I learned to pray for my children, others and me, instead of for reconciliation. I had no desire to find a new mate. I needed another man, like I needed another wheat field. I was learning obedience from the many things I suffered (resisted).

"Even though Jesus was God's Son, he learned obedience from the things he suffered." (Hebrews 5:8)

Dreams
Dreams are amazing. I awoke one morning feeling that Luis was home. Jyndia awoke at the same time and asked, "Mom is dad home? Where is he?" We were essentially having the same dream. Our dreams were difficult to apply correctly. A funny one showed Luis and me on a roller coaster ride at a recreation park. Just before the risky and dangerous coaster pulled off, Luis got off and said; "I'll see you at the end of the ride." He left me to ride the precarious, troubling, roller coaster alone. That dream was certainly an accurate analysis of Luis betrayal and duplicity!

In another dream, Luis took me through a beautiful mansion. It was his gift to me for being a good and faithful wife. All the decor and even the clothes in the closet were a soft sea green color. God used that dream to give me the deep feelings of honor I deserved. But the dream represented my true spiritual Husband Jesus, my Bridegroom. Jesus often represents the husband dynamic in good dreams.

Jyndia and I both dreamed about our family together, around tables at beautiful homes. We were often eating lovely meals and enjoying life. These dreams soothed and brought joy and comfort to both of us. Some dreams were loathsome. Often, Luis was mean and unhappy. He was once a monster with scars all over his face. Hum... an accurate account of a feckless soul state. The dreams stopped years later when I didn't need them anymore. Only God can judge their true significance. Dreams often give profound messages and wisdom. Our spiritual mind sifts them to help us ascertain truth. Dreams are one of God's most creative ways to get His life, image and goodness into our psyche. Jesus certainly wanted my heart to heal.

The restoration of our soul, (mind, will and emotions) comes in many curious stages. God uses Bible reading, dreams, visions, people, prayer, fasting, faith, and hope to establish us in truth. These dynamics are components that help us get back to the place we belong. In the healing process, we often need mental pictures that help our hearts go on ... The heart must go on ... Dreams seemed to be God's selected method to give me more insight and the emotional healing I so desperately needed. Some came from my spirit and others from my soul realm. Some depicted my personal desire for reconciliation and my belief that Luis was my lifetime partner. Those dreams were empowered by some of the prophecies I mentioned and my personal desires, which said, "hold on to the familiar a while longer."

At the beginning of our separation my sadness and grief were unbearable. I needed to believe that Luis was coming back. My understanding was so messed up. It was easy to believe the dreams meant that God was working to bring Luis home. God in His wisdom and mercy permitted me to believe those dreams for a season, at my worse time, until he knew that I could let go of them to look at what he was really offering me. He knew I had no other paradigm or model of life to anchor myself upon. Those dreams encouraged me, until I was strong enough to see and experience more of life and truth without Luis. God was working behind the scenes to develop truth and righteous comparisons. I needed distinctions strong enough to oppose the inner and outer lies.

Growth is precious
Feeling like I could look ahead, I began to grow and pray for strength to focus on my work and future. There was no more grace or need to pray for reconciliation. Thank God, You got me here! I declared, "Lord, I don't need the dreams or prophecies anymore either! Help me become a happy, contented, holy single woman and restore the hearts of my children!" I liked the fact that I was not trying to please a man anymore. I didn't need to alter my day for someone else or worry about where he was. I could work on projects, write, cook or clean when I felt like it. I loved being able to read as long as I wanted. I was surprised that I delighted myself in "this room called singleness."

Deep inside, I knew I could and would make it! I was changing my viewpoint and definition. I could finally see a prevailing, victorious, vibrant woman! One who through the power of Jesus, outlasted much adversity and persecution! I understood through my process of death and purification that I could really trust God. He would satisfy my life and sooth my soul! Jesus was really more than enough. I didn't think He could be, but He proved Himself to me. He was more than I expected and was the true lover of my soul!

The restaurant

Luis was certainly enjoying his singleness. He dated more than one woman and benefited from his popularity. Lacy wasn't the only one participating in his lust exchange! A group of ladies from my divorce care group and I decided to visit one of the nicer restaurants. Upon entering ... Behold! There he was, sitting in my new experience. I watched, as he smiled; charming and bedazzling his new victim! I knew all about that enchantment. It seemed that Lacy was Luis' private lover. He dated the more, demure and sophisticated publicly. What a disgusting web he had spun to serve his own flesh. Luis was still committed to himself at the expense and significance of others.

Luis' dating schedule often spilled over into Jyndia's visiting times. He had not been spending much time with her. When Jyndia looked across the room and saw her dad, her eyes lit up in excitement! She was so happy to see him! She attempted to leap out of my arms to run across the floor to get him. She wanted to have her Daddy! I helped her out by carrying her across the room to his table. I said, "Hello, how are you," (to the lady and the tramp) and put Jyndia in his arms! I smiled! Suddenly there was a stone-cold silence at his table! He held Jyndia like a hard-rock statue, frozen in place. I smiled again and left her with him.

I walked across the room in grand style to sit down with my friends. I looked great that night! What sweet pleasure! What joy I received! How bold and beautiful I was. I felt empowered and vibrant! I was the epitome of cool! (Thank God, I didn't fall in my heels). I was healing and it felt awesome! This was the courage-filled Dorothy I knew! My friends thought I was astounding! They were awestruck with my hutzpah! When I looked back at his table, he sat there as stiff as a hoot owl on a limb. That was good. He needed to see himself in the right light. I felt wonderful!

I had been passive and hurting long enough, but the lioness was emerging! Resurrection time was nigh! LOL! Of course, it was a small victory, but it felt good to take some measure of assertiveness. I knew that feelings of vengeance had to be given to God and acquiesced quickly, but they are a part of our healing process. They are normal at first, but ultimate retribution belongs to the Lord, the righteous judge! However, if I could only be God for one little minute, I would have taken care of him more than sufficiently! (Smirking)! "Lord, how about one or two small boils or a wart to begin with? - How about fastening him to a good-old, fashioned rough pole for a month or two in the dead of winter? That would be a great start!

I found this to be true: The German poet Rilke said: "A person isn't who they are during the last conversation you had with them – They are who they've been throughout your whole relationship." Amen!

CBS

Paying attention to my own purpose, I looked pretty good without Luis. Things began to move for me. I enjoyed life and who I was before the nasty diversion. My passion for impacting lives was still important. I began to study again and prepare for seminars. I was at a TV station talking about an event, when the right person saw me. Praise God, the director came out of her office and said, "You are really good at what you do. Would you like to work with our morning news show?" I answered, "YES I WOULD!" God ordained this! In no time, I was doing a "Parent Talk Show" with a CBS television affiliate. I so needed this new adventure! The idiosyncrasy was this: I had presented my program to television stations for years, but nothing came of it. Now, God's goodness and favor was marvelously shining through!

I had the favor of God on my life again! Who, can say no to God? I was grateful and delighted! Me on TV! Phenomenal! What a breath of fresh air! This wonderful new experience gave me hope and vision for my future. I felt God's breath, as I had known Him years before. Good news was long overdue. God had never left or abandoned me. I just needed to align with His plan and provision. When I moved back into place, I understood, the river was still flowing. It had never dried up. God had been fighting all the time for me. He just needed to win my heart again! Growth had taken place and signs of resurrection were sprouting and budding. I knew I could trust God! I was aligning with truth.

"For I will restore health to you and heal you of your wounds, says the Lord. They have called you an outcast, saying no one seeks after you. Because of that behold, I will bring you from the captivity of your tents. I will have mercy on your dwelling place. You shall be built upon your own heap and the palaces shall remain after the manner thereof. Out of you shall precede thanksgivings and the voice of them that make merry. I will multiply you and you shall not be few. I will also glorify you and you shall not be small." (Jeremiah 31: 17-19)

God amazingly brought me through water, fire, floods and that abhorrent wheat field. None of my adversaries had utterly taken me out, but I still had to watch and defy the emotional realm. There were times when I wanted to look back - old habits die-hard. You must stay aware that emotions can surface easily and need to be filtered immediately. I wish I could tell you, I got over the pull of the past quickly and sailed into sunny places, but I didn't. I had to move with God one day at a time, because we have an enemy who will always try to redirect us. Nevertheless, I knew the Talk Show victory would not have come with the disorder and derision of disobedience with Luis in my life. God's blessings only work in environments of righteousness.

We often choose to misperceive the devil's seasons of erroneous pleasure with God's blessings. The devil can't resist mimicking God temporarily, until he gets us where he wants us. His lack of opposing us can look and feel like blessings are occurring, even if we are living in the deepest pit of sin and insolence. Later, "Oops," his nasty payments are due, with interest. His mandates are taken out on our souls. We suffer many losses and regrets - sometimes forever. His counterfeit blessings are not righteous, good for us or free and must be detected at the gate.

Progressive lessons
Our beloved is wonderful, and dazzling in excellence! As time moved on, I enjoyed my God, children, job and myself. There was so much more to know and to live for. God and I enjoyed a breathtaking summer together. I grew in Kingdom Glories spending time with my Savior. I reached new heights, beholding His majesty and received immeasurable revelations and insights. My new conformity in the Lord was wonderful. He is unspeakable indulgence! When we connect with the King of the Kingdom, we can see life from the mountaintop. Looking into His eyes brings a gratification that is worth it all!

On the flip side, manifesting light will always penetrate darkness, and exhibitions of light, revelation and joy, create fear for the devil. He knows when we are really seeking and seeing Jesus, and when we see Jesus in His Glory we know who we are! We also see our authority, power and ability. When we know how to use our power and authority, the devil knows we can kick his lying tail coming and going! "Bam!" That's why he works so hard to divert us, leading us into wrong relationships and down disobedient paths that obstruct our growth. But, Bible reading, worship, time with God and prayer, create power and illumination that suffocates his rotten plans.

Satan prefers that we are busy and separated from God, into ourselves, others, work, erroneous relationships, depressed or miserable. These factors work to help him oppress us. He hopes we'll do anything else, but spend quality time with God.

By autumn, after my wonderful summer with God, the enemy had a new strategy in mind to derail me. In spite of my spiritual breakthrough and optimism, the bombardment of a new thought grew more prevalent in my mind daily. "It is so difficult to be on my own." The continual barrage was exasperating! Finally, I entertained the words and began to meditate on them. After weeks of hearing the thought, the veracity of the phrase "bushwhacked" my joy. Subtlety I was moving out of faith in God's ability to satisfy my life and subscribed to the enemy's thoughts, trying to understand my feelings.

The feeling realm can be dangerously observed from the wrong premise

I should have countered the phrase with the Word of God or with the fact that God was my constant fulfillment, love and provider. His abundance was available to help me, but entertaining the words; I digressed and wondered if I was missing something being on my own. The cares of life and the pondering, gradually stole parts of my pinnacle experience. The enemy had come for the light this time. I was waxing strong from spending serious amounts of time with God, and the enemy was threatened. He set in motion his diversion plan for a different reason this time, ultimately, he did not want me to move in God's might and power. He had to try to stop the power of my praise, Bible reading and worship.

I continued to spend time with God, but like Eve in the Bible; I stopped seeing what I already had in my Garden. Instead of focusing on "God would supply all my needs according to his riches in glory," I meditated more on my natural needs. I felt hindered and marginalized and wanted to move to another city. I wanted to move because Luis' visible lifestyle tackled me almost daily. I wanted no remembrances of my past life, but the devil made sure someone kept me informed. When I stayed in the presence of God, his lifestyle didn't bother me, but at times the residue from our bad relationship surfaced again. By now, Luis had put himself in a singles magazine to promote his availability and partied with twenty-year old's. Hearing about him on every hand was disturbing.

An artful enemy
I trusted that God understood my stress and expected intervention, but this is my point: be very careful, even when you desire a wholesome thing. You have an enemy that aggressively and artfully attempts to answer your request. He lives to mess us up again. His crafty solutions can look genuine, as he persistently attempts to mimic God's voice and blessings. If you succeed or fail; he is never satisfied and strives to redirect your path again. He is always plotting your demise. He is there to misrepresent choice A, B, C or D, and if we are negligent, he will accomplish it. <u>Never minimize your enemy</u>! Pay close attention to what you hear, see and feel. He is always endeavoring to work at the <u>same time</u> God is! How he loves to distort.

Remember, the devil will never stop trying you mess us up!

"Lord, increase our discernment and faith." Satan creates many kinds of scenarios to stop our dedication to God. He furiously hates our love, worship and allegiance to God. He wants it for himself. I want to tell you about his plan to answer my request. I traveled to see my mother and spent the night with a friend on the way. Judy thought I should meet an acquaintance. He was settled and had been praying for his soul mate. I wasn't sure, but perhaps this was God. I was certainly praying about companionship due to my constant thought. If this was God, I was interested and wanted to investigate a little more. I knew when we walk with God; He will bring us the desires of our hearts, effortlessly. There was certainly nothing wrong with wanting a good mate, from God, in God's season.

Judy called Robert and we talked a few minutes. Mysteriously, the same night, I dreamt about a mean and hateful man. I knew what that meant, but ironically, my pastor had spoken a word to me a month before. He said "Your husband is looking for you. He is a distinguished man. You will meet him soon." Pastor also said, "It is defilement to ever consider going back to Luis." Another minister told me years before, "Robert won't be able to resist your words. You will make a big difference in "Robert's life." Surprisingly, the man's name was Robert. He fit both prophetic words.

Now, I have my prayer before God, my dream and words from two trustworthy ministers in the mix; even down to the man's name. And I am praying about my constant thought, about companionship and moving to another city. Now, doesn't everything I mentioned look almost "perf" and amazingly accurate. So … I thought I should talk to him a little more to Robert. (Notice the - I) Over a few months, our talks evolved and the door opened to move. I decided I could at least visit him to see if the signs were right. After my wonderful summer with God; perhaps this could be a gift. (Does this sound like a replay)?

It wasn't long before Robert pressed me to move to his city, quickly declaring his ability to be a good partner and provider. He would be happy to help me make a fresh start there. Everything seemed to line up with my request and shouted, "This is it - This is God. Your life will be so much easier now." Even my pastor approved of the move. (Remember he saw him spiritually, even before I met Robert). Robert said, "God told me that you are one of his most prized possessions and I am honored that you will relocate here" … Sounded good …was this the mystical hand of God pushing me past the city limits and answering my prayers. I reasoned, (reasoning is dangerous, when we put intellectualism over our spiritual knowing), "Well, we are both legally single, and I would be marrying after the spirit, not the flesh this time … and I really want to move."

Doesn't all this look flawless? All seemed right with the world, except my dream and personal word from the Lord. My spirit knew from the moment I had the dream that Robert was a problematic man, but a more perfect solution had presented itself and I could leave town and that lecherous Luis behind once and for all. I would finally find relief from life's pressures and would not have to hear about Luis anymore! There would be no more of his suffocating presence, and no more of being totally on my own. My daughter and I moved there for three months … and all was not right with the world! All creation shouted, "You are in the wrong place and you know it! Get out of here!" My spirit revolted and came to a screeching halt. I could hear, "This is an absolute mistake! Run for your life!" … And I did!

Resolution
I was so happy I had grown in the Lord and was quick to correct my path. I was not supposed to be there and would not try to fit into Robert's life. Some doors should never be open. That was one. The relationship might have made my life easier financially, but he was absolutely "super wrong" for me and my life purpose. I want to tell you, there are a whole lot of things worse than learning to trust, suffer and lean on the Lord. No matter how important the pastors were in my life, my dream was right and trumped everything they saw and said. And of course, he really was a mean man - a control freak. The man had chief

codependent issues - off the chart issues. No wonder he was available! (Whew Jesus)!

I speedily decided, "It's okay honey. You are not supposed to be here. Don't give this muddled situation one more minute of your life. Your life and time is far more precious than this. God will take care of you!" I repented for my mistake, jumped into the arms of God and quickly changed direction. I was sorry I agreed with and entertained the enemy's words. I repented that I did not completely trust God for my joy, but still I refused to live disobediently again and got back on course. I had to be in the right place before God, no matter how difficult it was.

The old guilt-ridden Dorothy, would have spent years trying to change Robert or myself, but not the new spiritual me. I was proud that I was learning to <u>fully trust God</u>. I learned the devil's push to make me decide quickly about Robert was a clue that I was going the wrong way, along with my word from God. It didn't take long to realize that every door that opens is not a God door. If you feel stressed or rushed, it's not from God. It's almost always the devil pulling your strings, because he must work before you see what he's doing. Allow yourself <u>time</u> to move circumspectly. Speedy moves in relationship are a profitable arena for Satan, but not for us!

"But with too much haste all that comes is want." (Proverbs 21:5)

Line of defense

Opening the door to Robert resulted from first entertaining the enemy's words. The disorder began when I saw my cup half empty, instead of full. Secondly, I allowed Satan to plant unchallenged words in my mind without changing them to the truth. That was a big mistake. I needed to rebuke Satan's words and repeat what God said about my completeness. I also needed more wisdom in the natural realm to blend spiritual and conventional living. There are seasons when we can do full time ministry, but until then we must do all that is necessary in the natural realm to have sufficient income. My third line of resistance would have been having a strong income of my own in place and trust in God's ability to satisfy me. That sanctuary of soundness would have negated my desire to investigate the relationship past my warning signal.

Examinations past a word from the Lord to any measure always disappoint us. When God gives a dream, vision or word, we cannot take another apprehensive path. The dream was my fourth line of defense for protection. It was clear that I was not to allow a relationship to form with Robert. My correspondence from God at the gate was the clarity of the dream. God told me "Robert is a mean and unhappy man. He is not a blessing from Me." In the end my dream was truth, just as; "Luis is a womanizer" was true.
Yes, Men of God are to be honored, but we can never put their words above a personal word from God. God was right and they were wrong; no matter what

they saw. Whether the enemy answered their prophecies or not, the pastors were wrong concerning this Robert, but God's personal word to me was right! Just because someone is looking for you, doesn't mean you are looking for them.

I learned that being content in the Lord is far better than silver, gold or a human relationship. Our happiness comes from Gods Presence and doing His will. The right God relationship is great, if you both are blessing the Lord together, but no relationship can supersede what we have in Christ. I was happy I had grown and was willing to walk away from another illegitimate season, but of course not going at all would have been better. Robert was used as another set up, from you know who!! I did ninety percent better this time, but still did not entirely pass the test. I hope you are learning from my mistakes and will not dwell in a disobedient relationship.

The enemy of our soul is proficient in trying to answer our request to God. The devil will always try to stop us and will, unless we are more determined not to let him, by disciplining ourselves to know and quote the Word daily! The word builds a fortress!

Agreement with Words

We must learn not to receive negative words and feelings. When we listen to Satan, without challenging what he says, he can work out his evil schemes before we figure him out. Remember, he uses our good and godly desires to build his case. God's timing is best. He is our intuition, as we outstandingly trust His voice. The bible says, "All my needs were (are) met in Jesus name." The devil's words were not true. I had more than enough provision. My resources and treasures were full. I was looking at lack instead of manifesting God's fullness within me, in both spiritual and natural domains. I could have canceled Satan's words aggressively with the Word of God.

Fighting back as strong soldiers means we use God's thoughts and scriptures continually. Contending for truth means we know the Word of God and willingly to apply it. What we hear and allow is gradually conceived in our minds. Conceiving of the devil's thoughts give him permission to bring us counterfeit presentations and they manifest.

Since that time, I stop and cast down negative thought systems immediately with God's Words of truth. Notice, I was happy in the Lord, before I submitted to the enemy's illusive words, which seemed to come from my own mind. Those words were nowhere on my radar before. I wasn't looking for a new mate until the suggestions bombarded me after my summer fest with God. God's comfort was more than sufficient, until I refused to take authority over the contender's words. His words yoked me with the cares of the world again.

If we are anxious for a relationship, we are not ready... our season has not yet come. In God's time, our season is fully ripe. Yes, I wanted to move to a new city and put Luis behind me, but God could have made that happen better though my faith in His timing. I believe God will give a wonderful dream at that time, full of joy and knowing!

Meeting New People
There are hundreds of ways to get involved with people or groups to acquire more victory in joy and finance. God will not fail us. He is a brilliant business man. I could have done more to omit financial uncertainty and stayed in the spirit, concerning rumors about Luis. Perhaps my lesson was learning how to shut down conspirators, by holding my head up and burying my pride. Yes, God said, "It is not good for man to be alone, but this also means establishing rich friendships at Church and other places. Marriage is not the only place to enjoy life, friendship and growth.

Prayer:
Let's pray out loud: "God with your help, I will never hesitate to obey your unction's as soon as I hear your voice. Forgive me for not challenging the enemy and for compromising with Your warning signals. Help me to be less curious and more trusting of you. Make me strong enough to cast down negative words and listening to others. With your strength, I will not return unauthorized phone calls, because sentimentality is synonymous to vulnerability! Help me pass every test! In Jesus Name, Amen"

Stop spiritualizing everything
I have unfortunately seen hundreds of Christians miss the practical guidance of God, by spiritualizing natural components. We want the spiritual realm of the Lord so much that we miss His natural input. Remember, the "natural and the spiritual go hand in hand." The Bible says, "*The children of the world are wiser than the children of God,*" because we miss doing the practical, too often. Don't make that mistake. God will help you know what time it is, whether for your relationship, move, work, ministry or business. Don't resist what he is showing you. Don't over spiritualize the obvious.

Allow the maturity of time to come. Let your desires stay in the cave and hibernate until spring comes. There is a lot more you can do and learn before it is time. Spend more time with God. Work hard, take classes, read books or go back to school.

God wants you to flourish and increase
If you are open to growth, it won't be long before your life, career, business or ministry is strong and sturdy. Wait until it easily happens. There will be a right time - Let your dreams rest awhile in God's hands and trust Him. We need to grow and get the pride out of the way. You have nothing to prove to anyone. Rest assured, if God has given it to you, He will raise it from the dead if necessary at the best time. As a matter of fact, when it's time, your dreams or ministry will overtake you. You won't have a choice, but to run with it. You best get in shape now. Jesus prepared thirty years, for three years of ministry. You and I need more preparation time too; more than we can see. Yes, Jesus knows how to keep His desires and purpose within you in place. Have you noticed how well He holds the stars in the sky?

Serenity
Our best companionship and provision comes from the Lord. We must train ourselves to see His big picture and eternal view. No one else is responsible for you, but God and you. We can trust that God will do His part and He loves to redeem the time for us.

We need to stay in His presence and continue to identify every area of needed growth. We all need more light and revelation knowledge to take solid, calculative steps. Finally, make positive changes for a better future. Adjust and get off the wrong tract fast. Accept when you choose incorrectly, repent and quickly move back into place. Stay in agreement with God and stop when He says stop; go when He says go! Don't try to understand it, just trust Him. Just hold God's hand. Keep the faith by keeping yourself in His Word. Rejoice when you try to do the right thing and stop blaming yourself for trying to do the right thing. Just keep on following the Lord. If you miss it, practice hearing His still small voice better than before. He is worth it all.

Cottage in the City
Life was beginning to feel a lot less scary. I felt a sense of peace moving to Kansas City, at the request of my son. The new environment felt amazing. Spending quality time with James would be great. I was proud of his growth and grateful for his spiritual strength. Family connection was exactly what I needed. I had new stresses, but began to reinvent my life, keeping my eyes on Jesus. I was ready to embrace being an unmarried lady now. Nothing could be that hard when you have come through the fire and looked the devil in the eye. I Thanked God that Jesus had defeated him at every turn. Hallelujah! My long walk through the wheat field was over!!! I was gaining momentum and gusto now. It felt good to be thriving and growing again. And God blessed me to move after all.

A block away from James' house, I was blessed to find a great job as program coordinator for Special Olympics. I rejoiced that God was intricately involved in my life. Three months after relocating, my supervisor told me about two blocks from an elementary school. I called the landlord by faith, knowing my credit was in bad shape, but God was in control. The landlord said, "I have received over thirty calls today, but there is something special about your voice; you can take ownership of the house, and if you put the shades up, I'll waive your first month's rent." Yes, God loves to show us His favor! My daughter and I had our own space again! We were abundantly blessed and had a good time fixing up our own little cottage on the hill.

Our home was the smallest one we had ever lived in, but also the happiest and most peaceful. It was quaint, but decorated beautifully! We named it our "cottage in the city." We treasured our chalet. It was filled with light, love and harmony. Most of all God gave it to us. A year later the house was in my name. The landlord supernaturally signed it over to me. I was a legitimate homeowner. My mom convinced me to take it, even though I thought the house was too small. She said, "Now this is an opportunity to have your own property, silly girl." She assured me that people don't turn houses over that easily. God and my mom are great business people. Being in the right place, I could see the blessings of God unfold again. Before I moved, a friend tried to put fear in me about leaving Wichita, but I had finally learned to listen to God for myself. I knew I had His peace; my joy and home was evidence to stand on.

Empathy
When Luis came to see Jyndia, I could feel judgmental undertones. He was an image man and my blessing was not his ideal of prosperity. I thought, "Who does he think he is standing in all his grandeur? Was I supposed to ask for his approval?" But, I would not be moved by his intimidation. Luis was a small fragment of my past now, so he could keep his arrogance and image. Although, it can take years of negative intervals to resolve an illegitimate relationship, I would not be provoked. I could see that one of the reasons God attempts to stop us from erroneous connections, is that he knows the many hurtful phases necessary to breaking patterns and theories that affect us. The repercussion can infiltrate our emotions for years. The price of disobedience is far reaching.

I was surprised: God was cultivating compassion in my heart for Luis. He was really a poor and blind, pride filled man, who could not know God in his fullness. I hated what he did to me, especially the lies he told, but he could only give who and what he was ... and I was warned. If he had deeply known God, he would have been a better man. If he had been my true husband things would have worked out, but we all manifest darkness in our states of sin.

Sin had caused Luis to miss his greater potential in many ways. He may never know the measure in which he gave and lost his strength and destiny to women. Nevertheless, Luis' forfeited acting righteously, while those righteous acts would have given him, a greater destiny. We can never minimize this: when God says sin causes us to miss the mark, we can know that something was and is lost from allowing sin to reign in our lives.

Lacy, the ballerina and forgiveness
I purchased a beautiful ceramic ballerina doll for two reasons. The doll reminded me that by faith, Jyndia could be a ballerina dancer. It also served as a point of contact for me to pray for Lacy. I wanted to give God an opportunity to work goodness and love in my heart towards this woman too. I didn't want to hate or blame her anymore. Our paths had crossed for a reason. The least I could do was pray for her. It was tough at first, but I got past the bitterness. The prayers became easier because of the power of God. When I looked at the doll I would say, "Lord, Lacy is a Christian, so give her the real beauty that comes from your life. Forgive her and keep her in your hands." I continued to confess and declare by faith that she was blessed and holy. She needed the help of God, just like I did. We all needed more light from Heaven. Who was I to judge Lacy? We both disobeyed God and were obviously codependent. That was the reason we

allowed Luis (darkness) to choose us. We saw him as a "Savior," as one to complete our lives. We didn't know we already had all things in Christ Jesus. Their conduct was despicable, but God was giving me liberty to love, the way He does.

Not my town
After my challenging move; the news was upsetting! I could hardly believe my ears. Luis was moving to my town to permeate my new surroundings. I was working on forgiveness, but still didn't like his lifestyle or want him in my consecrated space. But, he was coming to finish his ministerial studies. I was okay with seeing him a few times a month, when he visited Jyndia, but this was a little much! He was the central reason I left Wichita, or better said, was driven out by the spirit of Jezebel! He was the last person on earth I wanted in my galaxy … That was until I looked at my Jyndia. When she learned her Daddy was moving to Kansas City, she was the happiest little girl in the world! Filled with joy, she would now have her Dad and Mom close. This was an answer to prayer for her.

Seven years old, was an important time to be with her Dad. Luis loved Jyndia in his own way; he just needed more power and freedom in Jesus. Jyndia did need more of his attention. This move would be about meeting her needs, not irritating me. He didn't have the faith to raise his daughters (Luis had an older daughter from his first marriage) in their rightful home settings, but he did see them as much as his dating schedule allowed. He might have been my biggest mistake, but he was not Jyndia's. I decided, if this was good for my child, my indifference and discomfort didn't matter. Luis' arrival would not invade my life and when needed, I would do my complaining to God.

Judgments
It wasn't long before Jyndia informed me that her Dad had another girlfriend (Eliza), Lacy was long gone. After several years, Luis and Lacy's reign of distortion was over. I was not surprised. Disobedience, adultery or fornication will not stand the test of time; not for any on us. Their lust was used to destroy our marriage, because it could be destroyed; but all the passion in the world could not give them substance or longevity. When sin used them up, it took their strength, dignity and purpose. It aborted them just as it does each of us. It abandons us in the shadows and on dark roads. It leaves us rolling with evil demons in the night and calling on God for mercy.

The Lord allowed me to hear that Lacy received a strong rebuke for her part in the destruction of my marriage. According to scripture, there are serious consequences connected to laying with a married man? Didn't she and Luis understand their adulterous activities and arrogant decisions were against God's principles? They were doing their thing to God, not to me. We never have a right to tamper with a marriage, even if the marriage is not God ordained. As Christians, we have to act with decency and order before God and man, no matter how much it hurts our egos. Lacy (and Luis) attempted to contort the truth, but the test of time and consequence proved they could not. The scars and pain of her disobedience (like mine) will last a long time. Sin, hurts! Disobedience always creates terrible and unsuspecting outcomes that negatively alter our future. We have no control over how, when or where it will seek revenge. Know this; sin always strikes back and demands payment!

"Therefore, all they that devour you shall be devoured. All your adversaries, every one of them shall go into captivity. They that spoil you shall be spoiled. All that prey upon you - will I give for a prey?" (Jeremiah 30:17)

Marriages
Thank God for putting a holy fear in my heart against dating a married man. As compelling as their stories were/are, we don't know the whole story. No matter what you <u>think</u> is going on, you must walk away. No matter what kind of picture they paint (man or woman), and some tell unbelievable stories, "<u>DON'T TOUCH THAT MARRIAGE!</u>" I say with great humility and thankfulness; I have never tried to take any one's husband. The penalty for this is monumental! Even in this century of great promiscuity, you cannot be that bold in the face of God.

I have heard devastating, hair-razing stories of people who tried and encountered miseries untold. Marriage is sacred ground. Interfering opens an area and level of sin not to be trifled with. Men and women woefully regret the repercussions encountered after partaking of this fruit. After the fact, it's too late to stop the effects of God's laws.

The media drags indiscretions, before the eyes of the world every day. Look at people like Tiger Woods, Jesse Jackson, Bill Clinton, Bill Crosby, etc. Nobody wins when a marriage is tampered with. No one breaks God's spiritual laws and gets away with it. Let God, in His Omnipotence and Supreme Excellency judge erroneous marriages for himself. And, until he (or she) is legitimately available, they are not worth the price you will pay for each and every kiss. What God has joined together, let no man touch or attempt to destroy. (Read the book of Malachi, Chapter 2 in the Bible. I will illuminate more on the topic of marriage in my book, "Marriages that Endure the Fire)."

The Harvest is real
God is God, all by Himself. His sanctions of blessings or curses stand and balance each of us. If the earth lasts a million years, nothing will ever change the infallible, indisputable principles of God. No one is big enough to break spiritual laws ... No one! They are engraved on the walls of God's balancing system, His universe. His universe backs up His every word he has ever spoken. And why would God waste His precious time warning us about sin and transgressions, if it were not important? God never talks just to hear Himself talk, like some of us. He means it when He says, "Obey Me." He's not joking. God is holy! He pays close attention to what we do and say. When God says,

"don't sin." don't sin, for your own good! It doesn't matter that our modern world calls sin a positive growth experience. Psychiatrists, doctors, TV hosts and spiritualists say, "Hey, everything is okay. Don't worry about it baby. You're okay!" The world proclaims, "Be comfortable in your misdeeds. There is no black or white. Do what you feel like doing!"

Hear God's cry; sin is darkness and it is not okay! The world's wisdom seems strong and right, but none of it has the ability to stand against the virtuous hammer of God's tough love. Just look at our pitiful world system. Judge it for yourself. It's intellectual and sensual rhetoric is filled with misery, suicide and death. It does not produce the happiness it promises. - Not at all!

The effectiveness of God's cleansing system, "HIS HARVEST, cannot be stopped." It has been set in motion from the beginning of the world. Until now, there has always been seed, time and harvest. Year after year, lifetime after lifetime, generation after generation; the laws of God's are proficient and they do their work. They are not overcome by public or popular opinion. His principles work for the great and small. They work for kings and queens and for the rich and poor. His grace is for holiness, it is not for going our own way or for doing our own thing. You will reap a harvest for both your sins and obedient deeds, being ten or a hundred and ten, grown or not.

Forgiveness from God and turning from your sin <u>will not</u> cancel your harvest.

"Be not deceived, God is not mocked, whatever we sow we do reap." (Galatians 6:7)

"Gold is tested in fire. God puts worthy men (women) in the crucible of humiliation" (Sirach 2:1-18)

Deception
I wish I could tell you not to be concerned with sin and sinning like some in the world do, but in good conscience, I cannot. As you can see, I didn't want to be concerned about the consequences of sin either, which got me in deep trouble. Only the mercy and goodness of God could get me out alive. Sin created a realm of darkness, I knew nothing about. God says we are foolish if we are not terrified with the power of sin and what it will take from us. I was miserable living through my wheat field experience. All my horrific dreams, shame, torture and manifestations of evil; had to do with my sin and disobedience. The assassin absolutely and immeasurably altered my world.

Can you imagine what I actually missed out on because of disobedience? My choices empowered and released suffering causing regret and so will yours. I never knew anything about panic attacks, clinical depression or a spirit of suicide, until I walked past God speaking to me!

The harvest is real. Do you want to personally know how well Satan will use disobedience to amend your life? You will not see him coming or even know what hit you. You will simply find yourself in a vortex of pain that you can't get out of. You will immensely care at that time. At that time, your forbidden lover will be as bitter as gall and a heavy vexation and sore. Under your weight of sin, your knees will bend and your tongue will confess, "I am sorry for my sins Lord." You will remember His voice then. No matter how much you pray for crop failure; our personal reaping and harvest will not be stopped. Your purification time will not be funny or pretty. The extraction will surprise you, as you come to see the demise of a relationship you compromised to get and keep. The repercussions of disobedience bring a harvest that often last a lifetime.

Can you really afford to agree with the lies of your enemy?

Lacy
Satan's beguiling gifts seem sensational, but they are there to penalize and ravage our lives. Lacy, would tell you, as well that their escapades were not worth the cost she paid. Why? Because we cannot build happiness against the Word of God and at the expense of another's unhappiness. A decision to bite the forbidden apple of Satan is a decision to bite into imbalance, pain and dishonor. The taken bite, must to be put back again and more!

Yes, we do emphatically reap what we sow! It doesn't matter if the reason is a good or bad one. Good excuses carry the same penalty as bad ones. I thought Luis was a blessing from God and disobeyed. Lacy thought she could step on others to get what she wanted; perhaps her reason was part of her own life concept or cup of sorrow, but neither of us could get away with our disobedient acts; and neither will you. Just because we are hurting or desire a relationship, does not give us permission to ignore God's voice or to break spiritual rules that cannot be broken.

"Be not deceived, God is not mocked, whatever we sow we do reap."
(Galatians 6:7)

"Do not let sin reign in your mortal body. (Romans 6:12)

"Watch and pray, the spirit is willing, but the body is weak."
(Matthew 26: 40-41)

Your Future
Yes, there is a Great King in the earth that reinforces good, but allows evil to be judged. Yet God designed a better way, which is listening and submission to His will. Let us accept His authentic love and way of doing things, instead of Illegal relationships that flee in the night. They leave behind life-time penalties. Thank God we now know that the devil's seemingly innocent and innocuous (harmless) words of, "God will understand. It's all right to do this. God wants you to be

happy. You won't have to pay for this," they are lies! These views are common, but we won't accept them again. We know who Satan is and we won't sign up for his realms of punishment. We don't have to. We know that Satan's gifts only bequeath insufferable wheat fields that cripple our lives and futures.

> *"But, God has called many sons to walk in His glory."*
> *(Hebrews 2:10)*

(Ephesians: Chapters 1-3 and the book of Romans). (Deuteronomy, chapter twenty-eight, strongly illustrates the blessings and the curses we can endorse).

Missing the mark
God is never happy about our miseries, maltreatment or losses. One of the results of sin is to miss the "best of God." Nothing is worth missing the best of God? We need His presence and protection more than anything? Ask yourself, *"Would it mean anything at all if I gained the whole world and lost my very soul?"* Of course not! Your soul is more precious than sex, silver or gold. Outside God's safety zone, your enemy waits to consume you. No matter how strong you think you are, is anyone worth choosing to proceed with into the depths of hell? Even the most rebellious of us is not that dangerous. Pray that you will never activate any part of Satan's devilish system.

Listen
Listen unconditionally to first impressions, feelings or words when meeting a potential mate or anyone. God gives insights and instincts for our protection. He is speaking and trying to prevent seasons of misery and loss for you, His beloved. Listen without reservation. The result of disobedience is not a place you want to visit, end up at or lose your life in.

> *"Whoever listens to me will live secure. You will have a good and quiet life, fearing no mischief". (Proverbs 1)*

Repentance
Study the word continually for love, strength and wisdom. Repent, change your mind, turn from evil, and get yourself out of anything that God has not endorsed. Repentance means to come back up to the top. You are a powerful, supernatural spiritual being in Jesus! You are not just a mere human being, so you can do this! Yes, you can help yourself. You can believe God. Come back up to the top. You have overcoming power! Explore all that it means to live His Spirit filled life. Let Jesus fascinate you and you will hit the mark!

Wonderful obedience
Obedience will change you and improve the quality of your life immediately. Even if you have to temporarily live in a basement, shelter, borrow food, money, or clothing. Just obey God. Humble yourself and see how quickly God fixes

things for you. If you submit he will soon elevate you. Humble yourself under the Mighty hand of God. Dismiss all pride and ask God to help you do what is necessary. Align yourself with the truth. No excuses! Missing the mark is dangerous! Be strong in the Lord and in the power of His Might, not your own might. Trust Your Father! He is faithful to you! The right questions to ask yourself are these: "What ripples are coming back my way? What seeds have I planted? How can I get righteous seeds in the ground to counteract and balance the disobedient ones? How can I line up perfectly with the will of God now, and stop all disobedience?"

"No one who continues in sin has either seen God or knows Him. If God's seed remains in us, we cannot go on sinning. If we have been born of God we know who the children of God are, and who the children of the devil are."
(1 John 3:6-10)

"Whoever exalts himself will be humbled, but he who humbles himself will be exalted." (Luke 14:11)

A prayer for those who want love

"Lord, thank you for helping those who want to be in love. Change our hearts and help us see your dimensions of love first. We want to trust your wisdom. We submit to your best and to deep relationship with you! We ask you to make us keen listeners, so we are not too trusting and gullible. <u>We will not extend unsanctified mercy to anyone with Your help</u>. Lord, change our negative dependency issues, permanently. Fill us up with Your love, completeness and security. We are ready learners and desire Your leadership! The popular tide of culture is not for us, but we believe You. Help us worship You today, as we choose life for our families and ourselves. Help us immediately turn away from every lying and conniving person sent to mess us up!

Lord, we stand on your Word to receive courage. We are complete in You. We are doers of the Word, not just hearers. We happily do the natural and spiritual. We accept that we already have everything right now, because You live in us. We trust your plan for love and rightness. We will not settle for temporary invalid pleasure. No disapproved or disqualified person in your eyes can enter our lives. You alone provide the knowing and success we need. We are successful now because you love us.

We refuse to quit believing you. Your authenticity is the answer for me. Thank You God for making us wonderful and supernatural beings in You. All is possible today for us; nothing is impossible. I love you, Mighty God! Your transcendent love and prosperity lives in me and is beyond comprehension. I rejoice in You Lord! I have it all, in Jesus Name, Amen." (Personalize this prayer for yourself and others)

God tells us to pray for those who spitefully use us too. Why? - Because they will need our prayers in the future. If we put ourselves in the middle of hurting others, marriages and wrong relationships, we will greatly need the mercy of God at some point. The retaliation will be far more than is expected. Every second of working out their personal harvest of willfully sown disobedient seeds will be excruciating.

A prayer for those who spitefully use us
"Lord, we ask that _____ yield him or herself to Your will and Voice. Keep _____ mind and heart steady and give _____ the ability to reap (go through) the harvest they have sown. Help them repent and seek Your face. Help _____ desire you more than anything else today and use him/her for your great Glory! In Jesus Name, Amen!"

> "Lord, Your unfailing love will last forever.
> Your faithfulness is as enduring as the heavens." (Psalm 89:2)

CONVERSATIONS WITH ELIZA Chapter 8

Because of God's goodness and mercy, I had endured the anguish and cruelty of the wheat field ... and then the break-through. The journey was surely long and grueling, all the way to the end. My affliction was over and a dark side of life no man or woman should ever see. I was happy to be sane and alive. Thankfully, the Lord was putting back in me what the devil took out. The radiance and life of God was my only stronghold and refuge ... and again my life went on, in joy and expectation. I still had the most important things, God, faith, me, my children, family, friends, ministry, church life and vision! But my past was still entwined with my now.

Jyndia mentioned she never saw Lacy or her children anymore, neither did she see Eliza, the newer girlfriend I knew of. This young ladies name was Chattel. I thought, not another poor woman beguiled by Luis! What number was this one by now? Four, seven or ten? She might be number twenty-two for all I knew! Now, Jyndia would need to be involved with another lady in her father's harem of women. Maddening! "Here we go again! "How many women would my daughter have to see her preacher daddy involved with? And what damage might this do to her perception of faithfulness between a man and woman?" (Help, Lord!) The image of an unstable man parading his lovers before his daughter's innocent eyes was wrong and disgusting.

Children so need to see a fidelity that helps them have faith and vision for their own lives. We are responsible to give them that. These happenstances truly hurt our children. When we open their hearts to multiple parental partners, it is confusing, degrading and destabilizing. Our children would have fewer obstacles to overcome if they could deeply honor their parents. There ought to be a solemn law against children having to see their parents involved with multiple mates, year after year. Until the parent is committed to marriage the other person should be kept away. But now, Jyndia would have to go into another measure of Luis' indiscretion and I would have to hear about it and try to comfort her heart.

Illegitimate relationships hurt our children and us. The effects can last a lifetime.

The Christmas call
I promised myself not to get overly involved, this Christmas. As usual, I juggled an avalanche of activities and now my phone is ringing persistently! But, I knew I needed to answer this call ... Picking up the phone I heard these words. "Hello, my name is Eliza. I am Luis' ex-girlfriend. I am calling to see if it would be all right to give Jyndia a Christmas present. I would also like to say goodbye to her. We spent a lot of time together and got pretty close." I felt, I was getting myself up off the floor with surprise!

Eliza's voice was husky, brisk and intelligent. I composed myself and trusted God for the adjustment I needed to make. Answering, I said, "Yes Eliza, that will be fine, but I thought you and Luis were still together." She replied, "No Luis and I are not together. Our relationship ended last August." After our short talk, we agreed that she would bring Jyndia's gifts by the next day. This would be a good time for them to visit. We politely said good-bye. I sat back to surmise the spiritual meaning of her call. Did this encounter really happen or had I imagined that I just talked to my former husband's, former girlfriend!?" I asked "God, what are you up to?

A meaningful dream
The dreams I held most precious were the ones I considered to be significant. The call immediately reminded me of a vivid dream six months before. The Holy Spirit showed me an event concerning Eliza and Luis. In the dream, I saw Eliza sitting on a park bench crying. She said, "Luis doesn't want to marry me. He said I won't be the right minister's wife for him!" The park bench represented her isolation and aloneness. Her words indicated that a separation had happened. Another time I dreamed that his family had not fully accepted Eliza. She seemed to be communicating her feelings to me. I knew she needed my prayers and I knew I would meet her.

The feeling of my dream denoted that there was resistance in their relationship, but, it was uncanny to see these various happenings of Luis' life in advance. That is why the call seemed to be a glance backward. In the Bible, in the Book of Acts, a lady opened the door to find Peter standing there. God had answered their prevailing prayers, but the people praying for Peter were baffled. They had trouble believing he was there. They had prayed for hours in faith, but could hardly believe their request transpired! They knew the power of God, but were still astounded to physically see Peter.

The first time Jyndia mentioned Eliza to me, the Lord planted the law of kindness in my heart towards her, two years before and two years after Lacy. I heard God whisper, "Pray that she won't be hurt!" God's love for her caused Him to move upon the most unlikely person to arbitrate. He wanted to equip Eliza and counter or neutralize a coming season of pain. It didn't matter to God that I was the illegitimate former wife. His comprehension of love for His children is far beyond understanding.

Now I knew the dream was true, so Eliza's contact felt abstract and far-sighted. Life was getting more interesting by the minute. Before my eyes was the manifestation of a prophetic dream, one that took place in July, the same year, before their breakup in August. I had dreamed about their breakup a month before it happened! Now, in December, Eliza is sharing with me that Luis had discontinued their relationship. I was mystified that I should know anything about Luis' personal life. Why should I be shown his relationships, years after our divorce? I didn't want to see his life in black and white or in living color.

Speaking to God, I said, "Why are you showing me Luis' life? I have my own concerns Lord! Luis is disturbing my sleep. I don't care Lord! I don't want to know about his significant other's. I want my sleep, please, without episodes!"

Bravery
Eliza was just beginning her journey to freedom. It took courage for her to call me. I'm sure she was filled with hesitation. I knew she was hurting and disappointed and looking for answers. Unfortunately, she had joined the club that failed to deliver its promises of happiness. I put myself in her place and knew the story. She was distressed from thinking she could trust him, but found out differently.

To her own detriment she learned of his cunning and shrewd ways. He had taken her to indispensable heights of mountaintop glory; and then casted her down into valleys deeply entrenched with dishonesty. She heard his words and believed she was the most important and wonderful angel in the earth. He told her, "There is none like you," and she trusted his words. Luis was among the most dynamic persons she had ever met, but in the end, he tortured her soul. She satisfied the hunter in Luis. He masterfully pursued, caught, and then killed his prey.

Jyndia's assessment of the pageantry
My daughter is a very perceptive young lady. When Jyndia met Eliza, she said, "Mom, she is tall and very pretty; she looks like Ce Ce Winans and we have fun together." Her overture of Eliza was different from Lacy's. With keen intuition, she said, "Mom, something was very wrong with daddy and Lacy being together, but Eliza is great." Jyndia never denied that she deeply cared for Eliza. Her heart was open wide to her love. Jyndia was always sad that I was left out, but she loved Eliza and their good times. Children relish the feelings of family.

Mom and Dad role models can sometimes give our disenchanted children endorsements of good thoughts, security and comfort. Jyndia got her proxy parental fix from spending time with her dad and Eliza. She loved feeling connected with family more than anything. (Don't we all)? That is another reason that God hates divorce. It leaves our poor babies so very confused about, "Who is who" and "What is what!" They are left to figure out too many kinds of feelings.

Children end up moved around emotionally like little unimportant chess pieces, trying to sort out who their parental figures and having guilt for liking all the new people in their lives. Unfortunately, this scenario is normal in for too many in our disobedient world. We have created illusive lives and surrogate relationships for our fragmented children. We then have the audacity to wonder why they rebel. We ask, "What's wrong with my child?" (No, it's not them, it's us)!
Jyndia was excited that Eliza was coming. My intrigue grew as well. What would it be like to meet someone from Luis' long line of women, (concubines)?

Although, I somehow knew of Eliza from several dreams, we certainly had another thing in common: the sting of Luis' betrayal! Would seeing her open old wounds, or would it provide a greater level of growth for me? Was I to be instrumental in helping her get over the same all-consuming experience I had entertained? ... And what was Eliza thinking, "Is Dorothy the insecure, villain Luis talked about?" Or perhaps she wanted to know if I knew about his new woman, Chattel. Had it occurred to her that Luis and I might be back together? She certainly knew someone; somewhere was occupying her old position.

Arrival
Knock—knock ... Jyndia opens the door. The two of them went for each other with big hugs and kisses! Eliza and I shook hands and were happy to meet. I was delighted to see that Jyndia felt loved and adored. She beamed with a double portion of energy! Jubilation filled the room as they discussed all they had missed. Jyndia was stunned to hear Eliza's relationship was over with her Dad. She suspected something was different, but wasn't sure. Luis told Jyndia that Eliza was working out of town; on a long assignment ...

Eliza and I shared pleasantries over a cup of tea and enjoyed watching Jyndia open gifts. There were moments when Jyndia looked at us curiously. How odd to see, two women she loved, who once loved her Daddy, in the same room, at the same time! Later that evening Jyndia discovered she would join Eliza's family and some of Eliza's and Luis' friends for New Year's dinner. Her cup of elation overflowed!

When Eliza asked to take Jyndia, I said, "If you're hoping for reconciliation with Luis, don't take her; not unless you're really sure it's over. I said, taking Jyndia to an event with his friends would public disgrace Luis' ego. It will also affect your relationship recovery." I knew that Luis' sophomoric definition of "manhood" would surely be offended. It was important to his self-worth and fairy tale mentality that all appear picture perfect, but Eliza had already decided, months after not hearing from him that it was already over. We absolutely know when someone else is the main actress/actor in our fifteen-part Broadway Show. (Even when we are in denial like I was).

A lot to talk about...
As confident as Eliza was, I could see that the breakup was hurtful and confusing. (Breakups hurt the best and most confident too). Her dreams of marriage and family were abruptly taken! She was remembering the words Luis spoke; they meant so much, just a few months before. She was not expecting betrayal or broken promises. His departure left her with millions of questions. I could hear her saying, "What happened to us? How could he leave me? How could he do that? I'm a good woman, a worthy woman, a smart woman." She also believed she and Luis were right for each other, because they related so well! She wondered, why she was added to a list of wounded and rejected people.

Eliza began the conversation by sharing how surprised she was that she received an email from Luis, stating he could not go on with the relationship. They had enjoyed a romantic event the weekend before; all was good, but just a week later, his report was issued. Of course, she was hurt and taken aback. They had been together a few years and were probably talking about marriage when this happened. She was amazed that he dismissed their relationship in such a cavalier, chicken-hearted manner. It was especially difficult to accept that this special, clean-cut, Christian man would do such a thing.

She realized too late that she had thought too much of Luis. He seemed like a man of God, a person with a pure heart and right intentions. She had fallen in love with the outside package and his promise of devotion. She said, "Some things just don't click for a woman, when the package is a minister! The thing most Christian women want." I certainly understood that dream; sharing with her, "That kind of man seems to be a reward for our good works. The minister piece is a big deal and men like Luis know and bet on it. This is how they hide their wolf's tails underneath their Bibles so well! This way their hidden teeth are difficult to see; especially when we want to believe in love and blessings.

Our conversations were deep and rich ... I shared, "unless we walk intimately with God, listening carefully, men (women) sitting right in the church house can easily deceive us. So many men just like Luis have some good outer qualities, but not the more important inner walk with Jesus. Many have no sincere praise or honor for God." I told her I was sorry she had been hurt and encouraged her to believe that God was just purging rubbish from her life. I assured her, it is His mercy that removes the wrong people and wrong destinies from our lives. (I asked God; how careful did I need to be to fulfill the purpose of our meeting? How much should we discuss or not)?

By the time Eliza met Luis, he was in seminary (cemetery) school, studying to be a pastor. He was farther along in his Christian walk, (trickery) than with me. But his heart was still full of adultery and womanizing. He was well defined by the fruit on his tree. Luis was still with Lacy, before being "wowed" by Eliza, he assured Eliza that he met Lacy after our divorce. *Now you know that bit of information really got my dander, way up high!* "What! How could he lie about their most unholy, hellish relationship, straight from the depths of hell?" I said, "Well, if he was engrossed enough to sleep around with Lacy, for at least two years of our marriage, he could at least be honest about it!" (Oh yes, I forgot; wolves don't tell the truth about their lives. They are too busy hiding their tails on the side of church benches and making their ex-wives and girlfriends look like raving idiots)!

I assured her, "Oh, they very much were together, like white on rice. Lacy literally was in my marriage, allegorically sleeping in my bed. Is that close enough?" Eliza suspected that Lacy and Luis had been together during our marriage, but chose not to see Luis in such a light. She said, "That liar! Luis swore up and down that he met her after your divorce. How many more lies did Luis speak into the night?" I said, "Only the Lord knows for sure!" And now he was lying about Lacy too! I was not surprised.

In the past Luis told me, he had been an excellent husband to his first wife Dixon, but she had serious insecurity problems. She constantly accused him of other women. (That's a no brainer)! He went on and on about her severe jealousy issues. Of course, she was; she was supposed to be. She had good reasons to feel jealous; her husband was sleeping with other women! If you are alive, and can see and feel that should make you jealous! Yet, Luis in all his crookedness, still found devilish strength to point an unscrupulous finger at each of us! (How do they do that)? Wow! The devil's self-protection ability through narcissistic people is real!

Eliza's encounter with Lacy
Lacy was not happy about her breakup with Luis. She tried hard to win him back. (But they deserved each other. Sorry that was my flesh). Luis told Eliza his relationship was over with Lacy when they met. The truth was; he was proficiently maneuvering both at the same time, at the same church, as long as he could, as one of the assistant pastors. (This was the same Church I encountered).

As time moved on, it was obvious to Lacy that Eliza was the one Luis wanted. She remained in the shadows and became the new me. (Her time was up. Satan had accomplished his destructive plan in her life). When Luis moved to Kansas City, Eliza learned that Luis was still communicating with Lacy. Eliza was devastated, and broke off her relationship with Luis; but he fought to win her back. (The enemy had not devoured her yet). To get her back, he had to tell Eliza why he was conversing with Lacy. He was providing her counseling and she needed his advice, because of a personal catastrophe. Eliza and Luis reconciled after his explanation.

Eliza and I agreed that without God's help it would have been difficult to care about Lacy's calamity. She and Luis trampled on hearts on purpose, without sensitivity. They continued to date behind Eliza's back and fully desecrated my marriage. Still, her ordeal was heartrending. Eliza and I hoped that Luis recognized that he was one of the reasons that door was open in Lacy's life. Lacy called him for reconciliation and comfort, knowing her suffering was a referendum on their relationship. She needed him; he was her cohort in sin and was accountable to share in her grief, not to treat her like a professional, after the fact. They both knew the truth and yes, he was partly responsible. …Again, we see the fallout from spiritually illegal relationships, which are indeed far reaching for each of us. No one wins with disobedience.

Wanting to warn
I told Lisa, I had visited with her mother at a local store, before she and Luis separated and appreciated her warmth. Her mom was trying to strengthen Jyndia and me. She understood what it felt like to go through a divorce. At heart, she knew I had fought to keep the marriage together. When she walked away I wanted to shout from the rooftop. "Tell your daughter to be careful with Luis. Their relationship is not going to work! Luis is a seducer and womanizer! He's a narcissist! Tell Eliza to protect her heart, and to run as fast as she can!" But ...how could a former wife say such things, without being labeled a fool? And, why should her mom believe me, when she thought her daughter's fiancé was wonderful? Eliza smiling, "Dorothy I wish you would have screamed it out as loud as you could!" (Funny)!

As our talks strengthened, I shared that the affair in my face was bad enough, but Luis' great lies were more hurtful. If Eliza was feeling like me, she wanted to leap out of the bushes and pounce on his head like a tiger. Her wounds, surprise and pain correlated with mine, but the new questions of "why," were regrettably hers now. What do you say to comfort someone who is hurting; when you know the man so well? – Someone God told you to pray for long before you met them ... But, telling Eliza about Luis' past life was not going to help. Calling him a "lying preacher type," was not going to help. Hurtful details of Luis' past piled on top of her present pain, was pointless.

When a person is feeling betrayed they want and need to hear something encouraging. You want to hear something hopeful about the person you still love. It's like an elderly person who realizes someone got away with their life's savings. You want to give them hope that the money is going to come back. Eliza's cut and pain was new and somewhere within, she still wanted to believe that her investment might return, just like I did years before.

In the first stages of letting go, there are glimmers of hope. The last thing we want to hear is ... go on with your life, or the best is yet to come. When we are hurting there seems to be no more life to go on to. Eliza didn't want to believe she had chosen that poorly or had been that "seriously played!" I wanted to ease her feelings of betrayal and offer comfort with wisdom from God. Luis' (Satan's) vanity and deep disrespect for others had again turned good times and high expectations into remorse. It is difficult to believe, but a player truly only loves you when they're playing. Will you allow a player into your life?

"Give not your strength to women or men, or your ways to those who ruin and destroy kings." (Proverbs 31:3)

Laughter for the soul
Eliza had the funniest things to say like this: "I'd like to wring his neck for cuttin' the fool with me, with his broke tail!" She kept saying, "I can't believe that Lacy had really been in the picture before you and Luis separated." With a comical

quirk, she said again. "Dorothy, He swore up and down he had been a faithful husband to you! That rat!" (Yes, that double rat)! When I told her how he peeked around the fence and ran back in the house after spotting me instead of Lacy, she laughed hilariously. She said, "No he didn't Dorothy! SHUT UP!" Thank God, we could laugh at him and ourselves. Although Eliza was careful not to repeat the hurtful things Luis said about me, I already knew the truth. He had verbally slushed me, in and through the mud. I would have been guarded if talking with Dixon too. (His first wife). After the fact, seeing the truth, she knew she had believed many lies.

Luis (being used by Satan) changed women, like bad underwear. Self-validation was the name of his song. The words were, "Dixon, Dorothy, Lacy and Eliza (and whomever else) were too insecure and jealous. They spent too much money and had too many issues. They offended my manhood." The truth was we didn't tell him he was wonderful as he relished other women in our faces. We didn't play dead enough and expected a faithful man. Of course, we didn't measure up to his worldly expectations of prestige."

Luis' commitment to one woman was an emasculation of his freedom. Wives, daughters, concubines, and girlfriends were superfluous stepping-stones to catapult his thirst for more of himself. One of the first things Luis asked me was, "Whom do you know that I can network with?" I hope you are paying close attention to these conversations. Satan is planning your demise too. Don't think he isn't! He has weak-kneed men or women with hidden agendas ready to stop your success. It's up to you to allow or disallow.

What are they looking for?
Immersed in another thoughtful conversation, Eliza questioned me, saying; "what is he looking for Dorothy? He's still out there! We are spiritual, intelligent, good-looking, and well-accomplished women. What does he want? What is wrong with him?" Perplexed, with his ability to commit, she wondered, how a man could change from, hot to cold. She said, "After spending two and a half years with Luis, how could he stoop to just sending me an email? How do you get reduced to an email?" I understood and agreed, "How coarse and uncouth the devil is!" She wondered, "Did I think too highly of him? How was I fooled? How could I be so wrong about loving a minister - a neat, polished, all American man? Why did I trust him?" Her soul searched for answers.

I smiled and said, "As wrong as he was Eliza, at least you got a pitiful, I'm sorry" from him. "The email was at least his awful attempt to offer you a little respect and closure. Luis never said he was sorry to me." I hoped the assessment helped to ease her pain a bit. I said, If Luis, as my husband had said, "I'm sorry;" he would also have to admit to his sexual crimes, which were beneath his public dignity and imaginary self-image. He had to convince himself that he was not doing anything wrong to stave off feelings of guilt. He had to psychologically justify his relationship with Lacy, to be a good man and minister who could preach on Sunday mornings and save souls.

I shared, "I was careful to tell Luis, 'I am so sorry I disappointed you in whatever way you feel, but I will not take responsibility for your affairs. They are not my fault!'" After humbling myself, I thought he might say, "I'm sorry too," but instead of taking responsibility he said, "I haven't done anything to you" and walked away. At the time, I felt as bad as being told the makeup on his shirts was mine! But, now I know, "A person, who can't say, 'I'm sorry,' has to be a scalawag!"- in need of prayer.

We must understand; <u>when we disobey God</u>, we allow a double-dealing spiritual system of darkness to overrule us. How can we expect anything more than a self-indulgent person maintaining colossal doses of animosity and sorrow to take center stage in our lives?

Chattel
Chattel, a young college student was Luis' next selection. He positioned himself securely with her before dismissing Eliza. He met Chattel at Church a few months before Eliza's sobering email. Eliza's first impression was that Chattel was just a college student that had gone to the same university as Luis, twenty years later. She took their meeting nonchalantly. Now, in her anger, she had a few choice descriptions ... you know, the things we say when we are hurting. (Anger is a stage of pain that must be lived out). We have no nice expressions for the new significant other for a long time. It hurts when someone takes our place. That new someone looks like the "ugliest person" in our universe. I certainly felt that way about Lacy.

Take a break
This is one of the most important reasons that a sabbatical is needed between relationships. When we overlap and compound partners, no one has time to heal or adjust. A season of purification, reflection, character building, and seeking God must happen before someone new is plunged in the middle of every one's dysfunction. We cannot be so insecure to need someone in our back pocket, before ending a relationship. The Lord requires that we are sensitive to one another, even when having permission to move ahead. Order and decency is expected by God, because forgiveness is a process.

For love or status
I met Chattel, perhaps a year after she and Luis began to date. Luis arranged that she and Jyndia travel together to a family reunion. I was initially surprised with Luis' new choice, but understood, we don't always know the true heart desire or motive of former mates. It seemed that Luis needed the younger-woman scenario to strengthen his own personal identity. Jyndia was embarrassed when church members assumed Chattel was Luis' oldest

daughter; they were close in age. Jyndia said, "Mom they look stupid together. Dad is old!" (Funny)!

Only God knows the true motive of Luis' heart, but you must be extremely careful when you have the means to be financially secure. Why? - Because some are looking for sugar mamas and daddies! Chattel offered Luis much more than being a charming young woman on his arm, but finally he could have the prestige and financial security he desired. I pray Luis' motives are pure -- God is the righteous judge. "Lord, help us each love and connect with others for Your righteous, Bible reasons. Purify our motives and intentions."

"They speak falsehoods to one another, with flattering lips and double-minded hearts. May the Lord cut off flattering lips and tongues that speak great things." (Psalms 12:2-3)

Pray this for someone you know
"God use ____ for your glory and help him/her love you. Make ____ a stable and honorable man/woman. Show ____ that life is more than status and self-seeking; but that true life is seeking Your face! Give ____ the true riches of life and help ____ grow. The world needs no more baby-mama-drama or self-exalted people! I forgive ____ again. Purify his/her motives and heart. Bless and protect his/her new mate. Help them bring you glory!

CERTAINTY Chapter 9

"Although God gives bread of adversity and water of affliction, your teachers will be hidden no more; with your own eyes, you will see them." (Isaiah 30:19)

The Word of God disagrees that negative experiences are essential for growth. The Word says that change and maturity should come through Bible instruction, prayer and maintaining a burning relationship with Jesus. God's first line of defense is a "strong personal relationship with Him and His Word." But, chastisement (correction) is also available in many other varieties for His stubborn, prideful children. We can learn through the Word and personal relationship or through suffering negative consequences.

"The foolishness of man subverts his way and ruins his affairs; then his heart is resentful and frets against the Lord." (Proverbs 19:3)

God works tirelessly to prevent harmful growth experiences and wants to expand our lives, without unnecessary misery. When we lean on and trust in God's Acuity and Presence, we become skilled and conscious in listening to Him. Our quality time with God establishes wisdom, shrewdness and obedience. A love for the Word and discipline to consume its realities give us insight and power for true joy and success in life.

Connection with God helps us make good spiritual decisions that deflect Satan's packages of woe. True spiritual maturity will not sign up for Satan's fabricated parcels!

Now I urge you, brethren, keep your eye on those who cause dissensions and hindrances contrary to the teaching which you learned, and turn away from them. - For such men are slaves, not of our Lord Christ but of their own appetites; and by their smooth and flattering speech they deceive the Hearts of the unsuspecting. (Romans 16: 17-18)

Taking responsibility

Eliza and I took responsibility for signing on the dotted line with Luis. Although his wooing and grandstanding was impressionable, ultimately, we were open to a spirit of flattery. (The Bible says if we can be flattered we can be deceived).

A man who flatters his neighbor spreads a net for his feet. (Proverbs 29:5)

For there is no truth in their mouth; their inmost self is destruction; their throat is an open grave; they flatter with their tongue. (Psalm 5:9)

Eliza and I refused to take ourselves off the hook and stood accountable. We were among those who chose poorly, leaning on our own understanding. Yes, God helped us outlast the onslaught, lies and dilemma, but He wanted more for us than deception ... our poor judgment got us in trouble and the mercy of God got us out. We gave the devil the opportunity to bite us and he did. We learned there is no magic from or in Satan's kingdom of flattery.

Even if Luis was an opportunistic man, it was still up to us to listen to God. We ignored God's rules of behavior and knew in our hearts "WHO" Luis really was. The spirit behind him wanted opportunity, sensual pleasure, promotion and self-celebration. We knew this through our own intuition and spiritual sensitivity. We allowed his manipulation and we empowered the player, thinking we had the ability to create an honest man out of him. We tried to take on the role of God and had to accept that Luis was not ours to perfect. Our neediness and lack of trust in God gave the devil power and permission. Knowing better, we were ultimately responsible for what happened to us.

Warnings from Dixon
I shared with Eliza that I had spoken with Dixon, Luis' first wife, years before. Luis and I had been married about a year when we visited Nia, his oldest daughter. During a shopping trip at the Mall, Dixon showed up out of nowhere. She had followed us there. I looked up from a clothing rack, wondering who Luis and Nia were staring at. The cold chills were all about Dixon; she stood there looking me over. Nia said, "Hi Mom." About that time this unidentified lady had my full attention! She put her hand out and firmly said, "Hello, I'm Dixon Elder!" -- Making it a point to add her last name -- the same as mine. She seemed annoyed. I said, "Hi, I'm Dorothy," without adding my last name.

Dixon proceeded, "I wanted to meet you. I don't trust just anyone to spend time with my daughter." I told her I understood her feelings. She seemed satisfied with my answer and me, and left. When we returned, Luis took Nia inside and Dixon brushed by him, coming out to the car to talk to me. This time she was softer. We shared kind words and then she told me how badly Luis treated them. She said, "Luis walked off and left us when Nia was about three years old." She looked at me gently saying, "I hope he won't do the same thing to you!" I was moved and startled by her bold comment. She wasn't being rude, but was trying to warn me. Our talk was short and awkward, but I was glad to meet her. Luis came out of the house within minutes.

Driving home, I questioned Luis about their relationship, asking. "Are you sure you tried hard enough to keep your marriage together?" I told him I could see the love in her eyes for him. "Yes," he declared! "I did all I could to make the marriage work. I was faithful to her! She was too difficult to live with!" Or, did he mean she would not let him play around with a smile on her face. He answered a few questions and quickly let me know he did not appreciate my inquiry or empathy for her. He didn't want to discuss their relationship or her allegations. Finally, I dropped the matter, but was concerned about Dixon's pain. There was nothing satisfying to know she felt abandoned and hurt. Knowing that bothered me. Something was wrong with their departure.

Former mates
When in a conversation with a former mate, listen to what the Holy Spirit says. You really can hear truth through their language. If the information is bad, don't just discount the information, but store it ... Or do you need to assimilate an escape plan. You will know the truth when you hear it. Dixon had no idea that her words would manifest, or did she? She had also known this man/spirit. I did feel the gravity of her words, but allowed myself to believe that he'd be different with me; after all we were married now. But during my time of crisis her words of warning incisively stood out. I knew they were God's way of preparing me for a coming day of sorrow.

Even before I would ascertain His heart; not wanting me to be caught entirely off guard, God was kind enough to show me the spirit behind Luis. Even when I endeavored to accept that everything was fine, God was consistently working to show me the truth. I also remembered, my nephew, who knew Luis years before I met him, told his mom that Luis was a very worldly man. You see God leaves many clues and crumbs ahead of time! We can't afford to ignore them.

Today I would say to Dixon, "Although I met Luis years after your divorce, I am sorry that I was in the picture and contributed to your pain. But I know God has blessed you and Nia despite what Luis did. Remember, you never lost anything that was good for you. May your joys be great, and thank you for the warning!"

I told Eliza, there should be a mandatory requirement before marriages can occur. The new mate should have to tolerate a personal interview with the old one. That dialogue would give us vital insights and solve lots of illusionary problems with a deceptive mate. (There are always two sides to every story)! The interview would make it much more difficult to fool the new mate. Masquerades might be snuffed out! ... Well, maybe not. Unfortunately, some of us would still refuse to listen, until we find ourselves in the fiery furnace of affliction. (Ouch)!

"God's wisdom is better than rubies. All the things you desire are not compared to it." (Proverbs 8:11)

Unfaithfulness causes insecurity
Luis always spoke of Dixon as an unhappy, angry lady. Of course, he failed to say her anger was justified. People in general are not angry for nothing. Dixon knew something about Luis that was true. It came from a womanizing spirit. She was not about to call her husband a "playboy" for nothing. Women don't do that. Dixon knew someone was zooming in on her space. She reacted like you or I would. A mate will and should feel the interruption and self-doubt of betrayal. When someone else is getting your smiles, affection, money and time, you know it. One of God's most amazing alarm systems is our sense of insecurity when something is wrong. True uncertainty warns us that our mate is unfaithful. The

disruption on the inside is confirming. I could always tell when the insecurity was coming from me or from Luis' lifestyle.

Luis told me, Dixon once threatened to send him "back to Mississippi on a mule." Funny! - But a mule ride is good ride for anyone who lies so well. The bumpy gallop might have made an honest man out of him, and helped him rebuke that womanizing spirit!

Fatherless children
When I thought about the unnecessary suffering Nia, Jyndia and so many children live through, I understood Dixon's antagonism. She was rightfully infuriated. Our girl's pain could have been prevented. She asked the same questions we all do in these situations. "How could he leave me to face the challenge of raising our child by myself? Where did the commitment go?"

Not only should you fathers be there to raise your children, but you should offer them daily strength. Nia and Jyndia needed Luis to be a real, face to face father, daily. Thousands of men need to go home and raise their children. If God has ordained your marriage, you must do what is necessary. If you choose to be faithless you are out of position and you know what that means. You cannot joyfully excuse yourselves to run free in counterfeit pastures when you have fathered your precious children.

You cannot forfeit your purpose. Your Calling is to empower your children, face to face, until they are fully grown! This is where the rubber meets the road. Faithful fathers are men who are separated from the boys. It's a simple question, "Is your lifestyle harming your children?" The ramifications are far reaching.

The effects of leaving your child are eternal. Just look at the evening news. When we hurt the most innocent we create tenuous and difficult places for our flesh and blood to walk through. Is this fair to our children?

Make every adjustment to create a wonderful life for your child. Long-distance parenting is an elusive lie. Weekly and monthly calls are not enough! Raising your child means you must completely involve yourself in their lives. You are a man, so be a man and hold your family and children up. Use your faith and raise your own child. This is the most important thing you will ever do! Your greatest treasure and legacy on earth are your children. They will far outlast a frivolous affair and a spiritually-illegal relationship. Do it! Establish love, honor, sacrifice and respect for your children. They need you. Your child is your eternal business. What you do with them daily will matter a million years from now. Commitment to your children will be your strongest Christian witness and will earn you a crown in heaven.

Your child should never have to face life without the physical and emotional support of you, their precious father. You are a god to them. Be there for them in Jesus name! You are needed. Will you let the punks and bullies raise and handle your seed, your business; your child? Who else will help them manage and maintain a positive, godly self-image? How can they rise to accomplish great feats without you? Who else will give them vision and pride? A mom is not designed to do that job alone; you are.

You represent the essence of God himself. Your calling is massive and vital! - The Kingdom of God in on the inside of you. You can do this! You are connected to God and truth! Keep your children close and defy all the statistics against them. You be the gate keeper! When all other lights have gone out, your children will count the most to you. As you grow older you'll be happy you treated them right and kept them near!

A powerful declaration
Stand and declare! "I rise up and say 'No' to every wrong, calamitous and sensual emotion. Wrong aspirations and acquaintances will not hinder God's authentic plan for my children and me! Devil, I shove your lying suggestion back in your face! Every time you try me, you will fail, in Jesus Name!" I declare doggedly, "Devil, you will no longer rule the details or desires of my life! You can keep your sticky, tricky duplicitous blessing! I won't receive your new tail adventure, guaranteed to annihilate me. I won't take it! You will not hurt me, my righteous marriage or my innocent children and damage my child's heart! Your lies are defeated in Jesus Name! Now go! Amen!"

Single parents
Loving my child, I was still extremely annoyed when I had all the parenting work to do, alone. Where was Luis when I had to drive Jyndia, here and there? Taking her to a Christian school, I drove an hour each way. While pushing her wheelchair up a hill on cold days, at times, I was fueled with anger. He should have been there to push too; at least sometimes. We needed help on those hot, cold, rainy, sunny, good, and hard days. I said to Luis, "She is our daughter, not just mine! You don't have a clue of how demanding real parenting is. You leave before the real work begins!" He so needed to know about the commitment necessary to raise his own children.

I mastered climbing ascending slopes while Luis mastered looking great and winning hearts. What a tradeoff. (But, God tried to prevent this!) What can anyone really know about true parenting when they show up every now and then? The detached parent can't tell the committed one how to parent, when they're sitting in the grandstands. We must parent from inside the arena, where it hurts, by choice. Dads and Moms, you must <u>be in</u> your child's life, not in another city or in another life. Pay the price to be a great parent. To call every now and then, is not true parenting.

I do understand single parents; your challenge is not fair. The absence of a non-functioning parent is not teaching your children anything good about family stability or endurance. Children don't need to see or learn how to leave their families when times get hard, or how <u>not</u> to stand on the promises of God. But you hold on by faith, your Father is with you! Get yourself and children into strong Christian groups and don't be ashamed to ask for support.

Prayer for children
"Lord, we pray, return the hearts of parents to their children. Heal them and heal the hearts of our children. Help our children forgive us for selfishness. We decree, _____ will not have to fight abandonment challenges! Peace and grace to their emotions and behavior Lord. Jesus, make that great difference for Nia, Jyndia, Jamul and for every child hurt by their parent's actions. God, I claim You will fill them with your liquid love, worthiness, value and light. Lord, help us each be great parents in Jesus Name! Help us especially plant Your Word in _____ heart! Your presence shall supersede and cancel every work of the devil!" Amen!

Eliza loved Nia
I was glad to hear Eliza connected with Nia too. She mentioned that Nia had had a difficult time being raised without her father present. She was hurt that she missed out on so much with him. Throughout the years, he had not helped his daughter heal well; this caused division between them. I had known Nia as an adolescent; probably during the time her mom was mending. Understandably, I represented the enemy, the one who was taking her Dad's time. In a child's mind, a few years after the fact, doesn't mean a thing. One thing mattered, "My Daddy is not close to me." She was right; I wish I had never been there at all. Nia did not deserve to grow up without a dad. He should have been there to tuck her in each night. She deserved to have her Daddy home, close to her, where Daddy's belong! "Nia, remember you have a Wonderful Father in Heaven. He will redeem your past. God, Himself, will make up for the time you lost!"

Healing for Jyndia
Eliza's visits were especially good for Jyndia. Her presence provided her with good feelings and bravery. Jyndia struggled more and more with peer pressure considering the Spina bifida. Preschool through third grade were satisfactory, but by fourth grade life was extremely difficult. Some of the children treated her cruelly as she tussled to be accepted. Some were ignorant and brutal. There are truly beastly children out there! I was more than livid about their meanness. I wanted to carry a big stick to school at times. Negative remarks were embarrassing, so Jyndia tried to hide her real feelings and stuffed her injuries. I wondered, "How do children get that evil?" How? The answer is, without good parenting; without Dads and Moms planting the Word of God in their hearts. Why? - Because, too many parents are too busy chasing self or sexual-

gratification, instead of teaching love and humility - that's why there are too many examples of bullies and evil acting children out there.

We are all connected and insufficient parenting affects our children and society.

I lived frugally, keeping household expenses low to keep Jyndia in private Christian schools. She needed protection and good male figures in her life. I would not allow her to be spewed upon even more. She was certainly as valuable as everyone else and was worth the investment. Not only was her heart shattered from Luis' decisions, but from her own pain too. I had to help her overcome a belief system designed to destroy her. (G.T.P.T.) Jyndia needed strength, value and comfort from both her parents. We often felt alone in our quest to stand and the expense incurred was mine to endure.

As a teenager, Jyndia could see the uncleanness of her dad's life. She developed a serious sour spot towards him. It wounded her that he went on as though he had not hurt or offended her. She felt depressed and perplexed, but of course she loved her dad. His oversight gave Jyndia even more to process. She needed to hear him say he was sorry for helping to create her personal battle. Years later, after her Dad moved away, she returned from a visit to say, "Mom, dad is still really flirty. His lifestyle bothers me!" She could see for herself the same old demon was using her Dad to mesmerize, entice and hurt women. His daughters were a part of that hurt too.

Exits of love
I was happy Eliza genuinely cared for Jyndia. I wanted my daughter to receive all the love and healing she deserved. They shared outings and talks throughout several years. She was like a special aunt when in town. Her support and interaction blessed Jyndia and helped her feel more beautiful and worthy. Eliza was a right on time gift to us! I'm glad she didn't just disappear into thin air. If Jyndia had not heard the truth, Eliza would have added another layer of pain to heal. Once Luis brought Eliza into Jyndia's life, Jyndia's feeling had to be considered and Eliza had a right to care and to stop some of the disjointedness and damage Jyndia felt. Eliza allotted a beautiful place of reference for Jyndia's sustenance and heart.

When a person is special to your child and leaves their life without a goodbye, the change can make them feel unworthy, rejected, and confused. An abrupt exit from a meaningful figure is never the best way to leave. It is wrong when the adjusting and processing is put on the backs of our children. No, we adults must do the accommodating when a relationship fails, not them.

I uncovered Jamul's heart to Luis; therefore, if he desired to maintain a relationship with Luis, the adjusting would have been on my part. When we bring a significant other into our children's lives, we must remember; at one time, we wanted our child to like them. Again, we must be big enough to help our children assimilate, in and out of the relationships we endorse. When the battle goes ill, the discomfort of the outcome is on us, not them. Our children often have a different actualization of a former mate that we do.

No more trampling on our children's sentimentality. Let them have the relationship if it was a good one for them. Let them have it as long as they need it. If Luis had ended his relationship correctly with Eliza; Jyndia would not have been lied to for months. She could have been made ready for the change, instead of thinking Eliza left town with not even a goodbye. Remember, these events trample on our children's self-value and solidity. Luis could have asked Eliza, when and how she wanted to say goodbye to Jyndia. We all could have helped her in understanding the healing process needed, with the truth. Let us assist our children with the goodbyes of adults they care about. It's not all about us. We owe them that because we caused the vulnerability. Their precious hearts are worthy of appropriate closures.

May our children always have peace and undisturbed composure!

"Do not provoke your children to wrath (pain or confusion), but raise them in the fear (respect) of the Lord." (Ephesians 6:4)

Grieving correctly
Eliza and I talked about the value of the grieving process, because disappointments hurt us. No one is strong enough not to feel the sting of a breakup and just walk away smiling. It is vital that we cry unto the Lord with all our heart. When we are hurting, pain and sorrow has to be released. Our emotions have to be healed, even when we don't understand the happenings of soul, mind, body and emotions.

It's important to find a good Christian support group and books like this one that help to direct the uproar and change. Grieve hard and long; your soul needs to release the pain, sorrow and disappointment. Your renewal is necessary; don't rush it. Gradually as you settle down to trust the Lord; you will see His illumination is there to guide you. Don't fight God's processes, just submit and the pain will lessen. Remember, it's all about love, obedience and purity for God. He is only harmonizing and stabilizing your life. The pain comes from the shredding away of sin and disobedience.

Although you are missing your relationship, try to grieve that you have fallen short of the glory of God, not because the wrong person is gone. Let God give you His light and revelation knowledge. He will help you rejoice and celebrate that the unlawful baggage of a cursed relationship is over. If you grieve for losing a sin in your life, the devil is able to enter again. Let Father, teach you how to let it be and how to trust Him. Cry unto Jesus; ask Him for truth. Ask Him to help you be more like Him and to love His word ferociously! Too much sadness can invite a spirit of depression, expressed in my experience.

Later, when I saw the truth, I was sorry I had grieved so grimly over an illegitimate relationship. It was a terrible waste of time, energy, focus and tears. I wanted something that was bad for me; something I never needed. God just wanted to align me (you) with authentic love, truth and joy.

Confirmations
Eliza and I understood that true stability comes from first maintaining a deep relationship with God. But, it is imperative that childhood perceptions be as unwavering and constructive as possible. Loving parents show us who we are. They help us see ourselves as worthy and in the Lord. With deep self-respect and vision, we are less accepting of emotional or physical abuse. A godly foundation helps us trust God more; then we are not afraid to step out of damaging relationships by faith. We also choose mates more excellently, when our identity and Word level is strong. Along with wholeness, we acquire the ability to maintain lifetime friendships and marriages.

During one of our last visits, Eliza could see that ministry was deeply embedded in my heart. She said, "Luis always said he was looking for the right wife; Dorothy, you would be the perfect pastor's wife!" I laughed, because that very desire became a tool for Satan and was why it was so difficult to let go of the relationship. I thought that being a pastor's wife was part of my calling and gave the devil a foothold to pull my strings.

I was touched that she recognized the call of God on my life, but was sad that a good desire can be so befuddled if we don't single out God's voice alone. I thanked her and said, "More than anything I really want to impact lives and teach the Word of God, but I can still do that empowered by God! His gifts and desires are who we are, and nothing changes what and who we are called to be and do!"

Your enemy will use whatever he can to stop you. Don't let what God told you to do be a source of misperception and pain. Your calling is operative anywhere you are!

Eliza could see that I was not the troll Luis portrayed. I was not deranged, unhinged or insecure, without cause. His propaganda had not worked. She knew the failure of our relationship was not my desire or fault. She acknowledged, "Dorothy, you tried hard to make your marriage work; be proud that you gave your best." I answered, "Yes, I did give my best, and you did too. We just caught the eye of the wrong person, barked up the wrong tree and got leaves in our mouths, instead of love. If Luis had been a qualified partner; God would have kept you or me with him."

We understood it was the grace of God that exorcised Luis from our lives. Father spared us from deeper ruin and blight. She teased me saying, "Well, at least he married you." I answered, "Yes, but with that, my expectation and pain was harder to defeat. You were spared much. Be very happy he didn't marry you! Marriage is not always a blessing ... the deeper you're in it, the more it hurts."

Eliza's friend Carrie was married to one of Luis' friends. Seeing his lifestyle, she felt led to write him a letter. Carrie talked to him about his weak testimony. How would he minister to hurting women, men and families as a pastor? She said, "Considering, you have been the perpetrator of so much pain yourself, shouldn't you reconsider your ways? If you really want to be an effective and holy minister, something more needs to happen." Prayerfully he took her advice and realized that no one is above God's way of doing things. I was happy to hear that someone <u>finally</u> confronted Luis, many years later.

Before they were

Eliza was far more independent than I was at the time of my divorce. She could look ahead sooner after their breakup and re-focus. Getting over someone has a lot to do with where you were emotionally and spiritually before the relationship developed. It's not that a breakup won't affect you to some degree, even with high self-esteem, but your ability to snap back faster, comes with God's sufficiency. Some people can cut their emotional losses quickly; and move on. Others get stuck like I did, because I believed incorrectly. I don't want that to happen to you.

Knowing who you are, before they were in your life, allows you to see exploitation better or the defeat of a relationship in a better light. A positive self-perception and personal self-value makes a great difference in your ability to look forward. <u>Break-ups show us who we are and what we really believe about God and ourselves.</u> When deep emotional pain knocks us to our knees, it is impossible to fake who and what we are. Do you know for sure what you have to work with on the inside of you?

Research shows, it can take one year to get over every three years that your relationship existed.

After nine years with Luis (one year dating and almost eight years of marriage), I was over the worse part after three miserable years of outlasting that ferocious wheat field. Yes, it was a hard press breaking away from holding onto false dreams; overcoming co-dependency issues and misplaced prophecies. With a misguided identity, I was up in the air, blowing in the wind of enemy's turmoil most of the time. I could not get centered. The core of my essence was boggled and distorted. Finding the truth was grueling, because I believed a lot of things that weren't true and held onto the relationship. Thinking, "surely, I was supposed to fight for it." (Lord Help)!

Why

The true question is this: "Why are codependents such gullible, dysfunctional people?" Why are we so good at attracting partners (spirits) like Luis? Why do we create environments that allow the player to survive? Do we choose to ignore God's voice, by thinking we deserve pain? Do we need the disruption and drama of infidelity?

We all have hidden characteristics that can destroy our lives. And we desperately need to know what they are. We need inner healing, assessment and wisdom in major doses to see relationships correctly. Our perceptions and beliefs must be right to have right relationships. We are what we think and perceive. Investigate and challenge your beliefs and acuity. It's amazing what we can't see and what we need to see. Ask about and purchase my booklets, "Self and Your Innermost Being", or "I'm Famous in My Father's Eyes!" I highly recommend that you read good books that help you identify areas of codependency. Believe me, we all have them.

I know, you don't think you are a "people dependent person," none of us do, but there is so much more you need to know to be free and powerful in Jesus!

Stand with yourself
Father God taught me, no matter who would not stand with me, you must stand with yourself! I had to love, nourish and honor me! I could not abandon me too. I learned that standing-alone is a maturing and refining accomplishment. If you are standing in truth, standing alone is a great test of virtue that will take down the adversity of Satan.

No matter whom or how many people leave you, you cannot forsake yourself. You are worth believing in! Trouble brings the right situation and time to love God and <u>you</u> more! If the world walks away, God and you will not. If we can love and support someone else, we can do it for ourselves. We are growing just like they are. Who can dare throw a rightful stone at us? God's way is to love yourself every day, with the same bigness and passion in which He loves you. You are full of God's essence, don't let him down!

Fully love yourself. You are God's marvelous creation. Meditate on your value with scriptures and firmly build His positive attributes within. Create a journal of scriptures that pertain to who you are. Read it continually. Soon, the regeneration of your soul's trials will be over; and wow - You will see a battle-hardened, sharply-honed person you love and respect far more. You'll proudly say, "No cage can hold me down!" Stop and spend some time loving you right now. Say: "I love you _____! I am completely worthy, valuable and sufficient!" God has made me good, therefore I am very good! ... And, yes you are!

Trust issues
Yes, we do receive harvests of thorns, thistles and vexation, from the deeds we planted. Every effort to satisfy ourselves is a lack of "trust in God" issue. We put our hope in a man or woman instead of God. We decide their offer is better than God's ability to make us happy. We can be rebellious, fearful and dishonorable.

If we are full of low self-esteem, we draw pain to ourselves pointlessly. Our actions are the symptoms and results of our lack of trust in God and His ability. We can't believe that God could really be our fascination and blessing. Faithlessness says God could not be more than a mere human being.

"Lean not on your own understanding, but trust the Lord with all you heart. In all your ways acknowledge Him and He will direct your paths. Don't try to be wise in your own eyes, but fear and respect the Lord. Depart from the evil of your own ways. It shall be health to you and marrow to your bones.
(Proverbs 3:5-8)

Whatever you compromise to keep, you will ultimately lose.

Remembering Eliza

Jyndia and I appreciated the refreshing times God gave us through Eliza. Eliza was thankful that the most improbable person was quickened to pray for her. The prayers gave her strength to move on with minimal wreckage. Our visits continued as long as we needed to talk. They were either robust and hilarious, or reserved and kind. God made sure we released self-blame and uncertainty. Our enlightening conversations were meaningful and important as God revealed truth and strengthened our hearts.

Did Eliza need to touch Luis again through Jyndia? Was she just curious about his ex-wife? Did she reach out to me to satisfy a need in herself? Or, perhaps we just needed the affirmation and laughter of each other for a brief time in history? Nevertheless, I was glad to see the hand of God through Eliza's life. Jyndia and I always smile when Eliza's name is mentioned. She settled the score in more ways than one … And, congratulations are in order. I was happy to hear the good news, Eliza is married to a man her mom calls, "The real thing!" May your marriage be a wonderful and strong, lifetime marriage; with lots of happy children around the table! Thank God, there are still godly and good spiritual men in our world. Those who are legitimately stable and available! Love to you Eliza!

"The fear of the Lord tends to life: and he that has it; shall abide satisfied. He shall not be visited with evil." (Proverbs 19:23)

Illegitimate connections

If you are in a relationship, this is a good time to examine its true origin. Is your mate exclusively from God? Has he or she faked it so well, for so long that you and they are out of touch with truth? Are they a great pretender? Do you sense they have a grandiose plan in process? Will their plans make you prey for their gain? Will you be hurt and pushed aside when they get what they want? Are you being used as a net worker or as a springboard? Does your mate really have the ability to commit to you completely? Are they only looking to fill their money bags at your expense? Is this person supposed to be in your life? Who are they? Deep in your soul you know the truth. Selfish ambition is an ugly game; will you allow them to play it?

Will your lack of trust in God create another self-inflicted ordeal? Or will you increase in your oneness with God and make His presence your best reward? (1 Corinthians 6:17)

Your authentic mate will be drawn from God's life and from truth. On your own, you will draw your own insufficiencies and beliefs of unworthiness. Your words of faith and truth, or defeat and desperation will create a worthy scenario for you. Your mate will come from your thoughts. The wholeness or incompleteness you exude will play an important role in the formation they receive. Make sure you are filled with happiness and competence. Completely know who you from a Jesus premise. Be self-sufficient and fully understand what is at stake first. Never depend on someone financially, but trust that God will take care of you. Expect the devil to be in the details. Expect him to try to insert his agenda. That's a given! Are you willing to wait for God to establish and connect you or will you move ahead of Him?

Satan's influences
Satan's' favorite impressions are these: "I don't want to be alone. I need more financial help. God brought them to me, or I don't want to try to make it by myself. It's too difficult." Listening to the wrong feelings and ideas, you assume you are prepared to open the door, but the devil's voice is not like God's. God motivates through wisdom and peace -- Satan agrees with "whatever" and engages your emotions. You must be prepared to stop him with internalized scriptures, before his thoughts can cross over into your thinking and rationalization. Stop him in his tracks. Tell him he's a big fat liar! Speak loud and clear, "I already have all things in Christ Jesus. There is nothing I want devil that you have! **Now get out of here!"**

Always see yourself winning and be prepared to walk successfully in the Spirit. Boldly proclaim, "No, spirit of deception, I'm going to trust God. He can take better care of me than you can!" Will you hit your enemy forcefully with an arsenal of Scriptures? Will you make him run! The devil is entirely scared of you, if you enforce his defeat in Jesus' Name. If you are serious about hitting the mark and saving yourself from years of misery, you will truthfully desire to <u>be prepared to stand</u>. Remember you are really looking for God in others. Why not just go to your original lover!

"They that walk in the Spirit will not fulfill the lust of their flesh, for the flesh lusts against the Spirit, and the Spirit against the flesh. They are contrary to each other" (Galatians 6:8)

"He who sows to his flesh shall of the flesh reap corruption, but he that sows to the Spirit will of the Spirit reap life everlasting.
(Galatians 5:16-17)

Presentations and Setups
Egotistical decisions and self-centered relationships have no substance; or ability to satisfy our heart. Whether in one day or forty years, disarranged relationships always abort and dissolve. Their annihilation signifies that the blessing of God is not with them. Your answer to an unqualified pursuant must be a polite and simple, "No thank you."

Passing the presentation test will mean that your priceless destiny stays on track. It will not be negatively altered. The wrong mate will not be allowed to pass or pollute your precious life. Hitting the mark, the bull's eye, is your goal in relationships. Hitting the mark represents God's best for you. Deciding to trust your teacher, you can and will quickly spot the "set up." You are a keen listener to God now and prepared to win!

Setups
Frauds manifest for the purpose of getting you off track. God only wants to give you love, prosperity and truth. I believe you will choose wisely and live a "fascinating life," ordained by God. You want the higher realm of total fulfillment, and more of God. Never count yourself as gullible or naive. You are not. Believe in God and yourself 1000%! The blessing of God's covenant promises belong to you. With His overflowing, powerful love, you can see your purpose, even from the portals of heaven. If you want to, you can easily see that certain relationships that are not God connections. The associations look and sound good, but not so. You will trust your Father and hit the mark!

Wisdom
I hope you will greatly utilize my life experience and conversations with Eliza to change every disobedient area of your life. If you have moved past the gate of decision ask yourself, "What am I doing that I must stop doing immediately?" Lacy, Eliza and I (and millions of others in different situations) shall never forget our anguish and bereavement; but these ruined seasons of shocking heartache are not for you. Every prohibitive relationship can immediately be cast out. If you have sinned and missed the mark, the wisdom of God is available to get you back up to the top. Repent now and allow Him to restore your life.

Will you accept His love and freedom? You can trust that He is your great reward. Your gift is not outside of you, but it is Jesus within you. He will honor and never leave you. Your Precious Creator gave himself as an offering for you. Who else has done such a thing? Fathers, redemptive hand through Jesus Christ is readily there for you, even all the way through your wheat field.

Hanging on the cross, bleeding and suffering is **what love has to do with it!**

Your spiritual joy is a high priority to God. Stay within the gates of love and give your strength and passion to your Lord!

"Let the beloved of the Lord rest secure in Him, for he shields you all day long. The one the Lord loves rests between his shoulders." (Deuteronomy 33:12)

"Listen to God with a broken heart. He is not only the doctor who mends, but also the Father who wipes away your tears." (Criss Jami)

Jesus and I love you!

SOBERING STORIES   Chapter 10

*"Lord, turn my eyes away from vanity and quicken me in your ways. Establish
your Word within your servant. I am devoted to your fear."*
(Psalms 119:37-38)

Attractions can be tantalizing. Attractions can magnetize and capture our essence, focus and state of mind.

I want to share a selection of stories that sadly demonstrate the aftereffects of disobedient attractions. I ask you, can our relationship with God overcome the biology that releases emotion and brain altering chemicals? - Substances that cause us to move past the voice of God. Can we learn to fear the outcomes of going past the voice of God, like putting our finger on a burning stove? Are the consequences of disobedience enough for us to stop permitting relationships that we know are not breathed on by God?

The murder of Precious Doe
In May 2005, the Kansas City, community humbly discovered that Michelle Johnson, the mother of "Precious Doe," was involved in destroying her own baby's life. Since 2001, officials looked for the person(s) responsible for her decapitation. A police officer found Erica's body.

The community named the girl "Precious Doe." An artist assembled a proxy portrait of what she might look like. The community wondered who would do such a terrible thing to a child. The truth was revealed; "Precious Doe's" stepfather had kicked the baby so hard in an evil rage, that he killed her. He tried to conceal her death by removing the baby's head with her mother's assistance.

When Michelle met Harrell, there had to be something within her that said, "I don't have a peace about him." Do you think she imagined helping a man kill her baby, with her assistance? Or that she would be a part of hiding this crime for years? Did she ever visualize that she would neglect, massacre and annihilate her own child? Don't you think for a moment that God didn't speak to her? He did, he always speaks.

Long before Michelle's husband influenced her mind and soul, somehow, she went along with Satan's enticement. Looking backward, we would see that somewhere along the line, she chose not to listen to the impressions in her spirit. She might have thought, "Well he's just something to do for now. Hum ... I like this bad boy or I want someone in my life. He's fun – He's somebody to do drugs with. Or, he gives me money and I'm lonely."

Michelle would have said, "Initially going past the voice of God felt innocent and trivial." Today she would tell you, "I couldn't put my finger on it, but I didn't have a good feeling about dating Harrell. I wish I had used more wisdom and power to follow my God consciousness. I never should have allowed him in my life. I had a feeling he would be bad for me, but hoped I'd get past that." He might say the same thing about her. Michelle would tell us today, "Those feelings (warnings) were not trivial or inconsequential. God was trying to keep me safe and away from evil. I found an unholy connection with him; a dimension no one should ever consummate."

Michelle will be tormented for the rest of her life, knowing she helped a man kill her baby – a man she will never have. By now, the thrill is gone. There are no more drugs or sensual pleasure to dull their minds, but Michelle will remember. Day in and day out, for the rest of her life, she'll remember and wonder how her life might have been better if this relationship had not materialized.

Erroneous allegiances are sinful from conception. They are built tottering. Sin is a word we don't like today but it still cannot be disregarded. Some resist being told that God's definition is right and should be employed. Therefore, disobedient coalitions are established in sin, pride, rebellion, self-desire and fear of loss. These relationships produce hurt, harm and death, because they have to. Everyone linked to them are infected, because Satan himself is the originator. Sometimes they produce penalties that last for a lifetime. In the sphere of sin and disobedience, we understand an empire called pain and shame. We understand that there is no escape from giving back what we took away. Disobedience will cost us in a way unanticipated; because we are not that different from Michelle. Sin does affect our lives.

Michelle's sad sanctioning can and will happen to anyone who won't listen. We are no better. When we go our own way, we align with darkness and everything wrong can and will happen. Here we become another person. We do what we thought was impossible to do. As Michelle lives out her life in prison, she will remember that the Holy Spirit tried to prevent such a day from occurring. She could feel God prompting her to go another way, but decided to take her chances in spite of her perception. God spoke to her many times. He never wanted such a day for His precious Michelle. He did His part and was grieved with the outcome. He didn't create her or anyone else to kill their child, or to live their life in prison.

Incarceration
If we asked our brothers and sisters in prison what happened to them, they would enlighten us with powerful first-hand testimonies. Some would say they were on the right track, until their eyes and souls met with a spiritually illegal mate. Then, they did what they thought they'd never do. They didn't realize Satan's unforeseen influence was hidden in the bait. They underestimated his detrimental enticement. They would tell us, "Humble yourself before the voice of the Lord. I wish I had." They would say, "Once upon a time my emotions and lustful feelings seemed so important, but now none of that matters. The

termination of my wrong relationship would have been easier than this. Now, my freedom, life and family are more important and I miss them."

Disobedience is sin, pride and rebellion. Each will utterly alter your future.

Will you realize too late that your purpose, life and family are far more important? What if at the end of your love adventure, you end up like our sister Michelle or worse. She did not escape her love adventure easily or happily. Michelle was not able to save herself or her own child. What if that happens to you?

Prayer
Do remember to pray for Michelle and for the thousands of Moms and Dads in prison. "Lord, richly encourage and bless every precious spirit in a penitentiary today. Restore their lives. You know each nameless face. Thank you that the Holy Spirit grieves with each one and can comfort their hearts. Help them repent and cry out for a new day, even in their infirmities Lord. Help them see and live that new day. Get them out as soon as possible in Jesus Name!" Amen.

Before emotions ignite
No matter how strong you think you are, going past the voice of God can be lethal! You are not stronger than Satan's entrapment on his territory. His catastrophes wrapped in beautiful people are real. Not everyone comes out with his or her life. Some jeopardize and lose love ones, their minds, millions or their purpose. Many in their waywardness are taken hostage in consuming, devouring ways

Sometimes suicide wins, when darkness consumes souls in godless relationships. - (Like the cheaters on the Ashley Madison website. They didn't know the devil would allow it to be hacked). Listen and believe God while it is day. Night comes, when no man can work or see truth. Make your decision now to obey God's definition of life and love. Decide to walk away long before emotions and desires ignite uncontrollable passions, and believe that Satan will make them uncontrollable. Don't allow insubordination to produce a work of sorrow for you and yours.

Sandra
A beautiful young lady featured on Larry King Live and Oprah's Show, seemed sweet and innocent. She initially thought her man's jealousy and control was a reflection of his love and passion. She recognized the truth of his soul-dependency too late. After irreparable losses, she understood that he was never ordained to be in her life. In 2003, her mother would be killed and Sandra's face maliciously shot off. She would need nine reconstructive surgeries just to gain some resemblance of a face. Sandra believed this seemingly wonderful man would make a positive difference for her, but failed to judge her reservation

enough. She never suspected his kisses would cost the life of her loving mother and her physical wellness.

She wondered, "Will I ever have another eye?" Her nose, mouth and right eye were completely exposed. The saline treatments used to grow her skin were incredibly painful. Her first surgery was twelve hours, the second four hours. Many others followed. Her challenges are still great as she lives life long past God's protective (voice) gates. Sandra had no concept of the horrific plan of the devil. We never do.

We must understand that wanting to please an emotionally sick individual is an impossible feat. It turned itself into a lifetime of calamity for Sandra and her family. This man came on the scene with serious behavioral and esteem issues. Sandra had no idea that he was a highly toxic, dysfunctional man, until too late; but God knew at the time of their introduction. God tried to transfer that knowing to Sandra during their first hello, but Sandra didn't take His voice seriously, enough. She unfortunately followed her own self-inspired desire and hope. She said, "It all began when he cut off all my friendships; even my male cousins could not come over. I knew I should have walked away then, (too late) but I didn't." Sandra had to change the way she dressed, and before long he began to slap her around. The beatings were next.

Sandra did nothing wrong but look in this man's eyes a moment too long, the first time they met. Boom! The trapdoor shut behind her outside the gates. The problem began long before his jealousy, demands, and sick control enacted. It began when she walked past the clearance of her loving Father's voice. Sandra gave herself away a little piece at a time after that, entering into his box of doom. She watched as the doors closed, knowing that her freedom and essence were cut off. His consuming jealousy and insecurity became her liability. God knew that when they met.

God's responsibility
It is never our job or obligation to improve the life of any adult. This is the job of the Holy Spirit. We are not God! He alone can change hearts and minds. We can't change or heal anyone. Again, we are not God! He alone can get into the innermost parts of our souls and the problems that began at childhood. <u>Our job is to pray for those we meet, as we connect them to clergy if possible. Then release them to God</u>.

I am so sad that Sandra went through such a horrific ordeal. Satan wooed and sabotaged her life by making her feel that this man was her responsibility. She never should have been there! It was not her job to please this very sick man absorbed in devilish dysfunction. His personality disorder was not hers to fix. She was not his god or subject.

Only God could help him grow, change or perceive life correctly. He needed a Savior, not Erica. A false sense of duty (unsanctified mercy), is one of the greatest ensnaring weapons our enemy uses. As I watched Sandra on television, Oprah said, "Why didn't you leave when you noticed he was becoming abusive?" I could hear the Holy Spirit shouting within, "*No, Oprah, it was too late then. It was too late when she ignored God's voice at the gate.*" It was too late one moment past obedience to God, when her and his emotions enacted. I wished Oprah had known the right answer to share with her audience, which is "The damage is done past obedience. By the time you realize they are physically violent, it's too late." Some people are obsessed with you, fifteen-minutes after a conversation, let alone dinner. By the time they move in and you are undoubtedly enslaved.

You decide
Considering Sandra's story, what will you do? Will you unwisely decide you know more than God does? Will you fool around a little while anyhow and open the gate to the devil's will and power? Will you allow his chains to clamp you down in iron? Will you become impressed with some one's attention, jealousy or control? Will you believe that bad behavior gives you more romance, sex and excitement? Will you try to jump through hoops to satisfy an "emotionally-sick," immature narcissist. Is that okay with you? Will you believe their evil perception and bleak view of life is right? Will you pretend their negativity is okay? Will you become the next statistic, or listen to God's loving voice?

To prevent emotional or physical injury from happening in the future, obey immediately. Move away unconnected before the wrong person is empowered. Stop the lying devil in his tracks! You don't need their attention; you can get your attention from God. You can busy your life, until He brings the right one. Walk away at the time of the handshake. No peace, no first date!
The bible says we can be taken with our eyes; so, protect your eyes and heart. Trust the Lord and don't look, wonder or think about it the second time. - Your spiritual eyes have already and immediately seen all you need to see.

Listening to God's voice is our highest form of vision and protection.
"I make a covenant with my eye's that I will not look (think) upon a woman (or man). For what portion of God is there in this? What inheritance will I have from Almighty God on High?" (Job 31:1-2)

Does obedience really matter?
If disobedience is not a factor in the failure of relationships, how would you explain the serious and painful consequences resulting from so many breakups, deaths and grievances? Some barely come through or die in the wilderness. What opened the door to their despair? You determine for yourself what is true. Are our stories just negative rumblings or is the Holy Spirit enlightening you? I pray you will receive truth, evidence and life that helps you prevent calamitous and reckless arrangements.

"Be not deceived, God is not mocked. What a man sows he will also reap" (Galatians 4:6-7).
"Present your body as a living sacrifice. Don't be conformed to this world, but be transformed into <u>God's Image</u>." (Romans 12:1-2)

Disorder
There is no real happiness beyond God's Word. His world is designed to respect order, obedience and righteousness. All disorder is cast out or falls away. Life works according to Him. I know, there is a way that seems right to us, but the end of our way is death to relationships and lives. Even if His ways seem old-fashioned and archaic in our modern times, you must know and believe His Words will come to pass. Nothing can stop God's laws. It's His planet, not ours; we must let Him do it the way He wants to.

Wisdom has demonstrated that bad things happen to people just like you! Have you watched the TV series, "Snapped" or "Deadly Attractions?" Do you believe those people are different than you are? Can you fight against God's laws and rules of life? Can you assume you will return safely from a journey of disobedience? What if your imprudence leaves your body burned, crippled, and sick, or your face destroyed? What if your outcome makes you more miserable than you could ever be by yourself?

He, who has an ear, will listens to wisdom's voice. We can absolutely be confident and happy in our Lord and in His timing with all of heaven support with and in us!

Let God fix people
You can't fix or change people. Some people won't grow. They don't have a clue on how demanding, unreasonable, narcissistic and dysfunctional they are. They are personally the last one on earth to think they need any emotional or spiritual intervention. The world is supposed to adjust to their jealousy, adulteries or fears. They will always blame others for their weakness or control issues. You will find they are good at being fun, romantic, sexy, loving, or passionate, but they are not authentic or God's choice for you. Their come to consume your soul. You are not here to help them love themselves better. Jesus is their answer. You are not.

True love gives as Jesus does
A taker is a sure sign that God has not sent him/her. God is not the taker, Satan is. Love gives, but a self-destructive mate subtracts from your very substance. It's easy to discern them, because they want to own you. You can feel their need to consume, mesmerize and overpower. Without hesitation, Run, run, run, for your life! Run as fast as your little legs can carry you.

Remember, our job is to say "Hello – Goodbye," and to pray for them. Your prayers are powerful enough for _____. But ... you are to pray in a safe place, across town, far away from him or her. We show courteousness and kindness to everyone, but we don't date and marry them. We are blessed people, who have more than enough of joy and connection through Jesus, we are not desperate souls. We are already life and prosperity! Our Father has already put everything we need within. And yes, we have His inside track of knowledge and knowing.

I can take the heat!
I knew and loved a dear Christian friend. She said, "Yes, I know I'm sinning by fornicating, (having sex outside of marriage), and I know I will pay for it; but you know what, when it comes you just have to know how to take the correction!" She was right to admit that she was in dispute with God's will, but was wrong to believe that she would just whiz through her time of repayment. She thought, "Because I'm a good Christian and have given so much to God and others, I will have an easy and tolerable correction, then it will be over!" Unfortunately, a few years later, Fatima suffered with a terrible form of cancer. She admitted she could hardly go on from one day to the next.

"The wages of sin is death," but the free gift of God is eternal life
in Jesus Christ. (Romans 6:23)

Fatima underwent extensive treatments. With pain and trepidation, she felt alone and abandoned. When every part of her body hurt, I am sure Fatima thought about what might have opened the door to her misery. (God is serious about our holiness). She had to wonder about her inadvertent harvest. I'm sure; she repented for her cavalier comments, and cried out to God in deep contriteness for healing and grace. According to the Bible we know that sin affects our lives and health. Only God knows the gauge of her situation, but did Fatima's sinful relationship permit this demonic interference? It wasn't long before she said, "If God is ready for me; I'm ready to go home." And she did. Sadly, the man she sacrificed herself for was nowhere to be found. I have seen these betrayals happen time and time again. what about you?

"No other sin affects you as this one does. Haven't you learned that your body is the home of the Holy Spirit who lives within you? Your body belongs to God and does not belong to you. God has bought you with a great price. Use every part of your body to give glory back to Him. He owns our bodies.
(1 Corinthians 6:18-20)

According to God's Word, did the issue of fornication open the door to the devil's arsenal against Fatima? Could she have fought a better fight of faith otherwise? Sin causes our hearts to condemn us; therefore, we cannot stand strong and hard against the enemy's tests and trials. If the devil can get us to agree with him through guilt, he can accuse us even better night and day for the sins we committed. When we are hurting, we think of our sins and wonder if they are the reason we are suffering. It is difficult to take authority over Satan when we feel accountable. Keeping our lives pure gives us more power to tread on the hater of our souls. We need the confidence of God that purity gives. The buoyancy of innocence helps us fight and stand stronger. To believe God in times of trouble is imperative! Did Fatima die before her time?

"Dear friends, if our hearts do not condemn us, we have confidence before God and receive from Him anything we ask, because we obey His commands and do what pleases Him." (1 John 3:21-22)

Adultery and fornication do affect your body
Sickness and disease in our bodies can often be the result of impertinent relationships. The Bible defines *Adultery and fornication as* sins against our body. They cause defilement in the eyes of God and magnify insolent behavior. One of the most penetrating scriptures in the Bible warns us to run away from all sexual sin like Joseph did in the book of Genesis, 39:12. Joseph tore himself away, running, but left his cloak in the queen's hand. The grace of God enabled Joseph to overcome temptation immediately. As you can see he was not ashamed to obey and to move quickly! He knew he could not fail God or jeopardize his future!

"His eyes constantly watch the behavior of human beings; he carefully observes their every step. No darkness is thick enough to hide darkness or wickedness from His eyes." (Job 34: 21-22)

"God will judge the good and bad for all their deeds." (Ecclesiastes 3:17)

Entitlement
As Christians, we know what it means to have high standards and morals. We believe we are worthy and deserve a good mate. Letting down our guard while expecting good from God, is one of the ways the enemy tricks us. We can also believe we are entitled and protected when making half-hearted decisions, but this is not true. God always expects us, as holy and keen soldiers to be aware; and to make righteous decision with the help of our helper, Holy Spirit!

For those of you who are living righteously with expectation; be careful not to agree with your senses during presentations. No matter how long you've been saved never forget, Satan is crafty and seductive. He lives to stop your momentum. Respect your enemy; he knows how to make your flesh feel good, even Christian flesh. He tells you to look at other Christians who fornicate and commit adultery and get away with it.

Think of the many pastors, in the middle of their third and fourth marriage or with mistresses. They have no biblical support to be out there. Satan will say, "Look, nothing bad happens to them. God understands; Go on in, the water is fine! The needs of your flesh should to be met."

Because it seems okay to fornicate or commit adultery in our times, is one of the most important reasons I felt driven to write this book. After all the world says,

"Who cares anymore? Isn't everybody doing it?" Well, God cares and will allow you to reap horrendous seasons of consequences for submitting to sin.

I am a witness that you will not get away with it. I did it and got pulverized - you will too! Agony and confusion is the price for self-gratifications for those who belong to Jesus. Wanting to believe that Luis was a blessing was wrong. I exchanged my glory for Satan's foot of crucifixion, and I never got what the double-dealing devil promised me. It never happened, but the desire to accuse God and stay in bed until I faded away did happen. But, like Joseph of the Bible, we can receive God's empowerment to run from suffering, by staying united in the oneness of God.

"Present your body as a living sacrifice. Don't be conformed to this world, but be transformed into <u>God's Image</u>." (Romans 12:1-2)

"Lord we pray and ask that we will never (again) propagate an evil harvest against You and ourselves. Help us choose to avoid pointless cruel results. Help us increase in love, trust, and devotion for you. We decide not to allow unclean relationships to touch Your holiness in us again."

Forbidden connections

Get your children hooked on the Word and Jesus, not just church. His Spirit is the only reason they will walk in wisdom and decide not to cross despicable lines. One of the stories on the series, "Deadly Women" demonstrated how pride goes before a fall. A very young lady was fascinated with a twenty-three-year-old Gothic man. Their relationship transformed her from a sweet Catholic girl into possession of a literal demon. When her family protested and talked to her about her new lifestyle, she and her boyfriend killed her parents, along with her eight-year old brother. She willingly assisted him.

Separately, she was a sweet church girl, but together they were two very wicked people. Wrong connections bring about frightening deeds and even deadly relationships. Think of the thousands of cases presented year in, and year out. Hurtfully, so many allow themselves to be mesmerized and possessed by the dark side and with dark people. Can we afford to believe we can play with evil to any measure? Isn't it better to give ourselves to God and His indescribable wealth and power? Shouldn't we make Him worthy and the passionate lover of our lives? We were created to love God.

"I make a covenant with my eyes that I will not look (or think) upon a woman (or man). For what portion of God is there in this? What inheritance will I have from Almighty God on High?" (Job 31:1-2)

Arrivals

We will know when our harvest arrives. We will know why and what we have done, because the Lord has talked to you about going another way many times.

But, the seeds we plant will return to us, good and bad. At that time, we will proclaim, God you are right; Your word is true. We do reap what we sow.

> *Be not deceived; God is not mocked: for whatsoever a man sows, that shall he also reap. (Galatians 6:7)*

Seemingly delicious yesterdays
Have you ever pulled the lid off your outside trash can in the summer to see that maggots have taken over your throwaway foods? Those foods were quite delicious yesterday. Disobedience is joyously sweet at first, but the seeds sown grow ugly roots, blades and then the full harvest. Finally, nasty insects manifest, multiply and overtake our desire. They dare to look you square in your eyes and say, "Ha-ha, by your decision I am here!" At that time, you realize you don't have happiness at all, but nauseating maggot lying vanities; that never give you what they promise.

Good and wonderful, long-term blessings come from obedience. Here we let God do what He does best. When the time is right, a pleasurable marriage relationship does occur, not a plague-ridden feast that eats away your life. God knows that tantalizing encounters are first conceived in our minds, and must be stopped in the emotional realm as well, before they take form. Disobedience changes our best course and shapes unconfirmed tomorrows.

> *"Your own wickedness will correct you and your backsliding will reprove you. Know this; <u>you will see it is an evil thing</u>. It is bitter that you have forsaken the Lord your God. The fear/respect of God is not in you," says the Lord of hosts. "Has the nation changed their gods? <u>My people have changed their glory for that which does not profit.</u>" (Jeremiah 2:11-19)*

Unsanctified mercy
A snake lay very ill in the bushes, trying to get to the other side of the lake. A turtle passed by. The snake cried out to him, "Help me!" He shared how sick he was, "I feel terrible. I believe I am going to die! Mr. Turtle, I know it is against your nature, but I beg you to help me. I've got to get to the other side of the lake. I want to be with my family. I can heal or die there." The turtle said, "No, no, no, I'm sorry, I just can't do that. To help a snake goes against everything I am!"

The snake continued to beg for his life. He persuasively promised the turtle he would not hurt him. He explained, "I just need help getting to the other side of the lake. Please help me!" Please help me!" Finally, beyond the turtle's peace and discernment, he hesitantly submitted to the request. Surrendering, he said, "Okay I will help you, but remember you promised not to hurt me." The snake said, "Thank you, thank you Mr. Turtle. I will remember your kindness!"

The snake leaped on the turtle's back and off they went to cross the lake. The turtle felt apprehensive, but continued to swim. He couldn't wait to complete the task. Inwardly, he hoped his uneasy feelings were wrong. The snake rode quietly ... All seemed well. The turtle took a deep breath of relief; he was almost there ... when suddenly! The snake bit Mr. Turtle in his neck! ...The turtle screamed piercingly! "You promised not to hurt me! You promised" wailed the turtle! The snake looking astonished and said, "I'm sorry, Mr. Turtle. I'm so sorry, I couldn't help it. I'm a snake and a snake has to bite you! It's my nature. I can't deny my nature, can I? I had no choice!"

Spiritual-illegitimate mates are sent to bite you. The devil can't help it; he has to try to mess you up. They seem to be very nice people, but because of the nature of sin, they can only remain nice temporarily. After winning your heart, they have to bite you, and you will wail just like Mr. Turtle! The dichotomy (contradiction) is this; chances are like Mr. Snake, they don't always know they've been sent to mess you up. They may largely have good intentions, but good intentions don't change the effect of the nature of sin. Mark God's Words, disobedient relationships bite! (Remember Luis prayed that he would treat me right. He initially had good intentions, but the devil still was given a right to bite me).

Too beautiful
Pride is being conceited, arrogant and having excessive high opinion of yourself. Self-leadership is pride and creates sabotage. Self-indulgence is the foundation of most problems in the world today. It's easy to think we are too beautiful, handsome or important to be dealt with by God's Word. We can think our intelligence allows us to make our own rules, but in the long run we realize we are not indispensable. Life has a way of teaching every person about their own insignificance and pride, which always goes before destruction. Self-leadership causes separation from God (Proverbs 16:18). Life on our own terms is the same as flagrancy. Exalting our human insight above the knowledge of God is bold-faced and impudent (disrespect). This is overconfidence that creates disconnection from God.

Humility
Humility, humbleness, and meekness are the opposite of pride. They are beautiful attributes and qualities of strength. Humility doesn't mean we are doormats to others, but it is total dependence on God for life, strength and wisdom. Humbleness is a wonderful characteristic that helps us initiate oneness, unity and relationship with our Father. With humility, we shout for joy and not in agony. We bolt and run like young rams in green fields of virtuousness and true blessing. Humility is the ability to discount what we think about the situation to obey God. Here we find ourselves hilariously happy and subservient to God's direction. Meekness provides access to God's Glory and favor. It never needs to say, "How I wish I had listened!"

"I Wisdom, share the house with discretion. I am the mistress of art and thought. I hate pride, arrogance, wicked behavior and a lying mouth. To me belongs,

good advice and prudence. I am perception. Power is mine! Through me, monarchs rule and princesses decree what is right. By me rulers and nobles govern lawful authorities. I love those who love me. Whoever searches eagerly will find me. With me are riches, honor, lasting wealth and saving justice. The fruit I give is better than gold, even the finest gold. The return I make is better than pure silver. I walk in the way of uprightness in the path of justice. I endow my friends with wealth. <u>I fill your treasuries</u>."
(Proverbs, 8: 12 - 21 and 9: 9-18)

I know enough
Have you compared God's wisdom to that of the eccentric, obsolete, gray haired, long bearded grandpa, sitting in a rocking chair? Have you decided He doesn't have the answers you need for today? But the world has the Cool answers regarding relationships and sexuality. You have taken for granted you know enough. Do you say to God, "I'm grown and I want to do what I want to do? You can't tell me to keep those old standards! Sure, I love You God, but You are outdated and not in tune with my savvy, modern enlightenment!"

Perhaps you have read books, mostly worldly ones or have listened to the philosophies of men. Perhaps you prefer believing the savoir-faire stars of the day. Their answers seem more relevant. You have subconsciously put the Bible in the other category, with old and repressive theologies. It belongs with the stuffy old mad man, the one who never wants you to have fun. You clandestinely (secretly) feel that God's techniques really won't work for you. The spirit of the age suggests that God's answers are rigid and not for you. What could He know about modern relationships and sexuality? The world's way is better and more exciting.

Society
A cosmopolitan society teaches us to pull the covers over our eyes, so we can't see the gun pointing at our head. It says; "Hey, do what you feel like doing. Follow your own mind!" Are they right? Let's look at Hollywood - the rich and famous. You would think with all their beauty, power, sex and money, they would at least have the power to stay together. But not even their glimmer or glamour holds them up for long. If you follow their lives, you find they are neither big enough to defy God's great principles. Their disobedient, illegitimate relationships and marriages/relationships always abort and fall by the wayside. They are affected and infected just as any other disobedient person. No class of people, Queen or King has ever escaped from the suffering of their disobediences.

God's blessings and consequences apply across the board. Wrong seeds produce wrong relationships. <u>A polluted harvest is the worse form of getting your own way</u>. Disobedience never ends the way you want it to. It's never all it's cracked up to be and people get hurt. The world says, "There's no problem when we sin;" but judge for yourself. Is God right or the world? What do you see? Do the ways of the world really offer happiness and longevity? When we look a little closer, the answers society gives always fail. Society offers a virus, a destructive bug that eats our flesh and takes our godly inheritance, one bite at a time. Offerings of sin and self; get us pain and trouble. The wisdom of the world causes us to trade our glory for contemptible microorganisms of maggots.

> *Where are the gods you have made yourself? Let them arise if they can save you in your time of trouble. (Jeremiah 2:28)*

God is eons ahead
In the old days, doctors didn't have a clue that washing their hands after serving each patient would save more lives. For hundreds of years people died unnecessarily for unknown reasons. Guess where the information about cleanliness and prevention from contamination came from? It was in the Bible and had been there for thousands of years. God always has the right answers! In generic terms, "God is bad, cool, all that and beyond!" Of course, the choice is yours to believe Him or not. Why not give yourself the opportunity to know Him and you will find that His presence and intelligence is matchless. <u>He can give you the information you want and need for happiness, more than the entire world put together!</u>

God knows more than you do! Just look at His track record and study His sensational historical victories. His train of victories; fill all of heaven. You will discover He has always, always, always, been right about everything. Who can be right about everything? He is worthy of your trust. His arsenals of successes have always surpassed every bit of opposition. I declare at the top of my voice, "God knows best!" There are immeasurable blessings for you when receiving life, Gods way. He will save your soul now and eternally. Our Father's words have been tested by fire. They always evoke the revolutionary truth you need! The status quo is not enough for you, but God is.

> *God laughs at the philosophies of men!*

God is always thousands of years ahead of us. He is more modern and relevant than your morning talk show or news. His Holiness alone makes Him the most amazing, savvy, omnipotent, intelligent and prophetic Person of the now and tomorrow. God is definitely in tune with you. He is the tune, sound and harmony! His satisfaction is wonder filled and enlightening! His techniques bring joy over bondage. Let us value the integrity of His living presence within us. We can emphatically know and believe; He does know enough. He is God! His peace is our umpire. We will not violate His peace!

> *"And Joseph answered Pharaoh saying, it is not in me: God will give Pharaoh an answer of peace." (Genesis 41:16)*

"All of heaven will praise Your miracles God. Myriads of angels will praise You for Your Faithfulness. For who in all of heaven can compare with You? What mightiest angel is anything like You? The highest angelic powers stand in awe of God. You are far more awesome than those who surround your throne"
(Psalm 89:7)

"Lord how manifold are Your works! In wisdom, You have made them all. The earth is full of your richness." (Psalms 104:24)

Your greatest admirer
Listen again to the deepest cry of your soul. You will find a significant and pertinent knowing about your creator. Can you find and hear Him? Ask God to remove wrong thoughts, feelings, attitudes and beliefs. Be willing to lay down what you think you know about love in exchange for His definition and preeminence. When you do, your spirit will witness with the magnitude of the God of scriptures. Never underestimate or undervalue the credibility and integrity of His living presence. His Presence is the difference that makes the difference. We thank God that we are an essential part of His enduring, eternal, and wonderful life. We matter because He loves us.

Declare! **"God you are more than enough for me!"**

"Come; see the glorious things that God has done! - What marvelous miracles happen to his people!" (Psalms 66:5)

"For as many as are led by the Spirit of God, they are the sons of God. The Spirit itself bears witness with our spirit that we are the children of God and if Children, then heirs of God, and joint heirs with Christ.

Declare: "I am a son/daughter of God. I am an heir of God and a joint heir with Christ. I joyfully confess my relationship with God. I am related to God as His very own child." (Romans 8:14, 16-17)

"God has delivered me from the power of darkness and has translated me into the kingdom of His Dear Son, in whom I have redemption through His blood, even the forgiveness of my sins."
(Colossians 1: 13, 14)

"For this I am confident, He who has begun a good work in me, will go on to perfect me in preparation for the day of Jesus Christ."
(Philippians 1:6)

As spiritual thinkers, we embrace and value only God-given spiritually and emotionally-mature people. They alone have received clearance from God. They are the only one's worthy of dating; otherwise we have allowed ourselves to be desperate and abandoned.

Prayer and declaration:
As spiritual thinkers, we embrace and value only God-given emotionally-mature people. They alone have received clearance from God. They are the only one's worthy of dating; otherwise we have allowed ourselves to be desperate and forlorn.

"Dear Lord, I ask you to forgive me for the sin of self will. I thank you for Your wisdom and preventative approaches. With your help and love, I will keep Your Word in my heart and before my eyes continuously. I ask You for a supernatural desire to be in Your presence. Thank you, for making me transparent to your will. I don't want to be impervious or unbending. I open myself to know you more! I ponder and meditate deeply upon You Jesus.

You are <u>my great investment and inheritance</u>. Thank You for giving me joy, good relationships and favor. Teach me how to manifest Your glory far more than I have. Help me to come up higher and maintain a deep consciousness of Your presence and goodness. Yes, I can trust you Father! Help me receive more light and revelation through Your life-valuing scriptures. I want to read Your word with tenacity. Make me an over-comer in every area of life. I want Your wisdom and not my own. Lord, I willingly surrender and allow You to destroy the works of the devourer in my life. I sincerely want to be free from self and fleshly desires. Save me from myself! Please remove my reasoning, pride and capacity to be deceived. Increase my discernment! Help me enthusiastically enter Your thoughts and new life daily!

Help me choose to live far above the hollowness of this world. I receive Your Kingdom (Your way of doing things) by force. I agree with You. I am a powerful winner and will act like it. According to You, I am more than a conqueror. Together we are unstoppable! I stand in Your faith. Thank You for keeping me away from spiritual ignorance and deception. Thank You for filling me with vision and holy imagination! Thank you, Lord for Your Presence, and for the good feelings I have through you! Amen."

"God does not oppress his people! Even though He is Almighty and exalted in power." (Job 37:23)

WHY DO THEY COME? Chapter 11

Why do the wrong mates present themselves?

They come because we are lonely and sad. They come when we think God is not enough to satisfy our joy. They come when we have suffered and when we rightfully believe we deserve the best. They come when we've been bad and good - When we are obedient and disobedient. They come when we are confident, feeling beautiful, handsome and strong. They come when we're looking for a mate and when our head is in the sand. Presentations happen when we are worthy and unworthy. Potential mates come when we are fat, skinny, ugly, cute, rich or poor. Shockingly, they come when we are absolutely in love and satisfied in God!

They come because darkness always tries to come - because evil lives and wickedness constantly tries to snuff out the light. They come because Satan gets high on your pain. He is an evil, jealous, hideous devil in the earth who hates everyone, especially you! There is nothing he likes about you, but your failures and his ability (given by you) to delude you. Deception and distortion are what he does. Darkness wants you to know, without a doubt that it desires to twist, pervert, test, execute and change your name. Evil simply wants to see if it can trample down your spiritual inheritance of holiness and life.

> *"He has called you through His gospel to obtain glory in our Lord Jesus Christ."*
> *(Thessalonians 2:14)*

Attractions
Are you spiritually prepared to keep your joy by continuing to walk on with God? If yes, you are ardently aware of God's glory, wonder and faithfulness. If necessary are you prepared to quickly say, "Hello and goodbye" as you move on with your sensational life! If not, will you pursue relationship with God for the strength you need to hold on in faith? Or give in to the first thing smokin? If you want love and affection from someone (like the majority of the planet does), will you look inwardly for the voice of God or not? If you haven't looked is it because you are not enjoying a blissful and intimate relationship with your Father?

> If you are not building a strong relationship with God and listening for his evaluations, you will most likely allow the wrong person to come.

If your level of wholeness is based on your wisdom, you are not going to be bursting from the seams with enough life or joy to choose correctly. Your discernment will be off. Therefore, you will not be observing with spiritual eyes and with a heart full of wisdom the wrong person will not have to stay away. Without wholeness, you are not ready for a healthy love relationship; however, you are hungry and ready to consume someone. This new person will be used to fill the cracks in your life. Your colors will show as the purchaser, taker and consumer. You are not ready to offer the right balance, but you are ready to "eat someone alive!" Like a people-eating, despairing cannibal, you will quickly devour your new mate's "vitality and substance."

The right one will come when **you need nothing from them,** and when your "singleness or unmarried-ness" has been spiritually satisfied! So much so that having a mate really doesn't matter. The glory of your illumination in your Lord is your authentic and necessary portion! You are already happy and free. You enjoy God and your own fullness so much that you are radiant and won't absorb your mate's essence. Ask yourself, are you sincerely prepared to bring an abundance of joy into your relationship, or will you bestow emptiness and hunger? Are you as "easy as Sunday morning?"

Has God filled all your wounds and breaches,
or will you engage as a ravenous predator?

Laws of attraction

We often attract parts of who we are. We also magnetize and pull towards us whoever or whatever experience we are internally asking for or think we need. This phenomenon happens at our deepest, most original level of desire. Look at who you are and how you think. How do you see life? What do you really desire? Who are you? What are your true characteristics? What do you really want? One way to know who you are is to look at the people you've allowed in your inner circle. Are they positive or negative? Spiritual or unholy? Are they emotionally dependent or healthy people? Those people are a lot like you at that time in your life. Ask yourself, is it time for you to experience more growth and inner healing to choose a better mate? What do you need to do to be all that God says you are? What changes need to be made to attract the right person? Do you secretly want pain and the wrong kind of attention? Are you afraid that someone will challenge your paradigm (self-concept)?

We often blame a bad relationship on our mate, before accepting that we ourselves have helped to establish the problem.

Negative spiritual request

Because we are spiritual beings, we talk with and through our spirits. Those we call into our lives can hear exactly what we are saying. They come to fulfill what we are asking them to do. Listen carefully to your deepest desire, soul thoughts and spoken words. Others hear our positive and negative callings, such as these: "I need someone to take care of me. I want someone to rule over me. I want someone with money; no matter what your character is like. I'm not worthy, so I don't care if you hit me, just keep me with you. I am so lonely and afraid, please come and help me. Make me feel beautiful/handsome ... I need you to be with me! I want your attention and recognition so badly. I am not healed or emotionally healthy, but I want your love and affection right now. Please come and rescue me and make me feel better about myself!"

Write down, what the words (messages) pulsations are that you are sending out? Your potential mate can hear you speaking. Is there a desperate plea within that says to a passer-by, "I need someone to complete me; please take some time with me? I know I look sophisticated, but would gladly take care of you. Give me a chance! Please take this loneliness away. I need you!"

Your thought life
The quality of your life and relationship is first developed in your thought life and then your physical world. Your world consists of your inner feelings, beliefs, thoughts and relationship with God. Your thoughts and words create sensations continually that go out into the world and attract desired illegal or legal connections. Then the experience of the trials you spiritually called into existence arrives, in the form of a personal presentation. You now are aligned to receive a blessing or a trial. Will it be a godly glorious happening or exist at your expense and consequence? So ... What are you saying and how badly do you want just anyone to come?

When they come, they already know what they can or cannot do with you and to you. The abuser and the enabler go hand in hand. When they come they already know what standards and boundaries are in place. Will you begin your relationship on a righteous level or will just any old thing do? Have you really decided that you will not tolerate a disparaging person with a hidden agenda or not? Your requests have gone out into the world. What are they? Who will hear, collect and answer them?

Let's hypothetically say, you don't like the way the man or woman you called into your life is treating you. Should you blame them for being a bad choice or is the true reimbursement from your own essence? Whatever we receive from a disobedient mate is always our responsibility. When we are whole, we call whole people into our lives, instead of sick, deceptive, implosive and needy beings. You do have control over who you allow or receive in your life. Your relationships reflect who you are. They are a reality of what you essentially think you deserve. The buck stops with you and your ability to receive perfected value, goodness and worthiness from God.

Are you spiritually calling into view the right God-ordained connection with your words and feelings?

"Refrain from illicit marriages and relationships" (Acts 21:25)

Are you whole?
If you are calling the wrong people into your life, the right questions to ask are these: "Why am I going beyond love's voice and against the grain? Why did I

allow myself to be a part of a decomposing and illusive relationship?" One of the answers is this: <u>You may somehow want the drama and pain involved because you think you deserve unscrupulous treatment.</u> Perhaps the energy spent is needed to keep you from working on the destiny God gave you to build. Perhaps you are afraid to really trust that God can get you there, the right way. Perhaps you haven't taken the time to renew your mind in the Word of God and you really don't know who you are!

Ask yourself, do I subconsciously need a problematic situation, because I am not healed, whole, fulfilled or focused? Do I invite people into my life that should not be there? Do I need more of God's medicine, vision and revelation knowledge to stop sabotaging my own life?" (Ephesians, Chapter 1)

> Your potential mate can hear exactly what you're saying.
> They know and sense who you are and what you want.

Positive spiritual request
The glory and manifestation of God exist in you according to your love for His presence and belief in His Word. Just how strong is your God-consciousness and trust? Do you relish the time you spend with Him and want more? Do you see what you really believe about God and yourself? Everything you do and feel comes from your own inner world of thoughts, feelings and beliefs, all of which initiate behavior. Your innermost desires of worthiness or worthlessness in life come from inside of you.

If your thoughts are spirit-filled, whole and righteous, your mate will hear you when you say, "I am happy, content, pure and whole. I could live unmarried for the rest of my life with God. I would love to meet you if you are also pure, content and whole. I have high standards and expectations so you must be a righteous person and well-adjusted, just like me. You must know who you are and be spiritually mature and free to run with me. If not, I can run faster with God and myself! I will not settle for less, so don't come otherwise. Stay away; I don't want to know you personally!"

They will hear you say; "You will need to love the Lord and yourself in a healthy way. I won't let you obliterate my life. You will not be allowed to devour my substance. You will not consume me. My life is not expenditure for yours. You must know that when you come. You must also be full of joy and knowledge and be well-qualified by God. We can share the intensities of God together, but I won't try to be your God."

It is also important that your mate hear; "If you are going to stress me out and not be able to love one person for a lifetime then keep on walking baby. The lights are off at my house! You can't come here!" They will hear your heart when you say, "You must be completely free from other relationships. If you are not, I will know and will not accept you. If I have the peace of God, I will allow you to enter my life, but you must be worthy of me. Your goals must also correlate with the ones God gave me."

If you are whole you won't desire a personal relationship with a depleted soul, other than praying for them. You'll run far and fast from an unbearable, immature, needy person. You won't carry someone else's backpack or take responsibility for their decisions.

I encourage you: keep standing on the foundation of God's righteousness. Keep knowing and feeling His worthiness, because He has made you a precious lion or lioness. Feel even more excited about who you are in God. You deserve the best and will get the best, because you believe you should. Being prepared and secure, you are ready for your authentic relationship long before the physical introduction occurs. When your definition of godly love and affection stands sure and strong before you, you will have drawn the good mate you deserve and desire, in Jesus Name! Amen.

The right one
If God has preordained a covenant marriage for you, you will surely see your permissible and godly mate emerge. The right person will come at the right time. You will be prepared with an inner substance to choose correctly, in patience and trust. This indispensable meeting will happen most importantly for the advancement of God's kingdom, not just for your throbbing heart. Your location, age, rank, color or size will not hinder this manifestation. This is a promise from God! You can count on it. You know you can trust your Father. You know Him, He lives within you ... And you were made for love!

God is more interested in your genuine happiness than you could ever be. When He establishes your marriage in honor, your obedience will assure a bright and powerful tomorrow. Through obedience you will rise to the highest standard possible. Your achievements will be impeccable. You will hit the bull's eye! God wants you to walk in that dimension, meticulously; together! You will plant good and righteous seeds for genuine long-term happiness. You will dwell where the living waters of prosperity flow. Follow well ...God wants to do you good all the days of your life!

When God says "No"
God only moves with a "YES and AMEN!" Please don't consent to a relationship without an absolute "YES" from God. You want and need His stamp of approval to get the quality of life you deserve. You don't want to end up feeling foolish, walking into seasons of stress and bottomless pits. You have decided you will not be part of some one's search for survival or growth research. You are far more honorable and valuable than that. Have you counted the cost? Ask yourself; are you truly ready for a "No" from God? On paper, your ideology for waiting sounds fine. It looks good on paper, but accepting a "No" from God must be consented to, long before the actual occasion. "A maybe" or an "I don't know" is still a "NO!" God always gives an emphatic "Yes; absorbed in peace!"

Remember: If Luis had been sent to be my husband, I would have heard an absolute affirmative word at the gate. We would have met at the right time and the right place.

Talk is shoddy. We can talk about what we will or won't do, but are you really willing and prepared to stand for the right person, come hell or high water? Are you emotionally equipped to go on with God? Will this be God's way, or your way? Have you established that your joy comes from the Lord alone and not from a human being? Settle it now! You have examined your heart and know that relationships are much more than trying to get attention, fulfillment, public acclaim, reward, approval, praise, applause or recognition. You already have all those things in Jesus. You are already famous in His Eyes. You are successful because He loves you!

Having no peace, joy or rightness was is an excellent indicator from God that we are not on His terrain. You will completely know when you have His voice. There will be no ambiguity, disbelief or faltering.

Wheat
When wheat is sifted, the real part of it falls to the ground. Wheat is solid and worthy, but the tares, debris, waste, and deficient parts remain in the sifter or blow away in the wind. The under-nourished and lacking parts still look like wheat at first, but then they float away in the wind. God gives us discernment to know who is "wheat or a tare," before a relationship begins. He also knows who will retain solid when the winds of life blow. The wrong one will propel away in the air streams of crisis, like Luis. The right one will standstill. Remember, you've got to hear an emphatic "Yes!"

"The enemy came and sowed tares among the wheat." (Matthew 13:25)
"Behold they are all vanity. Their ways are nothing. Their molten images are wind and confusion." (Isaiah 41:29)

God speaks at the gates
"And it shall come to pass if you hearken diligently to the voice of your Lord and observe to do all He commands this day, the Lord Your God will set you on high above all nations of the earth and all these blessings of life will come upon you and overtake you. If you respond to the voice of the Lord your God, you will be blessed in your city, with your children and through the works of your hands. The Lord will defeat your enemies and command His blessing upon your storehouses.

If you do not listen to keep His commandments and His statutes, which God commands you to do; all these curses shall come upon you and shall pursue and overtake you. They shall be upon you for a sign and a wonder. They will also be upon your seed forever, because you have not served the Lord your God with joyfulness and with gladness of heart for having the abundance of all things already. *Therefore, you shall serve your enemies whom the Lord will send against you." (Deuteronomy chapter 28)*

The information you receive when God initially speaks, is then in its clearest and purest form. This is the right time to listen clearly and act. Listen, concur, stop and respond immediately. Accept and know that your life is going to be far "more than it is" this way. God cries at the gate with all His heart. He knows, once you have walked past his voice, you walk in delusion, weakness and manifest your own desire. Your "good judgment" is overpowered by your own disobedience. God speaks to give you His protection, but God's voice of instruction will become paler and less significant as you walk on by. Decide that above all, you want to hear Life Himself speak correctly.

Happily, Unmarried
If you live in the revelation of Jesus' presence, you will find that your life is just as wonderful unmarried. The glory of God shall fabulously equip you to enjoy an equally, amazing life. If you are called to remain unmarried; God, Jesus, Holy Spirit, angels, family, friends and work will be more than enough for your realization of life ... And you will know this is where you belong. Those whom God gives you will be the intensity of support and wholeness you want and need.

Your self-actualization and assignment will be in Him. You will feel proud, satisfied and fulfilled this way. Your best line of attack and accomplishment will come from within this arena of freedom. You will know in your heart that no human relationship can ever truly make you happy. Even a wonderful marriage would not be substantial for you.

Your highest and most overshadowing desire and existence is in your devotion to God. He alone is your paramount of joy. Your most excellent position of status. Your truest, inner voice will let you know that you have a spectacular life as a dynamic, unmarried Christian. You will love sacrificing yourself to the radical agenda of life in "Jesus Christ." This is your calling. This is how He made you. This is why you are here. You already have a husband; (men and women), as the Bride of Christ.

You will live happily at the center of His kingdom business and reach others more effectively as an unmarried person. Jesus alone will be your high-octane source of life and pleasure – He is your "More" than enough!

"It is He who lies between my breasts at night.
He kisses me with the kisses of His mouth! (Song of Solomon 1:2)

"The laws of the Lord are perfect restoring the whole person. The testimonies of the Lord are sure making wise the simple. The precepts of the Lord are right and make the heart rejoice. The commandments of the Lord are pure and bright, enlightening our eyes. The reverent fear of the Lord is clean and endures

forever. The ordinances and protections of God's laws are true and righteous. They are desired more than gold; even fine gold. They are sweeter than honey dripping from the honeycomb. God's precepts warn his servants. They remind, illuminate and instruct us.

There is great reward in keeping God's laws! Who can discern correctly without having harmony and obedience with God? Lord, cleanse me from hidden unconscious faults, and presumptuous (arrogant) sins. Let not sin, and *self; have dominion over me. Then will I be blameless, innocent, and clear of great transgressions. Let the words of my mouth and the meditations of my heart be acceptable in your sight, O Lord. God make me a firm and impenetrable rock." (Psalms 19: 7-13)*

ASSESSMENT   Chapter 12

"God so loved the world that He gave His only begotten Son that whosoever believes in Him would have everlasting life" (John 3:16)

Ask God to show you how deep His precious love and acceptance flows for you.

You are loved and accepted by the King of the Universe. He loves you so much that He <u>gave</u> His only begotten Son. He did this so you might know Him. Giving is one of the best definitions of God's love. He so wanted to save you from sin, death and yourself that He sent Jesus. Jesus was and is the best God could offer you. Jesus came to us ... What a gift! Imagine, someone offered Himself to die and shed His Blood for you.

You are successful because Jesus loves you, and you must love yourself the same way God does. God's love, blessings and harmony cannot flow well through a vessel of self-hate, rejection and unworthiness. God wants to show you what it feels like to really be loved, by the very source of love. The world will give you many wrong definitions of "what love is," but acquiring God's best will mean that you accept the simplicity of His priceless gospel of love! He gave His Son for love.

"Confront the dark parts of yourself and work to banish them with illumination from God. Accept and give yourself forgiveness. Your willingness to wrestle with and defeat darkness will cause the angels to sing"

Consider the love God has for you. Love can help you rejoice when a wrong relationship fails. Love can set you free from the damage the relationship caused. God's love will help you discover truth and shine light on your great path of victories! <u>Only Jesus is worthy of defining you</u>. You are loved, accepted and adored. Your beloved thinks the world of you. You are written in the palm of His hand. You are connected.

Never abandon yourself
God's love will keep you from abandoning yourself. If God won't leave you, you can't leave you either. By the way, have you noticed how good you look without the previous disaster? The truth is you look wonderful aligned in God's will! You have nothing to prove. Stay in your lane and gradually life will show them who you are. Don't lift a finger to prove yourself. You won't have to. If you are hurting, remember that God is only bringing you back to love and to your rightful position.

There are women and men who have gone through dreadful trials and tribulations, but remained committed to each other. So, no more self-agony! Stop thinking you are a failure or a reject. That is a "boggish" lie, from your enemy. Don't receive the devil's hype in the least bit. Stay focused on the greatness of God and on who you really are in Jesus. You are not alone or separate from Jesus. By the way, who was that "You person," before the impostor infiltrated your life and attempted to take your name? You lost nothing. You still have all you did that was important before the relationship began.

Develop and look at your identity scriptures in your journal. If you don't have them written down or memorized, began the project today. You have to have them ready to go. You will need to use them many times, before they are imprinted on your heart and mind. Fight, the good fight of faith, for your identity every day. This way you will never abandon you! You are an important gift to yourself, from God.

"Keep your heart with all diligence, for out of it flows the issues of life."
(2 Corinthians 8:10)

I want you to see how easy it is to build a repertoire of image scriptures from nearly any book in the Bible. I choose to share these from Colossians, but you can create a vast journal for yourself. Why? Because, you have an enemy that seeks to take your name and identity, if you don't stand on God's truth!

Who you are
Colossians - Chapter 1
1. *I am righteous and filled with the knowledge of God's will!*
2. *I am filled with knowledge, wisdom and spiritual understanding!*
3. *I was born to walk worthily unto good works. I am worthy*
4. *I am fruitful and expanding in every good work!*
5. *I increase in the knowledge of God*
6. *I am strong with all might, according to God's glorious power*
7. *I have patience and long-suffering, which is long in resisting of evil.*
8. *I am joyfulness*
9. *I am wealth*
10. *I have the inheritance of the light with all God's saints*
11. *I am delivered from the power of darkness and have been translated into the Kingdom of Heaven with Jesus, God's son!*
12. *I am redeemed through the blood of Jesus*
13. *I am forgiven completely. I fully repent and stop sinning*
14. *I am reconciled to God*
15. *Through Jesus' death, I have been made holy, unblameable and unreproveable in Gods sight! (I answer to no one but God!)*
16. *I continue in faith, I am grounded, rooted, and settled in faith.*
17. *I am steadfast in the hope of the gospel of Jesus Christ*
18. *I rejoice in resisting evil or suffering in the flesh or human thinking*
19. *I have been made a minister according to the dispensation of God*
20. *I fulfill the word and work of God!*
21. *God's mysteries are made known to me - that were hidden from ages and from generations before*

22. *I have the mysteries of God and his riches of glory, which is, Christ is in me.*
23. *I have Christ in me the hope of glory!*
24. *I reach, warn, and teach every person in all wisdom—to present them perfect in Christ Jesus*
25. *I am perfect and perfected in Christ Jesus*
26. *I am a laborer, a striver, and survivor,*
27. *I have God working mightily in me; therefore, I am mighty and a magnificent person in Christ Jesus!*

Be filled with fruits of righteousness, which comes through Jesus Christ. Be filled in the glory and praise of God." (Philippians 1:11)

Mistreatment
When someone is mistreating you, cheating on you or breaking your heart, they are not the one. This is not truth. When someone walks away it is not completely your fault. Don't believe the rhetoric! Infidelity is a conscious decision, so never lose your sense of God, self and truth in the middle of the battle. Their resolution or decision to stop trying was made due to immaturity, lack of spiritual stability, lack of faith or the will of God. It was not entirely you, other than being in the wrong place! But don't you dare blame yourself for what they did! Give yourself some credit. You know when someone is hurting you and when he or she is wrong. You're not crazy or insecure. You know when you are being hurt. They would have done the same thing to anyone else, out of place.

People do what they want to do, based on their own idiosyncrasies, not yours. It's in them, not you. The end of a relationship does not change you or anything pertaining to your supernatural providence. You are still a noble, impressive and worthy child of the living God. Delight yourself in Jesus and let Him delight Himself in you. Nothing important has changed or is lost- not unless you allow the devil to distort your concept and imagination.

You are connected to life! You are still a winner and a wonder. He whom the Son sets free is free indeed! Tell yourself again about the champion you really are. You had power before you met them … didn't you? Of course, you did and you have power now! <u>They gave you nothing indispensable or imperative; God did.</u> His validation is more than enough for you. If needed, he will tell you what changes to make based on truth. Believe in the God in you. Believe He is worthy and reliable, and absorbs you into His great life! Don't allow your former mate, the circumstances or the mayhem to define you! Neither; give anyone the authority to know "you" better than God does. You belong to Jesus. You are the life of Christ!

Miscarriages
A miscarriage is defined as mismanagement, bad administration or failure to attain the right or desired end. When someone does not belong to you, you will never have a sense of serenity with them. You know in your knower, <u>you're</u>

dealing with stolen goods. You know you can't keep the embezzled funds. Sometimes we become more controlling, jealous or critical when we feel the separation occurring. However, in all our trying, we can't make the relationship conform to a lie. You or they will intuitively create problems to abort the malformation and deformity.

A miscarriage in a relationship is bad administration that creates premature expulsion. The laws of God work naturally for causing truth and righteousness to align; no matter what your personal cognizant wish may be. His laws are like a mighty ocean; they expulse and move everything in their way - out of their way. God cancels mismanagement and wrong directions to make crooked places straight again. He is the unconscious force that removes the lesser desire or our conscious will.

Finally, we must receive the knowledge that an erroneous relationship cannot stand. They abort because God is love and mercy. He moves wrong relationships to prevent untold tragedies from manifesting even more, grief, sorrow and regret. When you get to heaven you'll see the capacity of the why. God will say, "Now you can see it, can't you? You were just too much for _____. They were just not worthy of you." Accept His truth. Let His reality be a good enough reason now, through trusting Him.

Yes, something is wrong when a miscarriage happens, but after the healing, it makes the mother healthy and strong again.

Enemies promote us
We must thank God for every enemy because they help us grow. Some adversity we bring on ourselves, but we must let it create fuel for us. Enough fuel to move on beyond measure. (God had to allow Luis to be very hateful to me, before I could let the marriage go). Some opposition helps us see something we couldn't see before. We occasionally need a good enemy to push us over the top! Enemies make us fight better and make us run us into the arms of the Lord. They are useful. Stop and thank God for your enemies, even if he or she seemed to have done you great harm. Through antagonists and liars, your name will be known in heaven and hell!

David (of the Bible) was made known because Goliath messed with him and Israel. If David never had a foe, he would not have known that he was a warrior and full of faith! The world would have never known of David's great exploits, without a challenger. His tests were horrendous. It took worlds of faith to overcome, but look where his test of adversity got him. David is known overall, as a man after God's own heart. A man persecuted with suffering and much adversity; but he stood up to God's enemies. He also repented and turned from his sins quickly. With great remorse, he repented and sincerely mourned over his sins. That is the difference David made for the Glory of God.

David moved on with confidence in His God -- while most of us dwell in guilt and stagnation, never forgiving ourselves or seeing the bigger picture. David, put what God thought about him, over man's feeble opinion.

When we are whole, an enemy will make us fight against darkness, but when your self-concept is blemished; a foe will bring you down and cause you to fight against yourself. We can't allow adversity to make us fight against ourselves. That would not be from God. (Isaiah 54:17) If and when the time is right, God will deal with your enemies, or not. But, through your enemies you learn what you are made of; especially when the lion and bear come into your camp. Not to worry; in Jesus, we can't allow adversity to make us fight against ourselves. That would not be from God. (Isaiah 54:17) "No weapon formed against you can prosper and every word spoken against you, you will condemn."

By faith the walls of Jericho fell, after the people had marched around them for seven days. (Hebrews 11:30)

Shadows

When God said, no one could align against you, they cannot! In truth, an enemy is like a shadow in the valley of death. They are only a shadow. <u>They are only as powerful as you think they are</u>. Their influence is according to your big or small perception of them. Who can really be your enemy in the light of God's Mightiness – Nothing can stand! Like David said to Goliath. <u>"Devil, how dare you mess with the blessed of God!?"</u> Keep your eyes on your Father always and one day you will see that God (not you) has defeated every adversary.

Your Captain is world's stronger than they are; whether your enemy be human, financial or bodily.

Open doors

You will meet many kinds of people throughout your life, but few are meant to cross over the threshold into your inner court. When spiritually-illegal mates enter a consecrated life, we create pain together. This is another disadvantage of an illegitimate relationships and why they must be avoided. The people that hurt us are pain producers, but they only give us what they have within themselves to give. They give us who they are.

I had serious judgmental and anger issues to overcome from allowing Luis in my life. I couldn't understand why God would not deal with him for his adultery and his notorious, scandalous lies. Think about it … Why should God judge Luis in a way that I could see? Those dismal experiences happened to me, because I opened a door that God told me not to. I'm the one who put him on the train and tried to keep him there. God didn't! God was kind and said "My girl is in trouble. I have to help her put this man off the train." He could see my pitiful state of mind, lack of faith and inability to help myself.

In the light, I thank God for helping me. Father, changed the beliefs I had that permitted Luis to come in the first place. (I'd still like to have the total "essence of my time" back though). The truth was I owe Luis an apology for opening the door. We know that a dog, cat or snake will come into an open door, if we don't close it. Coming in is not completely their fault. The open door is the problem. Pain producers don't have the spiritual maturity not to come in, but it's up to us to stop them. Hurtful, harmful and deceptive people cannot and should not come into our house! And we are warned!

Allowances
If a wild animal gets into your living room and lies on your new white couch, will you put a blanket over it to make it comfortable or put the critter out? You see we don't have to be a rocket engineer to know what to do. If a deer destroys your new furniture and living room, whose fault, is it? The deer was doing an expected thing. You're the one who said come in deer! He/she felt the warmth, smelled the food and wanted it. It's you, the perceptive adult who must change the boundary.

I let Luis in and tried to make a play boy into a faithful husband. He could not be who he wasn't'. Allowing him in, caused both of us to be out of place. I should have said, "Scat. Get out of here deer!" I had the foresight to know better. I saw the door open and the deer on the couch. He did not. This is why I cannot judge him. God is the righteous judge. He will hold him accountable or not. He also knows why I feared not allowing Luis in my life, but allowed what I allowed. This is why, our identity in God must be prevailing. It is the only way we are perceptive and strong enough to shut the crazy door that allows strays to come in and out of our house!

Forgiving Luis, myself and everyone involved has given me the liberty to laugh and love. Until you get there, continually give God the hurtful experiences, anger and desire to judge. One day you'll discover that God has made up everything they did to us. Let him take the load again until every bit of hurt is gone. I claim what the great "Catherine Kuhlman" contended. She said, "Our erroneous marriage never happened. It was cast into the sea of forgetfulness."

Should Sharon - Stay or go
Is it better to go or stay, when a marriage is against God's will? My heart goes out to Sharon, a precious young lady who loves the Lord. She deals with many conflicting family difficulties that began from early childhood. Sharon let her family afflict and dominate her life many times over, which made confrontation too intense for her. The familiarity of her past contributed to her co-dependencies. She knew she was not a wanted child and went out of her way to make others love her. It was common for Sharon to go overboard in a relationship. Trying to prove and love herself, she loved others through excessive behavior, with too much cooking, cleaning, buying or doing. Sharon

has a great need to provide the evidence that she is significant. Her sense of worthiness came from bending over backwards and making others happy.

Sharon had not been able to get over a past boyfriend. She said, "Of all my relationships, this one is written on my heart. I can't get over him." She was a Christian at the time she began to date John. He was not. She felt convicted about their fornication and tried to get him to turn to God, but couldn't. This is a next to impossible task, when you're sleeping with a partner you're not married to.

Sharon was extremely patient and stayed with John through multiple affairs and venereal disease. A year into the relationship, she was hurt, several times in serious car accidents. It seemed that every kind of evil thing happened. She knew what this meant. God was dealing with her about her unclean, erroneous relationship. Sharon's feelings of endangerment were born from their illegal relationship. Those feelings were a clue that the relationship was inappropriate. Still she believed John was her soul mate. (Sin so deludes us). She put him above God and he continued to break her heart. Most importantly, he was not supposed to be a part of her life.

Finally, Sharon left John. She knew she could not risk more backlash suffered in the devil's camp. She had undergone enough difficulty and reproach. She forced herself to stay away, but continued to dream of John, even after she was married nearly five years. Sharon struggled to be affectionate with her husband. She said, "I married him, just because I was tired of being single." John eventually married too. His marriage collapsed three years later.

When Sharon learned he was available, she wanted to pursue their old relationship. She let John know she was still interested, but was married to a man that adored her. Sharon felt she should be honest with her husband. Thank God, John was a Christian by then, and did not feel the same way. Several years later John remarried and Sharon divorced her present husband. She is now remarried, but wonders if she missed the right man. Years later, she told me she was divorced again.

Rejection
Sharon's dysfunctional childhood was a big part of why she accepted John's rejection as normal. Depletion was a part of her internal and subconscious image. Self-denunciation played a big role in why she chose someone who continued to punish her. She needed the bad feelings he gave her. If God had ordered John and Sharon's relationship, they would have come together righteously with a Word from God. John would have had the same measure of strong feelings or knowing she had; and would have helped her love herself more. They would have had the strength and grace necessary to endure.

Sharon set herself up for more of the familiar pain she had known from childhood. Mistreatment was conventional for her. At heart, she knew John would not choose her permanently. She knew he would hurt her. Sharon needed a revelation of her own worthiness and value before dating. She needed a strong inner knowledge of her identity in Christ to balance her decisions. <u>But when we are hooked on the pain, derived from childhood, it's easy to subconsciously desire the same hurtful scenarios again and again</u>. If <u>we are not healed we want the pain and punishment that feeds our internal need for denunciation of self</u>.

Strong delusions

A corn seed will always produce corn, not an apple. Isn't it ironic that we expect God to break His own laws to make a bad relationship good or to bless a relationship he told us, not to get into? As God's holy people, stop fighting to make wrong, right! Call a lie, a lie, and a lie can never be the truth. Fabrications are never right, but if you want an illusion, God will let you have it. If you think that he or she is something more than God, God will let you see for yourself the ugliness of your selection.

"They will perish in all deceivableness and unrighteousness, because they received not the love for the truth that they might be saved. And for this cause God shall <u>send them strong delusions</u> that they should believe a lie, and they might be damned that believe not the truth, but had pleasure in unrighteousness. From the beginning God has chosen you to salvation (saving from suffering) through sanctification of the Spirit and believing in (God's) truth." (2 Thessalonians 2: 10-13)

Strange fruit

No matter how great your love or lust is; you must accept the fact that "great love" with the "wrong person" is still "strange love" and "strange fire" that smolders in the nostrils of God. Strange fruit is never recognized or blessed by God. It might be sweet to us, but it is sour to God. Why would the Bible say: "<u>What God has joined together</u> let no man put asunder?" <u>Doesn't that mean there is another kind of joining together that God is not part of?</u>

Our relationships and marriages are powerless, without the Excellency of Kingdom personification. Without His blessing, they die in the heat of the day. Our energy is spent trying to keep a spiritually-doomed relationship living and breathing. Our excruciating toil gives us nothing in return. We labor for naught, nor can we keep what we acquire.

Illegitimate transactions extract life from us and conclude in screams of agony.

Soul ties

You can see why soul ties are serious matters and are humanly impossible to break. Yielding to the wrong someone, spins confusing webs of delusion for a long time. Once we connect to an illegitimate mate, all manner of distortion is possible. According to God, when the devil convinces us to follow our minds and flesh, divorce and destruction is commonplace, even among Christians. The mayhem we see going on around us is not surprising. Still, all of creation groans in pain waiting for the manifest sons and daughters of God to be who we really are. God's universe still requires holiness. He mandates that we raise our standards, by resisting evil, self and Satan.

"If they obey and serve Him, they will spend the rest of their days in prosperity and their years in contentment! (Job 36:11)

Nothing was in Jesus

Remember, God never tests you with evil. Like God, we must possess a perfect hatred for the works of darkness. Keep hitting your enemy square between his eyes as hard as you can with the Word of God. Don't let him speak to you! Satan could not get the upper hand on Jesus, because Jesus only wanted the things of the Lord. There was nothing in Jesus for Satan to manipulate. "Lord, we want to be the same as Jesus. Create a clear heart within us."

"Be sober and vigilant, because your adversary the devil walks about as a roaring lion, seeking whom he might devour." (1 Peter 5:8)

Let them go

We are here to worship God in the earth! Your purpose for being alive is eternal and will last forever. It is more than just about living for another human being. There is nothing you need from them that you don't already have from God. If they leave you rejoice loud and long! <u>Why would you want someone who can't see who you are</u>? - Someone who doesn't have the sense or spirituality to want to be with you? - Or someone God is removing? If they need to leave, let them walk! - <u>Stop holding on to death</u>. You know from reading this book, they can't stay with you outside of God's will anyway. Your personal plan is not going to work.

Ask God to break the bonds. Give him a chance to do it. Yes, it will hurt and take time to do, but your relationship with Jesus is always the more. And you've got to have the more. The lesser will never be enough for you, but God's will, will give you everything you want. Release delusion, darkness and false obligation. You are far more than an illegitimate relationship. Let the contamination die. Let the past be a teaching tool and stepping stone for your victory. You are still a winner. Come back to the light of God and see.

You were created before the foundation of the world to extend His glorious life in the earth. (Ephesians 1).

Get lost in the higher purposes of Jesus. Worship is the greatest kind of interdependency. People can't always be there for you, but Jesus can and will. Don't give more credence to them than you give to God.

Forgive them. <u>They can only be who they are</u>.

"There is nothing more than Jesus to be gained, under the sun!"
(Ecclesiastes 2:11)

Rejoice! Rejoice! You never lost anything that was yours. You only lost delusion and disobedience. Who wants that?

Let life handle discrepancies
Sometimes we worry that God will not deal with people that hurt us. I felt led to share this story to remind you that God does not forget. People are dealt with when they hurt others on purpose. It is a serious matter to act disrespectfully towards <u>any</u> child of God. This is why you never involve yourself in some one's marriage, ministry or any life situation in a negative, <u>judgmental</u> manner. Don't make yourself an enemy of God. If there is a matter that needs to be addressed, pray first and then speak to the persons involved, respectfully and privately.

A few years after Luis and I divorced, Jyndia called me while visiting her Dad. She was upset and wanted me to know that one of her Dad's friends had been hurt in a bad accident. They were in critical condition. She said the person was a friend of Tina's. Tina was the lady that came to our home with Luis and her husband Carl, the night Luis packed to leave. That evening was principally one of my most difficult life encounters. The news was shocking for Jyndia and Luis. I asked her, "What is the person's name?" She didn't know. She only had parts of the story. We prayed for whoever it might be and ended our talk.

When I put the phone down, the most curious thing began to unfold. I hadn't thought of Tina or the events of that terrible night for years. God had helped me release her and the way she accused me in my own home. Now, (five years later) … when, I heard Jyndia mention her name, the strong emotions of that night reenacted.

I could envision and feel her in my face and how appalling she behaved. She was dreadfully impertinent as she judged me unmercifully. I cringed, remembering her antagonism as my heart was broken with Luis moving his things out of our house. She defended Luis in his sin, treating me shamefully. I was so defeated. The weight of our disintegrating marriage was unbearable and now this woman was telling me she knew what was going on in my home! -- I was the problem – not Luis' adultery! I thought about how I wished I had been stronger, but my oppression was insurmountable. I was in no way prepared for the demonic attack that came through Tina that night.

Before Jyndia's call, I was happily working on a project, but now, I felt torrentially troubled. Feelings of distress rapidly dismissed the pleasantness of my evening. These intense recollections of Tina unfolded, as if the event happened yesterday ... the stab in my heart was fresh again. I was so overwhelmed that I couldn't work any longer. I shut down my computer, went to bed and began to cry. My soul moaned and grieved with sorrow. I lay there saying, "Lord, I know you have blessed Tina to do well in life, but how do people like that keep prospering? They don't seem to care about bruising or hurting others. They don't fear or respect You, but they keep flourishing. Lord, I don't understand that?" (Tina had obtained a new executive position in another city, while hurting others).

A Tina mystery
It was as though I was emotionally transported backward to relive that terrible night ... I went on to tell the Lord again, how badly she and Luis hurt me that night. Their hatefulness and belittling was utterly uncalled for. The impending vision of their abhorrence increased and troubled my mind. My severe emotional change surprised me. I prayed and released the pain again and again, asking God to forgive me for my offense. I was sure I had forgiven her long before; at least I knew I had given it to God. However, this spiritual re-visiting was contradictory for me. Finally, I reached for my Bible for comfort. It fell open to a familiar scripture in Isaiah, which I had read many times.

"Fear not, I am with you. Be not dismayed for I am your God. I will strengthen you; yes, I will help you. I will uphold you with the right-hand of my righteousness. Behold, all they that were incensed against you will be ashamed and confounded. They shall be as nothing. They that strive with you shall perish. You shall look for them and will not find them that contended with you. For I am the Lord your God - I will hold your right hand saying unto you fear not. I will help you!" (Isaiah 41:10-13)

The Words seemed to leap off the page. The comfort of the Holy Spirit was real. I worshipped a while, and had no clue as to why I was so upset. Lastly, I felt relief and the peace of God. I relaxed and went to sleep. The next morning, Luis called to tell me the lady in critical condition was Tina. She was not a friend of Tina's. (Jyndia misunderstood). I was traumatized! Luis was noticeably disturbed! Tina had been in a one-car accident, but now the hospital would need to take her off life support. I had no idea that the person Jyndia told me about was Tina. I was perplexed, hearing such news and prayed for her recovery. I asked God to bless Tina's eternal soul.

I understood at that moment ... the Lord does work in mysterious ways. For His reasons, He spiritually reconstructed the incident. But, God did not want me to know why I was thinking of Tina. He was showing me something significant and reminding me that He does remember our pain. I don't know, but did Tina need my forgiveness again before she could cross over? I have heard that those passing over can see and feel how they hurt others ... As mysterious as the encounter was, I learned when God says to pray for those who hurt us; we must pray for them, because a future day is coming when they will desperately need

His mercy. I thought of Prophet Ratliff again, who said, "Pray for mercy for those who practice "use-abuse" against you." He said, "God will deal with them and those who used me for what they thought they could get." Time tells many things.

The Bible says it is a terrible thing to fall into the hands of the living God. Issuing out pain on purpose is treacherous and dangerous. God does avenge in these situations. We are personally dealt with in a variety of ways if we do this. Some die early for touching God's anointed. (Every Christian is God's anointed). An early death was truly sad for a lady in her forties. Only God knows what really happened and why.

I called to share my awe with a friend who wisely said, "Dorothy, Tina hurt a lot of people. No telling how many have prayed and asked God to change her before this day. You didn't will that for her and you didn't do it; so, stop feeling bewildered." As much as I hurt when Tina was in my home that night, none of it mattered considering eternity. Life on the other side is a real thing to deliberate, at all times. We each must be prepared to meet Jesus face to face. I trusted that Tina had time to repent for her sins.

Stumbling Blocks
There is a woe attached to our being out of place. We are given a lane that we must stay in. Remember, dishonoring others carries a high penalty. Getting ourselves mixed up in other people's relationships must be avoided. Remember, you don't know the whole truth. Ask God to help you mind your own business and be respectful if you are guided to talk to them. Don't judge another.

You don't know why people do what they do. Even if you think you know all the facts, beware and handle everyone carefully. Even if you think you know why they are going through a warranted, self-inflicted harvest, do not deliberately hurt them. You don't know the whole story. We are all important to God and God fights for each of His children, His anointed, just like He did when Job's friends judged him.

"As surely as I live," says the Lord, "Every knee will bow before me and every tongue will confess to God." Each of us will give an account of ourselves to God. Therefore, let us stop passing judgment on one another. Instead, make up your mind not to put any stumbling block or obstacle in your brother's way."

(Romans 14:10-13)

God lets us hear
I shared what I had learned about Lacy through Eliza earlier. God prepared my heart to pray for her, but He also let me hear about some others. In one example, the very thing a lady did to damage me, happened to her. She enjoyed my suffering and publicly attempted to embarrass me. It appeared that she and her husband had a good marriage, but a few years later they divorced too. She

told a relative, "I wonder if Dorothy spoke against my marriage? Perhaps, that's why we are divorced." What an odd thing to say.

I never thought anything about her or her marriage. In my state of mind, her marriage was the last thing on my weary brain. I suppose, she felt guilty for saying what she did to me in a room full of people. Nevertheless, we are dealt with for what we say and do to hurt others. We will also know when God is dealing with us about it. Hence, everything we give out will legitimately manage to come back to us, sooner or later! Never misuse anyone; we want blessings, not curses to come our way. Be very afraid to hurt someone, especially when it comes to their marriage. May God remember His mercy for us in times of judgment!

The fear of the LORD leads to life; then we rest content and untouched by trouble. God will not be visited with evil!" (Proverbs 18:23)

Every affliction works for my good. I have favor, position, and endurance, ripeness of character, hope and victory. (Romans 3:5)

"But unto you who revere and worshipfully fear My name, the Son of Righteousness will arise with healing in His wings. You shall go forth and gambol like calves (released) from the stall and leap for joy. You shall tread down the lawless and wicked, for they shall be ashes under the soles of your feet in the day that I shall do this, says the Lord of hosts. (Malachi 4:2-6)

HEARTS DO HEAL   CHAPTER 13

Healing comes from taking responsibility ...

The right questions are these: "What does God think about me? What do I sincerely think of myself? Who was I before they came?"

You have the security of knowing that God will heal your heart. Healing is yours if you accept it. There is a power for the righteous that releases the energy of a young calf, wherein you will leap in joy and happiness. Allow God to tread down the works of the enemy, but set yourself free. - All that is not well; will be made well by your Father. Allow joy and singing to arise from your heart!

All that pertains to life, praise and dividends of gold are yours right now. You have a wonderful boat to catch today and so many things to do. God has not given you a spirit of fear, but of power, love and a sound mind. His perfect love for you casts out all fear. Yes, allow His glory and light to fill your soul. Let the spiritual reimbursement of agreeing with God and godliness, bless your life.

Love God and yourself, until you are "You" again!

Hurting souls
For those who have experienced such times as I have, we have learned expensive and expansive lessons. When we came out of the wilderness, we were leaning entirely upon our beloved. Our vocal prayer was: "LORD, DON'T LET ME EVER DECEIVE MYSELF AGAIN! Help me want Your Continual Presence, Joy, Life and Ways." We have had enough of trouble, with the knots on our heads to prove our waywardness. We are convinced! We don't want another mistaken relationship again. We have learned obedience from the things we suffered.

But, if your wounds are open and you are hurting, I have a special place in my heart for you. I know how you feel and where you are. You are one of the most important reasons I wrote this book. The nexus of my heart is to help you see life from a better, more capacious premise. If you are hurting, let it happen. Let the phases of cleansing and bleeding come to pass. The sore will hurt, until it is purified. Let all the inflammation and contamination run out. Little by little, the pain will subside.

The healing process is a good time to reflect and challenge your viewpoints. Most of us found out the hard way that we don't know enough. However, if you are seeking God and pouring in mega doses of the Word, you will hit level ground quickly. Get ready for new heights of understanding. But, if you are looking at your situation just one-way, you are looking at a tree, (one thing) instead of the whole forest. You don't want to do that. This means that your

emotional perception is inaccurate. You must look at the whole of your life and being. The entirety of what has happened is bigger than just the relationship.
I know how you feel. I know how bad it hurts. At the time of my testing I couldn't see that God was putting me back on the right road either. All I could see was the pain and persecution. But, God has to remove the slant of the misleading relationship out of the way. The separation is like the medicine you should take to feel better. We often want to blame the devil when it is God who allowed the breakup. He did it because you are worthy and valuable to Him. Don't condemn yourself, but be kind to God's creation, "YOU." No matter who else has forsaken you, they just don't know any better; but you significantly matter to God and to many others. <u>Do not forsake yourself</u>. You are worthy of giving yourself friendship, love and esteem. <u>Give no one the power to make you hate yourself.</u> Nourish yourself as a friend.

God will help you create the right thoughts, feelings and actions

Don't dwell on what you needed to change then, which was not the entire problem. Nothing was wrong, other than being in the wrong place with the wrong person. Stop worrying; stop rehearsing all the bad things they did and said. Just surrender and let God do the perfect work he wants to do in you. You have encouraged others in the past, now encourage yourself. One of the greatest tests in life is to love "you," when no one else seems to. By the way, "You" are the greatest slice of life, He has given you to enjoy? Think about the goodness of God and you make yourself rejoice awhile for those great blessings! Just meditate and be grateful for the life that God has given you.

"Do not fear little flock. It is the Father's good pleasure to give you the Kingdom." (Luke 12:32)

Give yourself credit for trying to make the relationship or marriage work. Forgive yourself again. Get back up. Your life and purpose matters! Find a way to move forward just today. No one else can do it for you. You have repented, and you are still a good person in the Lord; nothing can change that. You are still blessed! Lift your head and stand tall in the Lord. Learn more about who you really are. Your negative life lesson is over now. You have come back up to the top of life, where you belong. One moment at a time, you will know that all things do work together for good for those who love Jesus.

The regeneration of your life has begun. Today, not yesterday is the beginning of your eternity. You are still worthy and wonderful in Him, your greatest measure of defense. Through the gentle love of Jesus, you will see the sun shining again. More than you have ever known. God's wonderful hand is working behind the scenes to restore you. He is spiritually taking the substance of your pain. His marvelous work of suffering on the cross makes up what they did to us.

Codependency, (emotional dependency) is allowing what someone else thinks of you to change how you feel and think about yourself.

Our foundation and childhood pain often caused insufficiencies to develop in our hearts. If we went out into the world looking for others to validate our existence, we began as depleted souls. Except for the intervention of God Words, we would still be diminished souls, but Jesus made the difference for us. He is still helping us understand that His love is the greatest fulfillment possible.

Rely on Him, not your own feelings. Feel what He feels and remember that good always overcomes evil. Your pain is Jesus' pain now. You will discover He has your cares in His hands. He is consuming every part of the misery. Later, you will know that He completely took it. Much of what has happened is just a matter of perception. It is important that you see life through God's eyes NOW!

Trails of purification are all about love

Your mate's negative response has nothing to do with your ability to love or to deserve love. It is common for the devil, through the perpetrator to blame and accuse the righteousness of the "accountable mate." But keep your spirit of faith active. <u>Your faith is not fragile</u>! Your God is strong! You will not break into pieces.

What do you believe about God and yourself now? You cannot allow them (demons) to make you think you're a bad person. If and where you need to make changes, God will show you how. He loves our spiritual and personal growth, but for the right reasons.

More Word! More Freedom!
There is no fragmentation in Jesus. God is with you, who can stand against you? Allow His healing balm to massage your heart repetitively. Love His presence. He is watching over you. You were born to dwell in Him. Accept His divine love. Meditate again on His presence and kindness. Can you feel the presence of the Holy Spirit? Make reading of the scriptures personal and mandatory each day. Continue to collect the scriptures that speak to you. Write them down and declare them over your mind, instead of sitting there listening to the devil's words. Fight for your joy and well-being!

Take the time to develop sections in a 3-ring journal. Add scriptures or powerful thoughts to each section. Keep your arsenal of supply close! You will be amazed that scriptures release the joy and vision you need.

Encourage yourself in the Lord, like King David of old did. Discipline and train yourself to invest in supernatural growth. Meditate and read those scriptures vigorously. Take them into every situation by force. Develop a glorious habit of saying them again and again; and they will give you the power, faith and vision you need to move in the right direction with joy. Rebuke Satan's spirit of depression, fear and rejection. He won't have a chance to work when you are in the presence of God. Make sure you develop a section on warfare scriptures too and declare them!

Still valuable
The Word will help you see how the devil is trying to hide the truth from you - **The truth that you have lost nothing but delusion, disorder and disaster!** How can God's child, who has everything in His universe, lose anything? Remember, Oz never did give anything to the "Tin Man," that he didn't already have and neither did your former partner give you anything you didn't already have. You were already someone valuable before you met him/her. You still are. You are more than fine. You are blessed! You've got plenty left in the tank, that's how awesome God create you!

Empowerment belongs to you. Keep the truth before your eyes and walk in the sensational light of Kingdom renewal. Jesus Christ is already healing your wounds; even if your process feels doubtful and dubious. Satan's spews of pain are only smoke screens of lies, but don't let him whisper even a word to you. Tear them all down with the Word! Believe in joy, life and Kingdom exuberance! Joy is who you are.

Your Father says, *"You are wonderfully and respectfully made in His image!"*
Believe that more than any other voice!

God, you are my justifier, because I believe. (Romans 3:26)

Great righteousness has come and great faith in God
(Romans 4:13)

No weapon
When we are whole, an enemy will make us fight against darkness, but when your self-concept is blemished; a foe will bring you down and cause you to fight against yourself. We can't allow adversity to make us fight against ourselves. That is not be from God. (Isaiah 54:17) When the time is right, God will deal with your enemies. But, through your enemies you learn what you are made of; who you are and who you are not, when a lion and bear come into your camp. Not to worry; in Jesus, we can never allow adversity to make us fight against ourselves. That would not be from God.

(Isaiah 54:17) "No weapon formed against you can prosper and every word spoken against you, you will condemn." 4.4.17

You are a warrior!
The negative beliefs we formed from childhood attach themselves to our subconscious minds. Maximum meditation on scripture is needed to change our way of thinking, believing and acting. If we work at it we gradually know, feel and confess who we really are. God's truth must be felt, experienced and touched

deeply at a subterranean level. To get there we build a personal relationship with Jesus. Loving Him daily renews our minds. Again, meditation on God and scriptures are keys to our success.

Will you take the necessary steps to fight for your preordained, phenomenal life? Ask God to help you warrior up. You can fight a strong fight of faith. You are contending for your identity, purpose, godly relationships, children, loved ones and to fulfill your obedience. Daily receive His Image anew and afresh, instead of a finite, limited mindset. Your true image will not come or remain easily; you will have to aggressively work to keep it alive. The truth must be known and declared. God knew and loved you before the earth began, before you knew yourself! Let Him awaken your heart to truth. Accommodate Him by aligning with scripture as a trusting child. <u>You are part of God's warrior Image right now</u>.

How can we be God's Kings or Queens, without daily renewing our minds? It will take measures of submission to God and faith building, to stop the defenses that are set up in your mind. It is more than a notion to pick up your sword and stand in position. Our God requires growth, maturity and more than great-sounding platitudes to be who He says you are. With work, your persistence will stop the resistance of the enemy. Fight to be the authentic you; the one God created you to be. Take what belongs to you! Let it be unto you according to the word!

"From the days of John, the Baptist until now the kingdom of heaven has suffered violence, and the violent take it by force." (Matthew 11:12)

"Be sober-minded; be watchful. Your adversary the devil prowls around like a roaring lion, seeking someone to devour." (1 Peter 5:8)

Therefore, take up the full armor of God, so you will be able to resist in the evil day. Having done everything to stand, stand firm! (Philippians 4:13)

Say this out loud: "I am part of the wonder of God! This day, I believe I can fly and accomplish anything through Jesus! There are no walls and no limits! I can see miracles happening all around me. Marvels are at my fingertips.

Together, God and I are the exceptional phenomenon's. I am loved, connected, valuable, necessary, and worthy! I always was! Thank you, God for removing defilement from my life. No weapon formed against me will prosper! Every spirit of witchcraft is cast out in Jesus Name! God and I cancel every negative word and assignment against me! Devil, you have no power against me! I am covered with the Blood of Jesus and I know the Word!" (Laugh at darkness in Jesus Name! Ha-Ha-Ha)!

Know and believe you are worthy and good enough. When you do your best in Jesus, you are the best! You matter to Jesus and He is walking with you!

Know and believe you are worthy and good enough. When you do your best in Jesus, you are the best! You matter to Jesus and He is walking with you.

The good fight resist disobedience
Being a devoted Christian is being a warrior. If you want a good fight, fully join God's army. Become a part of manifesting His Kingdom. Wield His sword of power and life to destroy obscurities. God needs you and the world does too. Help Him change this dying world. Deny yourself and go deeper into becoming a part of His extravagant life. Positive warfare will illuminate and heal your soul. The combatant's life in Christ, offers you the best fight in town. It will give you all the good resisting of evil you want.

Join the revolution! You have been given great power in the Lord. See His observation of life and be His essential difference. Greater works than Jesus you will do. Be like the mighty men and women of old who have gone before you. - They got hold of His supernatural promises, realizing they could make a difference too! They knew that living for Jesus was worth it all! (Read Hebrews the eleventh chapter. See how the world or old was not worthy of these mighty warriors).

Lord my heart is fixed trusting You Lord. (Psalms: 57:7)

Have I not commanded you? Be strong and courageous! Do not tremble or be dismayed, for the LORD your God is with you wherever you go."
(Psalms 41: 1-3)

Look ahead
What does your own natural, holy and happy state of existence look like? What are you doing now to reach your life purpose? Are you allowing anything to be greater than your own emotional healing and spiritual awareness? What is missing now that needs truth? There is so much more to know, to do and to experience in the "you" realm. What new truths have you discovered about your true identity?

God and you are remarkable! Let the force of your faith come out of your human spirit and live! Heal by activating spirit life. It will take eons of time to know the full capacity of God within you. But grasp onto Him now and stay attached. Stay connected. **He is not in another place. He is in you today**! No need to wait until tomorrow! Can you feel His comfort now? Hold your head up high in His love. Laugh in His happiness!

With the power of the Word working in you and the insights discussed in this book, you will make great decisions. You are an overcomer! <u>Keep</u> or releasing your former mate and yourself into God's hands. It's up to God now; you must rest in what He wants now.

Remember, your mate is also suffering from missing the mark. You were both disconnected from God by your dishonest relationship. They are not your enemy, the devil is. They simply were not the right one to coexist with you. Chances are they didn't stoop to hear God either. But, God's world and your purpose are much bigger than one, wrong, lousy experience. Your faith and obedience to God has put you in a place of favor and good return. <u>It's what you always had that matters most.</u>

God's love floods my heart through the Holy Ghost.
God has no anger towards me.

Don't count the days
Never disqualify yourself. You have not seen God's final decision. All the days have not been counted yet! Trust that God is working out something amazing for you. Embrace your journey and be a passionate praise unto your Mighty God. He is your King of Glory. If you want to feel something wonderful, feel unto Jesus. Feel His presence and His sound. Feel the breath that vibrates from the pages of the Bible. Feel the intimacy that comes from unlocking His treasures untold. Behold, observe, watch, and consider; you have the very best that life can offer. Stand firm in your faith and you will see the glory of your God.

What shall we live for
Hoist the blood-stained banner of Jesus high! What else shall we live and die for? Continue only in His Greatness and conquer all that besets (plagues) you. Know that you already have all things in Christ Jesus. Act like it. Use your weapons! Advance the Kingdom of God. You have everything you need. Go forward! Can you feel His love and abundance all around you? What a marvelous and grand finale yours will be. Be patient and don't count the days until everything's been made subject to the Name of Jesus. Believe! Your God has already exonerated you. You shall see the glory of Your faithful God.

"The wise grows wiser still. Teach the upright and he will gain more. The first principle of wisdom is the fear of Yahweh. Awesome respect and passionate love for and unto God is what His holy children want and practice. The wise know that doing it God's way is the only way.

For by God are your days multiplied and your years of life increased. Are you wise on your own recognizance? If you think so, you are not wise at all in God's eyes. Are you a mocker? When you laugh at God's instructions, you are foolish indeed." (Proverbs 9:9-12)

Set yourself free
The faster you drink from God's Word, the sooner you will understand, laugh, play and plan again. You are accepted in the beloved. Nothing can stop you; that is truth. You have everything you need to feel happy today. You are life and wealth, just like your Father. Everything belongs to you through Jesus and

everything is possible for you to do and to be. You don't have to go get anything. It is already there within you to unleash, unfold and discover. Liberate yourself from the minor. Take hold of the major, which is life in Jesus! The lesser was keeping you fastened to a lower spiritual dimension, but no more of the lesser for you!

Remember, if your mate was right for you, God would have salvaged the relationship. Let the falsehood fall to the side of the road. Let all the bad emotion and sin flush out. Let all the pain and confusion go. Your life is clean now. Everything is already all right. You owe them nothing. They owe you nothing. Jesus has filled in all the blank spaces.
Vindicate yourself. Hold your head up and enjoy God's freedom. You are accepted in the beloved. Just be with God ... Be with him mind, body and spirit, and you will see the forest! You are already the sunshine. They were not the sunshine. God and you were and are the illumination. One day very soon your wounds will turn to wings of joy. You will fly higher than ever before! Your obedience has already elevated you. God is continuing to create and reveal beauty to you. Behold! The ashes are under your feet; God is using them to introduce you, to the real you. - The precious and powerful you! Behold; His power will manifest itself in all you touch.

"Therefore, put on the complete armor of God so that you may be able to stand your ground in the evil day. And having fought to the end to remain victorious on the field, stand by fastening the girdle of truth around you. Put on the breastplate of uprightness. Put on the shoes of the gospel of peace, which makes your foundation strong. Take your shield of great faith and stop all the flaming darts of the Wicked One.

Receive the Helmet of salvation and the sword of the Spirit, which is the word of God. Pray unceasingly in the Spirit always. Seize every opportunity fearlessly and with unwearied persistence and appeal."
(Ephesians 6:13-19)

Don't accuse God
There is great profit in keeping God's ordinances. Serving the living God will never be a useless task. We must never attribute the evil or gloominess in our lives to God. He is our wonderful redeemer, and protector. He only manifests good to you. He is never the author of wrong decisions, pain or disobedience. Put the blame where it belongs; on the devils, back! Remember, God loves you so much that **He gave His only begotten son!** The King of Glory died for you on an old rugged cross in nakedness and shame. He died to give "you" life now and eternal life.

Speak honorably about the One who honors and promotes you. Your King and Queen-ship is from God. He works hard to prevent "harmful" situations and deserves our highest esteem. He tried to keep _____ from touching your essence, worthiness and value. He would never have chosen for you to cast your pearls before an unethical relationship. <u>God knows that something's aren't meant to happen. They are better hidden and should never be found by you</u>. Jesus died for your best and is never the one to blame. Blessed are we, who are not offended with God.

"Your words have been strong and hard against Me," says the Lord. Yet you say, "What have we spoken against You Lord?" You have said, "It is useless to serve God, and what profit is it if we keep His ordinances? You walk gloomily, as if in mourning apparel before the Lord of Hosts."
(Malachi 3:13-18)

Don't look back!
Strangely, Justin shared something with me; after Luis and I were married. He said; he had dreams that I was leaving him for quite some time. I asked him why he never told me - why hadn't he done something to change or stop it? He had no answer to give me. You see God was preparing him, just like he does each of us for inevitable departures. Justin needed to be psychologically and spiritually aware that our future separation and divorce would happen, because it needed to happen. God is good, down to the last drop. He is good to saint and sinner; and is always helping us prepare for future success.

Don't try to reopen the past. <u>Continue to separate flesh and spirit.</u> If God has said "No" concerning your former mate, you already know the relationship will not merge for long, even if you get back together. You know what to do … The answer is already sealed deeply in your eternal spirit. You know that the relationship should not reunite. Stand strong against future pain and don't push away the foreseeable hand of God.

If needed, God's massive, spiritual, nuclear, Holy Ghost power is available to explode every area of darkness in your thinking patterns. If you listen you'll hear the right words and see the right path to take. Let Him have _____. They belong to Him, not you. Allow the relationship to dismiss itself and expire. Praise God, the pain and imbalance caused by the parasite Satan is gone. Choose to see the truth and keep taking responsibility. The scales have fallen from your eyes. No more toil or worry. Rest in the Lord's power now. Your only job is to stay close to your loving Creator, in present time. All is well. *With intense faith, boldly receive God's promises with no staggering and unbelief. (Romans 4:20)*

Like Abraham, with absolute certainty, I believe! I boldly believe that God will carry out His promises for me. (Romans 4:24)

"Obey God. Worship the creator, not the creation and be healed."
(Luke 11:35)

Healing friendships
Keep yourself built up and well nurtured in the Lord. Choose healthy people who can love sincerely and to pray for you. (Believe me most don't have a clue about how to love and bless you). Develop <u>celebratory friendships</u> with people who understand how to strengthen you emotionally. And you become part of their strengthening system too. (Do you need to learn how to love and give better)? Good friendships are amazing.

Pray together. There is nothing like the love and care of a good friend. They are wonderful companions that energize and enrich your life. Ask God for one or two mature friends, mature enough to give you a wonderful godly hug when you need one. Don't hesitate to ask for a hug or an encouraging word when you need one. Don't lie about your state of mind. If you feel as lonely as a sparrow in the rain, say so; then pray, don't complain about it.

When you need support, call them, do it quickly. Cry out to God through the Word when you need to and then get back into spiritual thinking quickly. Make sure you have no dishonest sexual attraction to friends or them to you. You don't need any additional trouble or repercussion. Finally, do you have God's consensus before allowing these friendships the blessing of your inner circle? Choose family and friends, (not jealous ones full of back-biting), by using the same rules of listening to God concerning your mate. Be extremely observant of who you give permission to get close to you. (Friends can be sent to mess us up as well). After you feel the peace of God, get busy loving them back and see about each other!

Family
I encourage you to renew your family relationships. I know family can hurt you more than anyone, but God sent us to this planet together and that means something to God. Listen to understand each other and stop defending yourself, just listen and love. Write an essay about your family and give it to them. Let them know how much you love them, while you can! Sometimes our blessings are held up, because of broken family relationships. I thank God that He helps us improve family connections. Make sure you increase time with your parents, siblings, mates and children. They are a significant part of your life and mission. You will be glad you did. When they are gone, you will miss them far more than you think.

My precious mom did her best with what she had to work with. She went home to be with Jesus (at 84 years old) on December 22, 2007. I miss her and the love she has for me. Her frequent calls were such a blessing. Her concern for my day always meant so much to me. I would love to hear her fuss about almost anything now. If needed, she always had a way of cheering me up.

There is something so deep, golden and rich about the way your mother looks at you. She knows something about you; that you don't know. That information makes you aware that the "umbilical cord" experience (the oneness captured at conception), is a real thing. Mom's kind words helped me believe in myself. She learned how to show her love to us more throughout the years. We could see how much she approved of her children.

Mom learned that giving love was more important than toughness, rules, and regulations. She loved our hugs and kisses and looked forward to them. She checked on most of her seven children (plus two in heaven) several times a week. Months before she crossed over into Heaven, she had that far away-transitory look in her eyes. She was looking over into the New World and liked it better than this one. Now, she is free, young and healthy again. All her ailments and disappointments are gone and I know she is supernaturally happy with Jesus. I loved to hear her say, "You are good Dorothy." She felt my pain when Luis left but always said, "Honey, don't one monkey, stop no show!" She was so funny! Of course, she didn't like to see her children used or abused. Isn't that the true heart of a mother?

I love and appreciate my family. My sisters and brothers: Lois, Mildred, Larry, Walliah, Richard, and David are always bright spots in my life. Our brother's Craig and Robert have gone ahead of us to dwell with Jesus on the other side of the mountain. Thank God, our loved ones are in our future, in Christ Jesus. This planet is not our home, we are just passing through.

My children are also a great joy. James is thriving in housing. He and his wife have five beautiful children. They are flourishing in the Lord and strengthen their church and pastor. James and I grew up together, so I appreciate his love and words of strength. With God's help, we have stood together through many difficult times. He is easy to love and makes our family laugh a lot. (What a pleasure to see the duplication of God that produces grandchildren).

Jamul is quite the businessman. He is innovative, intuitive and an anointed leader. He washed my feet one day; I felt amazingly blessed. The experience was humbling, awesome and opulent. He promoted me spiritually. I love my Jamul and his awesome vision from the Lord. He is a good man and yes, he is quite prophetic.

Jyndia works in leadership with international House of Prayer, Hope city and helps her mom. She is also a prayer intercessor and is a great asset to the Kingdom of God! She is ambitious, moral, loved and a precious gift from God to others and me. Jyndia receives words of knowledge all the time, about her magnificent life. I have loved our priceless season's together and seeing God's goodness manifest in her body.

I thank God for church life and for a pastor that preaches the uncompromising, heavy-duty, end time Word of God. I am proud that he and his wife have the jewel of a one-time, covenant marriage, built on faith. I love and appreciate every friend, especially my long term anointed, prayer warrior sisters! Extended spiritual family is vital!

The gift of you
Loving others will help you increase your ability to receive a godly mate. Something special will heal your heart, when you give yourself away. Give the gift of you as often as you can and live beyond yourself. Leave Jesus' sweet fragrance everywhere you go. Give acceptance, validation and wisdom. Leave people better than they would have been without you being there. Help them become happier and more effective people. Don't leave anyone the same way you found them. Find a way to help them make positive changes too. They need constructive suggestions and wisdom. You are your brothers' and sisters' keeper in areas of love and prayer! The Bible says really love others and speak the truth in love. There are hundreds of things you can do to give life and joy away. Now is a most important time to do it. Look around and determine who you are supposed to minister to today and see how love and life fills your day in return. Someone needs your smile. You are greatly influential. God cannot fulfill his best for you until all hatefulness, fear and selfishness is driven from your heart.

Love your sister or brother as yourself. (Mark 12:31)

"Let us consider how we may spur one another toward love and good deeds. Let us not give up meeting together as some are in the habit of doing, but let us encourage one another even more as you see the Day approaching." (Hebrews 10:24-25)

We are us

God emphatically expresses, "we are one" in Christ Jesus. Our righteous acts toward each other are important to God. He knows there are always two sides to the story, but only His side offers the most precise and factual interpretation. He knows no matter how hard we try to be honest, no one has full possession of all the facts. Sometimes no one is right; both are wrong. God never takes sides. We must do likewise as we <u>listen to understand and not to defend ourselves</u>. God desires so much that we love and accept each other.

"There is one body and one spirit, by whom you were called to one hope." (Ephesians 4)

God watches to see how we treat those justly or unethically enduring hard times. There is never a right time to put your foot on some one's neck, or to mistreat them. If we judge harshly, we are storing up incrimination for ourselves. When we spit in the eye of another, we spit in our own eye. We tamper with and alter our own future. We are doing to ourselves, what we are trying to do to them. God will help you understand that treating someone poorly, is <u>projecting negativity upon yourself</u>. When we really understand this principle, there is more ability to issue out kindness instead of abuse and broken heartedness.

Understanding love as God does extends grace that covers a multitude of sins. Why would we need to be jealous, hateful, envious or afraid of each other? We are all the same in Christ Jesus, firmly linked together. We are all we have, as human-kind, together. We are built to need each other. God gives us the ability to love ourselves to love others. There is no person more dangerous than one that does not righteously love him or herself.

The Garden – Get connected
When Adam opened his eyes and beheld Eve, he said, "Eve, we are us!" What a beautiful revelation! The same is true for all of mankind. "We are us!" We must love each other as we love ourselves. We are connected. We can forgive and restore ourselves and others. "We are us." I am you, and you are me. Walking in this revelation helps us pray passionately and in the right context for others. When you understand they are the same as you and affect your world, you will be determined to love and forgive like Jesus does.

An interesting spiritual exercise to do is this one; when you hear about some one's problem, act like that person is you. Then, your prayers will be intensified. You will escalate in love and fear of dishing out judgment.

We are no more or no less than anyone else. Fear and competition or a Jezebel spirit is not part of perfected love and oneness. Changing people is God's responsibility, not ours. Trying to make people act like us is not fair. God crafted us to be an "encouragement and answer" for one another, not to judge or hinder with words. When we see the world correctly, we take our place in love and overcome the nothingness of the critic. We become "the love of Jesus" to hundreds of people around us. **Life is about walking in His realm of love and getting over the interruption of ourselves.** Jesus' cry was this, "Lord, help them become one in "every loving and supportive way." He is coming back for one church.

The view from eternity's balcony changes everything
Can you imagine standing in heavenly places; on mountaintop glory with Jesus? Seeing this helps you understand, life is far more than just your individual perception. But, your ability to love God's creation, the other "You's" in the earth, is what life is all about! - Loving others, shows your level of faith and ability to co-exist within God's purposeful plan. God's love for each of us is the same and gives incomprehensible joy that helps you say "Yes" to oneness. "Yes," to seeing the best in others and supporting them.

Pleasing your Father means that you recognize that others need help, just like you do in various areas. God needs you to give others (even the most unlovely), His eternal love and acceptance. He didn't go through hell and death, for us to keep the same ungenerous mindset. The world will know Jesus from the love you have and give. Love endorses the Kingdom of God and can never be destroyed.

Yes, we are one in Christ Jesus! We consent to His precious prayer by saying "Yes, I will become one with my brother and sister. I will love Jesus, myself and my neighbor, as myself." (Study: John 17)

"If anyone does not love, he does not know God; for God is love. God showed how much He loved us by sending His Only Son into the world so we might have eternal life. This is real love. It is not that we love God, but that He loved us and sent His son as a sacrifice to take away our sins. Beloved, if God so loved us, we also ought to love one another."
(1 John 4:8-11)

A word from God
Shhhh … Don't worry says your Lord God Almighty, just be with me and listen. I am He who appoints the sun to shine by day. I decree the moon and stars to shine by night. I stir up the sea so that its waves roar. I hear and see all that happens. I'm going to turn it all around and make everything beautiful for you, just in time. (Jeremiah 31:35 and Zephaniah 3:14-20).

Your powerful declaration
Say this forcefully! **Say it in the spirit of faith**! "I am fine. I am made in Jesus' image. I will not shed another tear of sorrow over _____. I accept that _____ was someone who was never supposed to be a part of my great life in the first place. I declare that no one unsuitable can attach him or herself to my excellence and kingship again! I will express my emotions as much as I need to today, but declare my tears will be full of happiness and cleansing only. My best friend God is walking with me and catching every tear. Thank you, God for trying to prevent the relationship from connecting.

God, You are removing all my sorrow and sadness to make room for the happiness. I will not suffer unnecessarily. I will not take the devils shame and pain; that belongs to him. Lord, I do receive your forgiveness and restoration. I am happy that the greatness, joy and truth of Jesus can return to my life now. The toxins are leaving me now. I know I am better off now and accept that.

Today I will enjoy and trust You, God. I am still a dynamic person. I won't waste my time and emotion on _____ any longer. One day soon, I'll wonder why I felt this way at all. I accept that _____ was not supposed to be in my life. _____ is not worth an ounce more of my precious God-given energy. Right now, I practice being happy, free and feeling protected. I am connected with You God and all that is good.

I decide not to miss a beat of enjoying my wonderful life. I have important things to do for and with You God in this season. People are waiting for me to bless and help them. I feel great and love to study Your Word. I am not my forsaken past; neither can my old deeds and life define me! I am more than what happened between _____ and me. Much more!

I existed successfully with God long before this relationship began. I am not my pain. I am the blessing and Jesus life! I am connected, important and valuable. I won't miss my sacred purpose again and move forward trusting my Messiah. I am a winner right now and will continue to make a difference! God and I are the great adventure I am looking for.

My success is based on Jesus' love and respect for me. Yes, I remember who I am today. I remember I was going somewhere when I met _____. He/she will not stop me from going toward my destiny now. I am far greater than the pain of my mistake and I haven't lost anything! God is my life; the relationship was not my life. **The gates of hell will not stand against Jesus and me. Amen!"**

READY FOR LOVE   **Chapter 14**

Eyes have not seen, nor ears heard; nor has it entered into the heart of man, the things that the Lord has done—for you!
(1 Corinthians 2:9)

We are receiving a Kingdom that cannot be shaken. Let us with grace, (God's enabling power) serve God acceptably, with reverence and godly fear. "All that cannot be shaken will remain. For our God is a consuming fire."
(Hebrews 12:28-29)

"Take hold of instruction and never let it go. Keep her for she is your life."
(Proverbs 4:13)

Christian dating is well defined. The Bible indicates that we are exclusive and uniquely created by God. We are special in His sight. We are God's conception of life and far more than sexual objects. Our relationships are designed to be a <u>part of our worship to God</u>. The Christian attitude toward dating is best summarized in, 1 John 2:16. It states, "The world, the cravings of sinful man, the lust of his eyes...comes not from the Father but from the world."

The precedent for Christian dating has its roots in the following biblical principles. <u>You must have confirmations of peace, joy and righteousness along with obedience, and a word from God</u>! These give us the green light to walk on in harmony, until vows are exchanged. Paul writes, in 2 Corinthians 6:14. "Do not be yoked or put together with an unbeliever. Of course, righteousness and wickedness have nothing in common." 2 Corinthians 6:3 states: "Put no stumbling block in any one's path, so our ministry is not discredited."

Accepting a wrong relationship does become a stumbling block and dishonors our lives. As Christian, we should not marry anyone who would cause us to sin. A Christian marriage is a union that takes place between two Bible believing, obedient, mature Christians. Marriage is for praise and worship unto God and to serve Him better. Marriage is an extremely sacred union, entered into for the glory of God. It should never be impulsive or after our own personal desire.

Careful consideration and prayer is needed; even after we receive God's endorsement. The tradition of the ancient Hebrew custom was to be engaged at least one year. It takes time to see each other in every probability of life.

Dating
Christian dating is only designed for the possibility of marriage. If you are dating someone, your expectation is high. You're hoping this is the God sent one. Not to burst your bubble, remember to slow down and examine what God is saying. He will speak through your spirit, feelings and emotions. Remain fully submitted

to His voice? What is the word, insight or knowing you received from God? Are you trusting Him with your future or feeling desperate? Remember your first meeting is the best time to accurately judge what God is saying. Your first quickening is your key to act positively or negatively. - Deciding to follow God later, will be too late.

Later, God will have to pry the man/woman out of your spellbound fingers, when you're passionately and emotionally gripped in love or lust. At that point, it will take divine intervention and hard circumstances to snap you out of it - (Like a slap in the face). But nevertheless, you know when and what to listen for now. Always, reaffirm what you heard, felt or know and take the information seriously. Remember not to change or downsize what you hear, feel or know.

It is critical to know if you can go forward or is this the best time to escape? If you are not experiencing peace, do the right thing before an emotional investment begins.

"Get wisdom, get understanding and forget it not; neither decline from the words of God's mouth. Forsake her not and she will preserve you. Love her and she will keep you. Wisdom is the principal thing; therefore, get insight and in all your getting, get understanding. Exalt her and she will promote and profit you. She will bring you to honor when you embrace her. She will give you an ornament of grace and a crown of glory. She will deliver you." (Proverbs 4:5-9)

Prepare for deception
Are you prepared to meet and embrace your new potential mate? Settle before you date that you will not go past the question mark or check in your spirit, no matter how cute or charismatic they are. You will not allow your thoughts or feelings to set you up for failure. Settle it ... no quick reactions, not until you know. Remember, darkness will talk to you with phrases like this: "Well, everyone else is having fun. One or two dates won't hurt anything. God wants me to enjoy life. I'm tired of being lonely, depressed and rejected." But ... you know the devil's words are poison and his minions are out to get you!

"Enter not in the path of the wicked and go not in the way of evil men. Avoid it. Pass not by it. Turn from it and pass away. (Proverbs 4:14-15)

Make every wrong thought bow its knee, because the wrong path is evil! Live by reading the Word daily, with prayer and a fasting lifestyle. This way you will not entertain carnal and limited feelings or relationships beneath your purpose. The Bible says, "Cast down every imagination and every word that attempts to exalt itself above the truth."

We demolish arguments and every pretension that sets itself up against the knowledge of God, and we take captive every thought to make it obedient to Christ. (2 Corinthians 10:5)

The thief has come as a roaring lion to steal, kill and destroy, but the violent take him down by force! (2 Corinthians 10:5 – Matthew 11:12)

Before the date
Are you saying, "You've got to be kidding? I should be afraid of a little romance, a candle light dinner or something nice to do every now and then? A nice conversation won't hurt me ... Getting all dressed up and flirting a little bit is fun. Life should be fun!" You may also believe that he or she is just a friend that needs an encouraging word. What could be wrong with that? You may justify yourself by saying, "As a Christian, it's my spiritual duty to be a friend. I am anointed and appointed for this. They need my input. My support is necessary and I would like to have a buddy like them - someone nice to hang out with sometime!"

Are you thinking, "How am I going to get a mate, if I don't date around? Do you feel that way, because God can't meet your physical needs and you have a right to look for companionship? After all God certainly understands my aloneness! It's just old school to believe that an innocent date could get me into trouble." Yes, I am boldly saying, as a lover of Christ you must submit your physical and sexual needs to God; until He confirms that you can date a potential mate and marry him or her.

Remember, it will be the little foxes (our acts) that spoil the vine. The little things will gradually ruin multiple seasons of your life. Yes, I am saying that a little romance is not a little thing at all. Think of the stories I've mentioned. What about the people you know as well, some regretted just one single date. If you listen, you will see that God has given you your own race to run. You are not going to allow yourself to be reckless or easy.

The right person can only come when you are whole. Completion means that nothing is broken, missing or lost within you. If you are whole you will remain confident and satisfied with God, life and self, even in the midst of storms. You will understand it is the glory of God that attracts and keeps your righteous marriage in place, not you. If you really want to do it God's way, don't even exchange phone numbers, until you know. Something as simple as a date for a wee cup of tea could strongly activate the flesh. Peace and confirmation must be in place first, without question. Put everything on hold until you receive your God-clearance. If you don't have 1000% peace of mind, don't proceed.

Hanging out with Jesus will cure your need for romance, until it is time. If you really get into Him, the fun and enjoyment of Jesus is all you'll need. Don't worry, if you are patient He will confirm the right one, at the right time. The best thing you will ever do is awesomely fear and respect what the Lord says to you. Make "self and ego," obey your Mighty Spirit Man. Let God's love and Holy Spirit confront and acquit you. Your respect for God's timing is a wonderful thing.

When Jesus speaks, listen …

"The thief comes to steal, kill, and destroy, but Jesus (the Gift of God) came to give you life and that more abundantly." (John 10:10)

Depleted souls
A depleted soul brings about negative attributes; such as devouring a mate by requesting that he or she give you the love and emotional security you need. If you are a female, are you chasing him or is he chasing you? Are you allowing the man to be the hunter? Is your relationship in order? Are you injecting your own words into God's equation? Are you a happy person with God and you? Do you look inwardly or outwardly for good feelings? Do you have integrity and a strong character? Do you know how controlling you really are? Can you pay your own bills? Are you looking to your mate for money?

Do you really care about other people? Who do you encourage or minister to? Do you love God and your neighbors as yourself? What is your purpose? Can you listen to others without butting in to talk about yourself? Do those close to you think you are whole or deficient? Can people tell you how they feel without you defending yourself? Are you insecure?

How do you deal with rejection? Can you listen to understand others or do you attack? Do you follow through? Are you dependable? What are you willing to do to stay true to God? Will you sellout -- when a mate appears? Will your affection and passion for God grow and remain true? How deeply are you established in truth? Will you forfeit it all for a mate?

Find out what you don't know about yourself and develop emotional stability in every area. These traits greatly affect your relationship. Childhood pain must also be addressed, respected and resolved; otherwise mistaken feelings and perceptions employ desperate and possessive emotions that get us in trouble. Take the time you need to receive inner healing before embarking upon any relationship or prepare yourself for more pain. If you are not healed, you are not ready to date. Your love and self-concept will be out of balance. Your aim has to be; to own personal wholeness and freedom, not a person.

Emotional healing
Until God completely heals your heart, you will be the invisible offender in your relationships. You won't even recognize that you are extracting factor. You will deplete your poor mate's essence. When you are emotionally incompetent, you are a pain seeker and your own worst enemy. Emotional neglect causes, more emotional rejection. Your malnutrition and emotional neediness will hinder God's best for you. Self-denunciation and guilt will keep repeating itself.

A new mate will not have the ability to heal you, only God can. Putting pressure on someone to do so, overwhelms and dislodges the relationship.

Unless the Lord builds the house, the builders labor in vain. (Psalms 121:1)

If we built the house, then brick by brick and thought by thought,
we are trapped in it with the devil!

Dangerous not to know
God's image and belief system creates equilibrium and resolve for us; but co-dependencies affect millions of people and their relationships. Some of us never take the time to heal emotionally. We decide we're okay, just like we are. Have you ever looked at a comparison guide on foods or vitamins and minerals? The guide shows, which ones have quality ingredients and which ones are of inadequate substance. Being properly equipped for a relationship is the same and requires deep value. Some of us have quality substance within, and some of us have deep inadequacies.

It's okay not to be ready to date, but it's not okay to stay the same. You are responsible to explore your emotional status to know if you are healthy. You need to know where and how you can grow towards wholeness. Your goal is to become complete, well-adjusted and perceptive, before you date. Growth is a good thing. Getting ready for love is being open to self-knowledge and discovery.

When you were a child you were willing to learn new things, to find out what you didn't know. What about now? Are you willing to humble yourself again to be all you can be? You will have to be teachable and not a "know it all," if you're going to remove dysfunctional blockages. An old adage says, "It is too dangerous not to know what you need to know." It is prideful to believe you don't need to grow. Are you afraid to look at yourself to see and know the real truth?

In a perfect world, if God had been our earthly Mom and Dad, we'd have a perfect perception of who we are. Not having that comparison or assessment creates human insufficiencies. These deficiencies cause us to look for what we are missing in other people; instead of looking within God and ourselves. We look for life through people that can't give us the joy we need. These shortages create more lack and doubt. Therefore, it's easy to misunderstand and look for love in the wrong ways and places, but, the one who holds our eternal and internal waters is the one with authentic joy and fullness. He alone has the thrill and vivacity we're looking for! (Otherwise the thrill is gone)!

Qualities
If we are healed, the attributes we like in God are the characteristics we like in others. If we are not healed, we have no concept of goodness and draw people to ourselves that treat us in ungodly manners. We can subconsciously believe we need to be treated poorly. This is why God re-parents us through our reading the Bible, church life, great inner healing books and workshops. Christian counseling can be good too with the right person and supportive friends can

help us overcome dependencies. We all need help; we can't see the back of our own heads; by ourselves. Find out what you don't know and then you will see what you cannot see. The same old mindset cannot see or solve the problems.

Become devoted to a meaningful prayer life; otherwise, you will continue to attract unrewarding and short-lived relationships.

"Make sure of your own soul's salvation. Know for yourself and understand the measure of excellence. It is God Himself whose power within, creates both the desire and the power to execute His gracious will." (Philippians 2:12, 13)

Beware of undiscerning friends that mean well
Onerous and new prophecies continued a few years after Luis and I divorced. The prophecies worked to throw a wrench in my healing process. I asked, "Lord, are the insights and my persistent friend, right or wrong? I don't want to miss you!" I did want to please the Lord, but remember; I never, ever had a direct word from God about reconciliation. I simply tried to accept what others said. (You see, the devil keeps using the same old tricks on us; but within different scenarios).

I'd say to God, "This prophet said, Luis and I are supposed to accomplish great feats for You." Or that one said, "God will bring you and your husband forth in a ministry anointing for marriages!" Lord, another one said, "God wants to work a miracle in your marriage, obey and let Him do it." Someone else said, "It will take a long, long time, but God will use you and your husband together." At times, I was royally confused about God's will. "Hum; Lord, are these prophecies really supposed to come to pass?"

The words were impressive but worrisome, and some of the dreams continued, not to mention a pestering friend. Deb, my stubborn tenacious friend was a big pain in the neck. She urged me to ask Luis, if the Lord had spoken to him about some of the prophecies we received years before. She pressed aggressively, "Dorothy, don't let your pride or the devil prevent you from talking to Luis." The prophet said that Luis needed to be reminded. You must do this. What if God is dealing with him? You have to cooperate with the Lord; how else can He have His way in your lives." Doggedly, she nagged me daily.

While spending the night at Luis' home, Jyndia had experienced a supernatural occurrence. She awoke and saw a vision of me sitting in a chair in his living room. It was so real that she went through his house looking for me. She said, "Dad! Mom is here!" He said, "No Jyndia, your mom is not here!" She felt the vision suggested that I was supposed to be there. (I'm still not sure why she saw me, unless I was watching over my baby's soul through a state of prayer).

I asked, "Lord, what is going on with all of this?" Did God really have a new pre-ordained destiny for Luis and me, after our divorce? The prophecies, dreams and visions strongly suggested something. What if God really wanted me to act, as one of the prophecies indicated? Was I supposed to step out in faith? Did God want to do a new thing, now that Luis had moved to my city? <u>I did want to please the Lord, and did not want to disappoint Him</u>. Finally, I thought I should do something, even without a personal word from God!!!

Notice, all I had was lots of maybes; knowing that God clearly instructs and never tries to baffle us! Think of Moses, when he went in to deliver the children of Israel from Egypt. He was not at all perplexed. He knew exactly what God was saying to him. Perhaps he had learned how well the enemy uses good people and lying situations to pervert truth, even when we are minding our own business.

Not having the discernment needed, I decided to try to reverence the prophecies. I wrote Luis a spiritual letter, putting aside the probability of being persecuted for doing so. I reiterated the past prophecies he knew about and asked if God had spoken to him about our ministry over the years; through dreams, visions or prophecies? I reminded him of a dream he himself had during our marriage. He walked on an extremely narrow path around a mountain. He said the path tapered in, step by step and grew constrictive. He frightfully moved slowly with one foot, in front of the other. (His dream meant that he should walk circumspect and guardedly before the Lord. According to God's will for him, he knew he should not look to the left or right).

The letter was kind, as I carefully explained its purpose. I said, "If God has spoken to you, should we be obedient to do the ministry God ordained for us to do? Should we attempt to please the Lord for His kingdom purposes?" I thought I did a good job explaining the deep importance of the letter, but never felt peaceful doing so. I humbled myself to give him my sacrificial offering; Jyndia gave it to Luis during one of her weekend visits.

Observations
I wanted to get this arduous assignment over with as soon as possible, but never received an answer from Luis. I doubted that he read the letter. As the years passed, I knew I had missed God's voice again and forgot that I had reached out to him, until I talked to Luis about a bad time Jyndia was having. She was going through an angry and depressing time related to her father's departure. I emailed Luis to share her suffering and feelings. She needed to hear him say he was sorry for the pain in her life. I explained that she resented being raised without a father. She needed him to understand her and a cycle of grief and hardship. I talked to him about the power of healing words.

The email angered Luis, but he was not about to take responsibility for Jyndia's feelings. He replied, "Those are your words, not Jyndia's." (As if a twelve-year-old cannot articulate feelings, whew!). "You are blaming me for this, because I didn't take you to Texas with me!" Now ... that is how I understood that Luis did read the letter and what it meant to him. In no way, shape or form had he seen the spiritual significance of my martyrdom letter! My (insubordinate) attempt to be obedient was reduced to ... I wanted to go to Texas with him. My letter was not spiritual to him at all. It had only spoken to his super ego, and I learned a hard lesson again! Looking unto the Lord, I said, "How many times around this mountain!" **When would I learn to follow His voice alone**? (I hope you won't mix things up like I did).

Wisdom is the reward you get for a lifetime of listening, when you'd prefer to talk.
(Doug Larson)

I emphatically say to you! - Learn this lesson and <u>do not act without a personal word from the Lord for yourself!</u> No matter how right all the indicators look, don't do it! Don't give the devil opportunity to trample on your godliness. I so regretted trying to share spiritual bounty with Luis; religiously, but not spiritually being lead of the Lord. He was right to walk on. How could he have revelation of ministry with me, when I was out of place? My actions were not from God; no more than a cat has ability to be a squirrel! Being out of order, I should have read a book like this one, before I wrote it. (Smiles). But you have an opportunity to act precisely, within your relationships and associations. If it's to be, let God do all the leg work. If he said it, He will perform the actions needed. He does not need our help, letters or mishaps!

My sheep know my voice and a stranger they will not follow. (John 10:5)

"Be not unequally yoked together with unbelievers, for what fellowship has righteousness with unrighteousness, and what communion has light with darkness." (2 Corinthians. 6:14)

God inversely uses us
At a seminar, I discussed areas of deception thorough religiosity, prophecies, visions and dreams. The group deeply enjoyed the insight and wisdom. Afterwards, a precious lady said to me, the prophets were right in one way Dorothy. I asked her what she meant. She said, "You and Luis are changing thousands of lives and marriages through your book!" Wow! Her perceptiveness startled me. What a way to look at the prophecy and how God is touching lives through my difficult story.

The Lord does work in abstract and mysterious ways; His wonders to perform! Her revelation meant the world to me, because I knew, we were somehow supposed to bless lives! My soul and spirit celebrated. God had conceptually given me the desire and the call of my heart, His way! He had even used my path to nowhere. God doesn't like to teach us through disasters, but he will use them. I learned, just because the standard bearer's changes, the standard and call does not.

Kingdoms are lost
The devil is cunning. Even through well-meaning people, he projects his lying specters to repeatedly, pervert truth. If we are not committed to God's voice alone, we receive compromising, confusing, and deceptive messages. Although we are still growing, we need keen discernment to knock him off his perch. There are good solid rules that help us learn to do so.

Absorb the stories I have mentioned and look at your own evidences. From this day forward, we must act only with a personal word from the lord? In no way was I supposed to contact Luis or you _____! I acted on the words of others and got slammed doing so! My reasons were very good reasons just like yours are, except they were/are not authentically from God. They were derived and inspired from the enemy tinkering with my soul realm. We could say, well, wanting to save your marriage was a good thing, but disobedience is never a minor thing. Refusing to hear God or not waiting for instruction are very serious matters of insubordination. Read the entire chapter of 1 Samuel 15, and see how seriously God takes the instructions He gives Saul.

For rebellion is as the sin of witchcraft, and stubbornness is as iniquity and idolatry. - Because thou hast rejected the word of the LORD, he hath also rejected thee from being king.

My friend and beloved of God, don't act on anything without a definite word from God, and when you get it, do exactly and immediately what God says. Satan is not a weak strategist. He's not just going to give you a meager temptation. It's going to look grand and salacious. Deception will even look reasonable, but look at the losses invited and suffered from disobedience. God is watching to see if you will trust him enough to obey wholeheartedly, or will your sensual, five-sense realm or human knowledge win the case? Lord, we desire to apply wisdom, during every test of life.

Dejected, Saul lost his Kingship from not following God's instructions! Think about it ... He lost his Kingship! This is how serious disobedience is to God is. Kingdoms (time, energy, life and substance) are lost from noncompliance! Deciding not to follow God's instruction is grave! This is the way we work ourselves into Satan's hands in every area of life. But, when it comes to relationships, we excuse ourselves by looking through a murky glass of self-desire or religious protocol.

We create human laws and idols that appease us; instead of respecting God's voice. But, this is vanity and disobedient, even when we try to make it a holy thing through our own might and strength. It can be a woman who stays with an abusive man to (so call), please God, without his Voice -- Or a man who works four jobs to keep a greedy woman happy. We feel better when we tell ourselves that we are pleasing God. We are befuddled because there is no peace in our decision and lack of trust in His voice. We suffer valuable loses; just like Saul.

And Saul said unto Samuel, I have sinned: for I have transgressed the commandment of the LORD, and thy words: <u>because I feared the people, and obeyed their voice</u>.

Now therefore, I pray thee, pardon my sin and turn again with me; that I may worship the LORD.

And Samuel said unto Saul, I will not return with thee: for thou hast rejected the word of the LORD, and the LORD hath rejected thee from being king over Israel. (1 Samuel 15: 23-26)

Grace
In the "New Testament," we live under grace through the sacrifice of Jesus Christ, not the law. Grace gives us power to live holy and good lives through the righteousness that Jesus provides. We are not obligated to kill a ram or walk on glass to cleanse ourselves. We are made clean through accepting Jesus and the powerful work He did on the cross. Through Jesus' Blood, God is pleased to dwell with us. We live right and work hard with God because we love Him, but we don't go out on some obscure limb of penance or self-punishment to please the Lord. Yes, there are times we are called to suffer for God's Kingdom agenda, but you will know this through a word from the Lord.

It is God Who builds and maintains our lives and marriages. If they are not sanctioned by God, they are going nowhere. Too many of us fight hard to keep the unattainable, including people that just don't belong to us. This is one of the reasons many marriages die in the heat of the day. Through mental and religious ascension, we end up losing again and again.

Lean not on your own understanding, but trust in the Lord with all your heart. In all your ways acknowledge Him and He will direct your paths.

Self-punishment and enabling
It is easy to think your faith is strong enough to maintain a non-covenant or disobedient marriage/relationship; but, it is not! How can you fight to keep together, what God is not fighting for? Without the blessing and faith of God, you only walk in vanity. There is no God-reason to allow a person in your life that is hurting or misusing you. By becoming an enabler, you permit an aggressor to subside and exist in your life.

Have you ever heard the adage, "If you find a fool, bang his head against the wall?" Yes, that's a bad thing, but the devil does it through someone's ignorance daily. Right now, somebody is physically or emotionally "banging" somebody's head against a wall, and someone is allowing it to happen. The enabler and the banger subconsciously think they need each other to accomplish their inner craving for punishment, power or control. The "permitter or allower" is driven by fear of loss, while the aggressor loves to punish, exalt power, fear and control over the permitter.

Too many of us distort God's will for our relationships. We say, God wants us to endure harmful people through good and bad times, through punishing or abusive times, but this is a lack of knowledge and faith. God calls you to walk in peace and does not give anyone the right to abuse you on purpose. If you are allowing this, ask God to change your level of wisdom and stop allowing an illegal relationship to rebuke you. No, God is not punishing you for past sins, which is one of Satan's most famous bondage-keeping lies. Remember, when you repent, Jesus takes the reproach of your sin away. Your Father is a blesser! It is Satan who loves to punish and abuse you. No, you are not supposed to suffer persecution in a man-made situation or dance like a monkey in high heels to please a nut! This grossly disfigures what God expects of you. The enemy is your accuser and belittler; he's always waiting to destroy you. God brings you up and out; but Satan takes you down into his web of lies.

> Remember, the Blood of Jesus is enough to cover confessed sins. Never try to work out your own salvation, without surrender to Jesus Christ. Jesus is the Savior; you are not. In no way should you be involved in penance, abuse or crawling through glass!

Programmed for failure or success
Your ability to love correctly is based on God's love for you. Your worthiness is based on Jesus' worthiness, not yours. Our self-value or self-hatred creates disharmony with God. He cannot work through disagreement, self-hate, unworthiness or a failure complex. They are not part of His nature or prominence. God's will is only life, right feelings and joy for you. He is a good God, and, if you want His blessing, you must come into agreement with the King's attributes.

A spirit of unworthiness sets us up to fail. We assign collapsing missions to ourselves, desiring to fix or increase our pain. You may not be in touch with your internal desire for pain because of unworthiness, but desire shows up; especially in relationships and life selections. Personal growth means that you stop avoiding inner healing. Facing your fears is easier than you think with support and prayer. Unworthiness cannot just be stuffed away, <u>it has to be felt, grieved, released and replaced</u>. Our Father is there to help you every step of the way. You must resist impulses to belittle yourself and meditate on truth.

Persecution should not be induced by you or your mate. Knowing this requires wakefulness, vigilance and wisdom. Opening your eyes means spending quality time with God through His Word. The power of His Word changes everything; your feelings, beliefs, examples and outcomes. Thousands of scriptures are available to tell you who you really are. You must learn them.

Every unworthiness issue can be overcome. Renewing your mind and heart takes work, but it's worth it to stop wrong beliefs and self-abuse. You have a responsibility to move higher into His realms of understanding, consciousness, vision and inner healing. Act! Your life is in your hands. You have a choice: You can live in "World A," the beautiful Garden of Eden that God-ordained for you or "World B," the one that is full of abuse and Satan's lies. Get healed and walk in truth! It's time for you to live, laugh and enjoy the best! You deserve it in Christ Jesus!

When you act, God enforces the defeat of the enemy!

Religious protocol
Do you remember the point of my dream about the angel in the basement? I was using the one and only scripture I knew, defectively. The scripture was "God hates divorce." I put myself under the law, trying to do the right thing, not knowing the totality of what God really said. I thought I was pleasing the Lord, even though I was steeped in bondage to a disrespectful, negligent man. I thought I was supposed to suffer and stay there no matter what, even though the Word of God said differently.

My little bit of knowledge was dangerous, but when I studied "Malachi 2: 10-16," and the many other scriptures, I could see the big picture. I learned that God hates a lot of things, and especially wives crying at the Altar of God, because of their husband's adultery. In my book, **"Marriages that Endure the Fire,"** I thoroughly discuss the depth and complexities of marriage and divorce.

I can change him or her
We can believe it's up to us to change to appease an "out of place or immature, silly mate." The "allower" can believe that God wants them to suffer to some degree (little or much) for a variety of known or unknown reasons. But, even in covenant marriages, God has ordained that a separation can happen if someone was abusing another. Settle it! God never endorses penance or self-punishment. That school of thought is demonically inspired. Repentance and obedience is God's way to self-actualization and contentment. Nothing but His Blood, cleanses sin. If we honestly ask Him to forgive us for our sins and turn from them, in exchange, we are given His grace, help, provision, realization and love.

The propensity and perplexity of self-induced suffering comes into play, when you choose not to grow in the Word and when you don't know who you are. You, the "permitter," will have no idea that your perception of life and love is wrong. Twisted beliefs can become an acceptable narrative from childhood, through the works of Satan. His lies add fuel to preconceived negative feelings. If you are one that is susceptible to cycles of pain and dysfunction, remember this is never okay with life and God, but you are only helping Satan rejoice! With

God, you can stop these cycles of defeat and change the negative dialog of the devilish critic in your mind.

In truth, you don't want to reinforce or reproduce negative behavior and experiences that create death. If you are addicted to pain and failure, you need help! And that's a good thing. When you see the realities of the sunshine within you; you'll be glad you acted! Along with this book; churches, books and counseling are available to help you change these demonic beliefs. <u>God has made you good and worthy and you deserve good!</u> No matter how much you love this person or what they are providing; ultimately compromise will only get you what you cannot keep. No more pain or rejection for you.

Self-flagellation belongs to the devil; give it back to him right now. It is not yours. Let God fight for you and show you a wonderful dimension of life that you have not seen. A dimension of light, real love and worthiness!

Remember, godly persecution has nothing to do with allowing a mate to devalue or disrespect you. The difference is this; when God allows you to suffer for righteousness sake; He is not talking about a disobedient relationship. He is speaking of suffering for a <u>righteous cause</u>; one that advances His Kingdom.

Trust issues
Every disobedient issue is a lack of trust in God issue. I did hear God say, "Luis is a womanizer," but I also didn't believe or trust His Voice enough to walk away. I chose to believe in an erroneous hope, instead of a precise trust in God. Developing trust in God is crucial, but only happens from spending time with Him. More than anything, <u>God wants to be trusted by you</u>, just like you want to be trusted and loved by your children or someone you care about. Let us trust in our Father's love and plan for our lives. God delights in blessing His children. He knows you better than you know you. When a potential mate looks your way and says, "Hello," your reliance on God will make the difference. You will be listening and trusting His voice, won't you?

God will gladly open your ears to the sounds of Heaven. His reverberations are the difference between life and death. Lord, "We exalt your voice over our senses and mental opinions. We keep Your Words before our eyes day and night. We submit and understand that faith comes from hearing Your Word and solid Bible teaching. Amen!"

Subconscious purification
My depleted, non-affirming childhood, concealed truth from me; I added to my pain by marrying Justin and Luis. Marriage caused me to lose more actuality and trust in God. I thought I was doing everything possible in my young world to be a good Christian, still I saw few positive results from my prayers. Since God would not answer, I decided I must be a bad person and bad people need to be punished.

After Justin, it was easier to take my life in my own hands and attracted more familiar pain with Luis. I felt that I deserved it, because no matter how hard I tried, I wasn't blessed. And of course, the devil was happy to bring me as much unworthiness and pain as I wanted. Intuitively, <u>I knew Luis would take from me. Unquestionably, I allowed it</u>.

But, how could I be objective, with preceding wounds and emotional baggage? Not loving myself and feeling like I must be a bad person, permitted me to be a displaced person. That is the reason I forfeited my Raytheon business, my honor and value. I fought to keep my business and marriage, but they were built on the shaky ground of codependency and an unworthy relationship. It wasn't that God refused to bless me; the problem was I was not in the right position to receive my blessings. I had to learn to be in the right place, at the right time.

I stress the importance of inner healing because I believe bad relationships come to us when somewhere deep within we want and need a <u>sentence of chastisement and pain.</u> We give away our goodness believing we are bad, unworthy or insufficient, because childhood feelings must be irradiated. We need more godly truth, vision and value to prevent attracting the instability of a Luis kind of deadly relationship. A love that is small, selfish and full of pain!

The gift of you
Thousands of God's children do the same thing repeatedly. We are not equipped to stop the vicious cycle of failure, unworthiness and pain. We often become a shield against our own success. We forfeit responsibility by refusing to grow; and negate knowing who we really are; through knowing God. God has ordained seasons for us to know, enjoy and love ourselves, in Him. Those seasons must be lived out, from beginning to end.

God wants you to experience and appreciate the joys of you, as a gift from him. He waits for order and growth to occur. He delays relationships, until the capacity of our substance is full and overflowing. Many are not married or seldom acquire good relationships, because they have not appreciated the gift of themselves. Loving and honoring you; allows a precious and priceless mate to come your way.

> *There is no fear in love, but perfect loved drives (expels) fear or punishment. Fear had to do with punishment. The one who fears is not fully experienced in (God's) perfected love. (1 John 4:18)*

Let God define you
Be proud of who you are and dance with your own destiny. Put the color of Jesus back in your cheeks; grow and change! Enjoy God's maximized definition of you. All by yourself, you are a significant wonder! God made you that way. Why would abundance of life ask anyone for a piece of bread, for significance, or for a definition? You and God are the only ones allowed to share in your

explanation of beauty! No more introspection is needed - Just look at Jesus, not at the haters or insignificant. Look until you see yourself as worthy, blessed and honored. When you see Jesus shining brightly within; you are ready to see a mate worthy of your essence, if you want one.

"I will praise you for I am fearfully and wonderfully made. Marvelous are your works and my soul knows right well." (Psalms 139:14)

My resurrection
Through it all, I acquired something beautiful that I never want to lose. In the fires of transformation and renovation; I gained a godly truth and inner strength that wrought clarity, purpose and wisdom. I will always cherish the experience of God's all-prevailing, sturdy and lovely presence. He did walk with me, all the way through that insufferable, unbearable, ungodly wheat field. Through it all, God changed my past concept of dependency on a relationship, to seeing His eternal beauty. I learned the best pleasure in life comes from Jesus.

Luis, or the terrestrial winds of Satan, did not destroy me; neither did his lies or persecution, and all the haters he used. I found that God does make all things new again! To be found in Him, is the consummation of joyful and marvelous living. His presence is better than silver, gold, love and "shoe shoppin" all day long! "I'd rather spend one day in the Courts of our Lord than a thousand elsewhere." Taste and see that the Lord is great!

How spectacular to discover Jesus, instead of striving for meaningless rewards and the hardships of an illegal relationship, I appreciate the more important matters of spiritual destiny and inheritance. Now, I'm looking at the right thing. Thank God that I have found and love the real Dorothy. She is exciting, funny and a powerful Kingdom changer for God!

Remember who you are
In the movie "The Little Princess," the young girl said something quite valuable: "All girls are princesses! Even if they live in tiny old attics, even if they dress in rags, even if they aren't pretty or smart, or young; they're still princesses - all of us are! Didn't your father ever tell you that? Didn't he?"

God saw all that he had made, and it was very good. (Genesis 1:31)

The "Man of Honor," movie is about Carl Brashear. The Navy Diver knew who he was and would not be defeated! He completed the twelve steps required, because he knew he could. He became the first amputee in US Navy to return to full active duty. He was a man of faith, power and honor and God backed him up!

I am far from oppression, and fear does not come near me

Declare these scriptures:

- *I am complete in Him Who is the Head of all principality and power*
- *I am alive with Christ*
- *I am free from the law of sin and death.*
- *I am born of God, and the evil one does not touch me.*
- *I am holy and without blame before Him in love*
- *I have the mind of Christ*
- *I have the peace of God that passes all understanding*
- *I have the Greater One living in me*
- *Greater is He Who is in me, than he who is in the world*
- *I have received the gift of righteousness and reign as a king in life by Jesus Christ*
- *I have received the spirit of wisdom and revelation in the knowledge of Jesus, the eyes of my understanding being enlightened*
- *I have received the power of the Holy Spirit to lay hands on the sick and see them recover, to cast out demons, to speak with new tongues.*
- *I have power over all the power of the enemy, and nothing shall by any means harm me.*
- *I have put off the old man and have put on the new man, which is renewed in the knowledge after the image of Him Who created me*
- *I have given and it is given to me; good measure, pressed down, shaken together, and running over, men give into my bosom*
- *I have no lack for my God supplies all my need according to His riches in glory by Christ Jesus*
- *I can quench all the fiery darts of the wicked one with my shield of faith.*
- *I can do all things through Christ Jesus*
- *I show forth the praises of God Who has called me out of darkness into His marvelous light*
- *I am God's child for I am born again of the incorruptible seed of the Word of God, which lives and abides forever*
- *I am God's workmanship, created in Christ unto good works*
- *I am a new creature in Christ*
- *I am a spirit being, alive to God*
- *I am a believer and the light of the Gospel shines in my mind*
- *I am a doer of the Word and blessed in my actions*
- *I am a joint-heir with Christ*
- *I am more than a conqueror through Him Who loves me*
- *I am an overcomer by the blood of the Lamb and the Word of my testimony*
- *I am a partaker of His divine nature*
- *I am an ambassador for Christ*
- *I am part of a chosen generation, a royal priesthood, a holy nation, a purchased people*
- *I am the righteousness of God in Jesus Christ*
- *I am the temple of the Holy Spirit; I am not my own*

- *I am the head and not the tail; I am above only and not beneath*
- *I am the light of the world.*
- *I am His elect, full of mercy, kindness, humility, and long suffering*
- *I am forgiven from all my sins and washed in the Blood*
- *I am delivered from the power of darkness and translated into God's kingdom*
- *I am redeemed from the curse of sin, sickness, and poverty*
- *I am firmly rooted, built up, established in my faith and overflowing with gratitude*
- *I am called of God to be the voice of His praise*
- *I am healed by the stripes of Jesus*
- *I am raised up with Christ and seated in heavenly places*
- *I am greatly loved by God*
- *I am strengthened with all might according to His glorious power*
- *I am submitted to God, and the devil flees from me because I resist him in the Name of Jesus*
- *I press on toward the goal to win the prize to which God in Christ Jesus is calling me upward*

For God has not given me a spirit of fear;
but a mind of power, love, and soundness!

THE PATH OF THE RIGHTEOUS GROWS BRIGHTER Chapter 15

The path or the righteous is like the light of dawn. Its brightness grows to the fullness of day. The way of wickedness (disobedience) is as dark as night. They cannot tell the obstacles they stumble over.
(Proverbs 4:18)

"And if the Lord is pleased with us, He will bring us safely into that land and give it to us. It is a rich land flowing with milk and honey. He will give it to us."
(Numbers 14:8)

Loving God

We can choose to ride the waves and winds on the high seas, they will always blow in our lives, or we can plan to fail and sink when presentations come. We can grow, love and change for the better or die in the heat of day. We can learn to be sensitive to the voice of God or harden our hearts towards truth. We can ask God for love to love Him back, or never experience the joys of obedience and agreement.

I learned that my average love for God, was still love, but I wanted it to be more -- a great and deeper love. Even if you feel your love is small, it is still love, and little trust is still the beginning of trust, but it will grow if you want it to. Years ago, I felt discouraged because my wounds kept me from loving God the way I wanted to. I didn't believe Jesus really loved me or could adequately satisfy my soul. When I began to develop in the Word, my ability to love God grew enormously! His constancy lifted me up and off the ground; into the breakthrough and possibility realm.

Being off center and out of position affects our ability to love well, but deep passion and intimacy with God is always possible. We are empty and vulnerable without His intimacy. Living outside of God's love and kindness cannot be allowed!

"God, we pray that you will manifest a burning fire for Jesus within us. Help us know the secrets of life in you. Make Jesus the object of our success."

Let God get them

It's true, we need nothing more, but God. When we get God, <u>He gets our mate</u>. Blessed is he who has total confidence in God. Blessed is he who is poor in spirit. This means we understand we are deficient, apart from God. We are not a self-sufficient people, but we are built to be God-sufficient, inter-dependent people. Without His presence, we are insignificant human beings. But passion for the Lord makes us "Supernatural Giants!" Then, we can practice being in His presence and wait upon Him like we would a lover. We can be zealous for His presence and can fight a good fight to be with Him. Just like we would energize ourselves to be with a favorite person; we can get closer still to our God … and kiss His face!

Don't limit God

If you were short of money and prayed for God to make a small payment for you and He did; you'd wonder why you didn't ask Him to pay all 30 payments instead. So why do we limit God in our lives when He wants to prosper us, mind, body, soul, health, family and financially? But, He knows that our life of prosperity begins with loving and wanting Him close; then we are full of faith and a powerful blessing to Him, ourselves and others.

How do we limit God?
- By not spending time in His Presence.
- By thinking He cannot give us what He promised. Luke 17:14-16
- By refusing to believe by faith, unless we see it with our own eyes.
- By misrepresentation - thinking He can't do more for us.
- By not fully obeying His commands. John 4:24-29
- By not obeying immediately.

The transformation

When Jesus said to Peter, "Let down your nets;" Peter only let down one. That is why; it was a net breaking load of fish in a small boat. But, what if all the nets and boats were made available? -- If Peter had not limited Jesus, he would have had many more fish to sell, eat and give. The right perception of God will have everything to do with how well you thrive in life. Keep your insight, intuition and realization focused on His true reality and capability. <u>Everything will depend on how well you know and believe God!</u>

Nothing is wrong with you or your righteous situation that Jesus can't fix. Just take the limits off God and let the "Son" shine through. You will see and know, all you need to see and know.

When you can say, "I trust you Lord" the transformation will begin. Leaning on God's unlimited ability makes life tranquil and sweet!

Loving you, through Jesus

Today, I thank God for every agonizing progressive step that brought me back to peace, purpose, love and freedom. I fancy being centered and on the saddle, and back on track in purpose. I needed to get home to His light and glory again, back to my destiny. I am here, on earth to be a supernatural believer and minister of God. (We are all evangelist).

I was not supposed to be somewhere else, daunted and changed into an ordinary person, fighting to fit into a life, lesser than my objective and purpose. I was way over there and out of place in someone else's world. I was missing the mark by trying to find Jesus and purpose in a man. When we try to love ourselves through a relationship, we pursue the worst kind of falsehood and misery possible.

Not to worry, God will help you maximize. Our alignment opens us up to the goodness of God. His kingdom principles will help you recover your time and focus. He is full of timeless possibilities and wonder. His name is possibility! After all, we are forever young and blessed in Jesus. In him consequences are fixed and time losses are redeemed. He loves to give us more than we would ask or think. When we get back into place the part that remains after the shaking, is the only part serviceable to God. He doesn't want the sinful part, but the residue that is left – the gold, is the vital part to God. He will gladly use the ashes -- the best part.

Remember, there are no losses in God. Don't look back or go back. If you choose to live outside of God, you will create and plant more failure and regret. Receive His rewards of life and joy instead. You have God-given power to positively change everything you touch, if God has given it to you!

Remember, your life and trials are more about cleaning the clutter out, so relax and say, "Work a-way God!"

Judge all prophecy
All prophecy should be a confirmation of what God has personally said to you. If a prophet says a storm is brewing, you will already know it in your spirit. You won't be surprised when you see the rain clouds forming. Too many individuals prophesy out of their soul realm, in pride or for money, rather than giving us the truth. Some try to make you feel better about your situation, even if it is not God. Before you apply the words of a prophet to any degree, make sure you have your own personal Word from the Lord.

A prophet's words should never be the only confirming directive you follow. Their words should line up with what God has spoken to you. Let the Holy Spirit be the witness that judges their words as true or false. If they are right, you should feel a quickening of joy, peace and righteousness. Their words should fortify your faith, if they are true. Never follow the words of any man/woman without a confirmation from God first!

We need a "Thus says the Lord," not the unction of a man. A prophecy should corroborate with what God has said to you. Prophecy is a confirmation that you are hearing God correctly.

Clarity
It is true; that a real prophet can see certain aspects of your life, but a directive should never be a new revelation for you. If it is God, you will receive a resounding yes, in your spirit and soul. You will know that you know because the information is not new! Listen carefully to the Lord, before you accept any word as truth. If the Holy Spirit does not move you, don't receive the prophecy. Dismiss it! I wish I had!! You can see how much trouble prophecies got me into.

After a prophecy or word of knowledge, If God says the same, consider it or put it in your future. If it is right, put it on the back burner and let God increase your vision for it. He is the one who will bring it to pass; even then, let God breathe on it. Put it totally in His hands, (Write no letters like I did). Again, let God bring it to pass. Take your hands, mind and pen off it. Never force your mind and heart to accept something beyond God's voice and your faith. When God is speaking, He will unfold each detail and authenticate your path and timing. You will know what He is saying, as much as you know that you are short or tall. (God speaks to you from within).

After my adventures in wisdom, I learned to discern more carefully. Some of the words people gave me aggressively went in one ear and out the other. They were so wrong, a thousand times over. One man, after giving me an elaborate word, said the prophecy would only work if I gave a large offering. When I didn't, he made a negative comment about me in church. I do agree that a prophet can speak some things into existence, but something is wrong when you don't have a witness to give what the prophet is asking for.

Another lady told me I would get a miracle for my daughter if I joined her church. She was wrong; Jyndia gets miracles all the time and we didn't have to join her church to get one. God told me to leave and to never go back and I obeyed. A few years later, her church was televised in a heartbreaking legal ordeal. The city was shaken when abuses were discovered. God knew all of this would happen when He told me not to go back. I was learning to obey and was so glad I listened!

Another person told me to move to a certain city or I would lose Jyndia in court to Luis. Jyndia is a young adult now and has always been with me. Luis and I have never had a court battle concerning Jyndia. Thank God, I never moved for those reasons. I'm glad I followed the unction of my Holy Spirit for myself. That night, I hung the phone up, rebuked her words and went back to sleep.

When I was going through the separation with Luis, a so-called lady prophet said, "Dorothy, we rebuke the devil off Luis. I decree in the Name of Jesus that he will come back home!" A month later, when she ran into Lacy (Luis' girlfriend), the lady told a friend that Luis and Lacy really had it going on. Lynn, (the so-called prophet), said they were the perfect couple. She was impressed that he was so good to her. Then she said, "Well, Dorothy should not have put him out." In a month's time Lynn had changed her words to appease us both.

A visionary prophecy about a move, work or ministry will resonate in your spirit if they are true. Although, I have received confirming prophecies and words of wisdom, they are few and far between. No matter how good the person's intentions are; you must watch and pray, because the devil is.

Words create
Sometimes through words spoken, a prophecy can conjure up things that are not from God, like rubbing two illegitimate sticks together to make an unholy fire. Example: The pastor who said, "Your husband is looking for you," which helped to create the words that drummed up Robert. Remember that Satan will always try to answer words of prophecy, desires and prayers. Be extremely suspect; that a personal prophecy might not be from God, but from a man's heart. Follow God's voice only! Do not enter uncertain, ambiguous prophecies, or you will end up shipwrecked. Following man-made prophecies create confusion and always mess you up. I certainly had a bout with them. I can tell you one thing, now my discernment is keen and I listen well.

We are all prophetic or intuitive at times. When I hear God say something about a person, place or thing; it always comes to pass. One more thing, beware of those who say their church is the only place you can be blessed. God is an enormous God and He is in many places. He is never confined to just one movement.

> *"Let us grow up in Jesus who is the head of our lives.*
> *He is the Christ." (Ephesians 4:15)*

We agree
Let's agree that we won't have to learn any future lessons the hard way. We won't give the enemy opportunity to trample on our godliness. We accept, listen to and concur with God's will alone. We give Him what he wants! We agree that even the smallest "yes" or "no" is gigantically significant. We fully understand that we will incur losses and pain if we act half-heartedly. We accept only Father's confirmations. No matter how intelligent, genuine or necessary the person seems, we won't take the bait in Jesus Name! We won't end up riding alone in funeral Limousines, grieving over mates lying on road sides, grappling with demons.

> *God stilled the roaring of the seas, the roaring of their waves*
> *and the turmoil of the nations? (Psalm 65:7)*

Choosing to be unmarried
I especially enjoy not having to use the energy to focus on the needs of a husband right now. I don't want to worry about, if the wrong mate is playing around on me or if we are simply making each other miserable. In this season, an invalid husband would change the dynamics of everything, but the right one would fly right beside me! The wrong one would take my time and substance. I wouldn't be able to explore God, me, or to write wonderful books. Being with the wrong person marginalizes our lives. But, this is a great time for me to do special projects with my children, grandchildren, family, business, church, associates, participants or staff. What could be better?

Now, I love exploring the room called singleness. Jesus is here and with Him all is wonderful! I'm determined to pursue God in this season and choose not to date. I don't have to. There is nothing I need from anyone. If there is someone for me, Jesus will work out the details. He is capable of arranging the meeting and marriage. He will get our man or women for you men. As an unmarried woman, I discovered something that I didn't know; I found that I love spending lots of time with God, studying, writing, winning souls and just being me. My life is supernatural, transcendent, rich and rewarding!

My precious Holy Spirit helps me see what I need to see and hear what I need to hear. With wisdom from my past, the self-denial trials are much easier. I don't want or need the pain that comes with them. I am careful not to return wayward phone calls or to dwell on flattery. I give it to God. I don't have to lose myself in another person's goals, motives or purpose anymore. Thank God, I am not who I used to be and He is moving me upward and forward.

This is so funny: A man, continually asked me out that was not to my liking, and I was proud to say, "I bless you as a friend, but please find a lady who likes your pony tail and your jokes, because I don't!" For me, getting the wrong man is like getting wet wood drenched in manure. My life is exciting and fun without adding just any old somebody to God and me. It's interesting to look back at presentations and how I've been blessed to discern them correctly. Yes, abundant living is far better than a raggedy, destined-to-fail, relationship!

For the Spirit, which God has given us is not a spirit of cowardice, but one of power and of love and of sound judgment. (2 Timothy 1:7)

Marriage is not for everyone
If marriage was mandatory, God would be responsible to provide spiritual mates for all his children. From birth, some will never give marriage a serious thought. They simply don't desire it; others never get asked or accept an invitation. Some decide not to marry for Kingdom reasons. Many are not ready to live the married life, knowing that marriage requires great sacrifice. Knowing your personal will must die within its walls. You and your mate must come into a oneness, which is not an easy task.

Do you think Adam in the Garden of Eden felt a lack of fulfillment? He lived in the presence of God, so Adam was content and complete with God and himself. There is no indication that Adam had any perception of aloneness, not at all. <u>He knew he was not alone</u>. Marriage was God's idea for partnership and procreation, not Adam's. God is the one who said, "It is better for man not to be physically alone." God could have allowed Adam to be content eternally, just as he was; except He wanted mankind to birth a race of holy children to propagate the earth. You see, God wanted an extended family to love for Himself.

When God said, it's not good for man to be alone, He didn't mean that marriage was the only way to have deep fulfillment, but that people need people. We need family and spiritual friends that love us; and we need to love them. A spiritual family is imperative. Marriage will never satisfy us completely. We are ultimately here to know Jesus, to love and be loved! God is love and a wonderful spiritual husband, for men and women! God has a purpose for each of us and loves to see His children entrenched in rich, rewarding, celebratory relationships, but not necessarily marriage.

> "Some are made for the Kingdom of Heaven. He that is able to receive this let him receive it." (Matthew 19:10-12)

Marriage won't solve your problems

Are you complete in God, as Adam was? Or is your perception of life, one of aloneness? If your answer is aloneness, you have not embraced truth. You are not aware of the oneness you already have in Jesus. Until you have soared as an unmarried person and have seen the joys and provisions that God offers, you are very much alone and no relationship will provide fulfillment for you. Your time has not come and a relationship will only create problems for you. It will only be as great as your contentment in God can be.

I have seen too many people pretending that they are fulfilled, but if you are "faking security," sooner or later your co-dependencies will show up like a pronounced pain in the neck. Neediness will cause you to join in; with the statistics of those who put too much weight and misery on their partner. When the relationship goes under, you'll end up requiring that someone else help you feel good about yourself, again.

Good singleness (unmarriedness) means you have learned to be happy in the Lord, because you will always be singularly defined in some ways. Even within marriage, you should be interdependent; not soul dependent. You cannot put all your weight on a mate, but you are designed to walk hand in hand, blessing each other. Marriage doesn't change the fact that you will have different opinions and goals. It won't magically create or cure anything. Marriage is hard work; at times, it will feel like it's just dishes in the sink and shelves of laundry to wash. Marriage, in no way blends you and your partner into a magnificent creamy milkshake, except in spiritual realms of life!

> "One thing I ask of the Lord, this only do I seek. I desire to dwell in the house of the Lord all the days of my life, to gaze on the beauty of the Lord and to seek You in Your Temple." (Psalm 27:4)

Mesmerizing glances

Eye contact is not at all trouble-free. Think of how a rudder controls a mighty ship in the ocean. In the same way, small acts critically control the big picture of our lives. Compliance, disobedience or yielding, becomes the rudder that turns your life around and allows your ship to go astray. When we look where we shouldn't look, the authority of that glance, can steal us away. Eye connections have a penetrating power with the ability to deceive and defeat us. We must respect the dominance of what we look at, knowing that sight arouses feelings and feelings arouse actions. It all begins with a look. (Study the book of Proverbs and see what the architect's observations are).

"I make a covenant with my eyes that I will not look (or think) upon a woman (or man). For what portion of God is there in this? What inheritance will I have from Almighty God on High?" (Job 31:1-2)

Keep yourself innocent at every age. What we look at can be perilous. Looking away from what God is not looking at, prevents the bang of the trapdoor. Like ancient oriental fighters who perceived without sight, we must trust ourselves to see with spiritual eyes. With proper use, we are not taken away captive. Subduing or conquering the power of a glance will pulverize sin immediately. God knows that glimpse can inspires us to go on beyond the gate door; therefore, he told us what to do to stop the devil in his tracks. Our job is to shut down the flesh by looking upon Jesus. He is our magnificent alternative.

"Wisdom calls aloud in the street. She raises her voice in the public squares. She calls out at the street corners. She delivers her message at the city gates. "Simple people, how much longer will you cling to your simple ways? How much longer will rebels, rebel in mocking and fools continue to hate knowledge? Pay attention to my warning. I pour out my heart and tell you what I must say, but you have refused me when I have beckoned for you. You have not taken notice. Since you have ignored all my advice and rejected all my warnings, for my part I shall laugh at your distress.

I shall jeer when terror befalls you like a storm and when your distress arrives like a whirlwind. When ordeals and anguish bear down on you, you will call, but I will not answer. Although you will look eagerly for me, you will not find me. You have hated knowledge. You have not chosen the fear, respect and honor of Yahweh. You have not taken notice of my advice.

You have spurned all my warnings and you will have to eat the fruit of your own way of life, and choke on your own scheming - for the errors of the simple lead to their own death. The complacency of fools, work their own ruin but whoever listens to me may live secure. You will have a good and quiet life. You will not fear mischief or trouble." (Proverbs, Chapter 1)

You are looking for Jesus and yourself
No human being can touch you like Jesus can. God knows that your deepest feeling and level of significance comes through entering His Empire of Glory and Love. During the happiest times of my marriage, neither, Justin or Luis could touch the part of me that Jesus alone could. Many nights after the family slept, I

found my Bible and a special place to eagerly behold and embrace my Jesus. I had to discover more about Him. Being alone with my Savior was the highlight of my day. Marriage was nowhere close to His depth of intimacy and heavenly presence.

Flesh can never gratify the real you. Your authentic happiness will always come through spending time with Jesus. <u>He is the Spirit of Life and Truth</u>. Exhilaration is right under your nose and in your own backyard. Never put anyone in the dire position of having to gratify the needs of your soul. It is not their responsibility. <u>Your covenant mate is or is not, an extension and connection with, the happiness you already have from and with God.</u> They will not fix you or change your life assignment, but will walk hand in hand with you to take ground for Jesus, or not. <u>They can't tell you who you are, only God can</u>. He is the only one who will ever completely satisfy your soul. He has the goods, joy and the light you need. With great pleasure, you will wonder why you ever looked outwardly for love!

"Be strong and of good courage, do not fear nor be afraid of them, for the Lord your God, He is the One who goes with you. He will not leave you, nor forsake you." (Deuteronomy 31:6)

"His Faithfulness is your shield and rampart. (Psalm 91:4)

<u>*Remember you are weighed down with glorious purpose*</u>*!*

When you know God says "Yes"
If God ordained marriage for you, you will surely hear Him say, "Yes this is the one ... Walk this way!" When you hear the "yes" word from God, you are on your way to connecting with your potential mate. Congratulations! Your lifetime, legitimate, spiritual mate has arrived. This is it! God's fullness of times has arrived for you. Your God-ordained covenant marriage will be an essential part of your future and purpose. What joy! Your husband or wife is on the scene. You will know without a shadow of a doubt that you have a PERSONAL WORD FROM GOD FOR YOURSELF. This will be a signal that your life is in order.

Hilariously receive your new marching orders! Go forth and enjoy your wonderful life-partner; with God being a witness to your holy relationship and marriage. If God gave him/her to you, you can keep your relationship forever. There will be no putting him or her off the bus. This partnership will endure every test of fire. "Congratulations," indeed are in order. Keep your dating period holy and don't open your gift before it is time. You want purity this time, and the true blessings of God. Remember the value of your body and your obedience to God. Keep your hands on the Bible and off each other, until you say, "I do!" If you know God has spoken positively, ask Him for your wedding date, proceed with caution and rejoice together!

"Do not awaken love until it is time. (Song of Solomon 8:4)

"Do not throw away your confidence; it will be richly rewarded. Persevere so that when you have done the will of God, you will receive what he has promised you." (Hebrews 10:35-36)

God expects husbands to have faith for their marriages
Marriage is a precious God ordained institution that harmonizes the dictates of natural and divine inspiration. It was designed by God as part of an integral ingredient. Marriage fulfills God's plan, even from the Garden of Eden. Marriage is an essential part of society. It heightens and perfects the pure, fresh and joyful life of the Garden. Marriage is a scene of beauty and the temple of God. It has been preserved to this present hour as a human and social blessing. It soothes and sustains, amidst depressing and difficult circumstances in a fallen world.

Covenant marriages are supposed to stand the test of time and fire. When God puts His children together, He gives them faith and power to work on their relationships; until death separates them, one from another. How can individuals give up on their marriage when there is faith available to change every circumstance? There are couples, who have done every manner of evil to each other, but they stayed together and God renewed their love!

We know that non-covenant relationships become disconnected with no support from obedience. They are built on human desire and will always war against God's will to alter righteous paths. Have you noticed how easily people give up on marriages today? They don't want to suffer or resist anything. They think their marriage should be like a TV comedy. However, in Malachi we see that God expects His children to have faith for their marriages; and faith to develop and endure difficult times. God puts the responsibility of covenant marriages at the feet of men. <u>The keepers of family life</u>.

Malachi 2: 10-16, says, "Have we not all one Father? Did not one God create us? Why do we profane the covenant of our fathers by breaking faith with one another? Judah has broken faith. A detestable thing has been committed in Israel and in Jerusalem: Judah has desecrated the sanctuary the LORD loves, by marrying the daughters of a foreign god. As for the man who does this, whoever he may be, may the LORD cut him off from the tents of Jacob--<u>even though he brings offerings to the LORD Almighty.</u>

Another thing you do: You flood the LORD's altar with tears. You weep and wail because he no longer pays attention to your offerings or accepts them with pleasure from your hands. You ask, "Why?" It is because the LORD is acting as the witness between you and the wife of your youth, because you have broken faith with her, though she is your partner, the wife of your marriage covenant. Has not [the LORD] made them one? In flesh and spirit, they are His, and why one; because He was seeking godly offspring. So, guard yourself in your spirit, and <u>do not break faith with the wife of your youth.</u> "I hate divorce," says the

LORD God of Israel, "and I hate a man's covering himself with violence as well as with his garment," says the LORD Almighty. So, guard yourself in your spirit, and <u>do not break faith</u>."

Jesus covers covenant marriages with a distinct holiness and grandeur. He sees them as a blessed estate. They are clothed with honor and magnificence. He ratifies these contracts and guards His obligations, with His Own Precious Blood -- But foreign wives (or *disobedient relationships*) are not from God. In Malachi, the disobedient husbands, gathered to themselves wives of their flesh; wives not ratified by God. Often men and women try to make unsanctified relationships holy and esteemed, but they cannot be.

God still expects men (His children) to have faith to nurture their marriage and to build them up. His grace releases strength to do so. God considers struggling and hardship as a part of our lives. We are built to overcome adversities, even if it takes a lifetime. We are made as hard and strong soldiers, not as mama's little biscuit eaters. With faith in God, we can help our covenant marriages stand. If your marriage is ordained by God, you will know that it is and you cannot let what God has blessed, default. What God has joined together, has the power to stay together. Let no one put it under!

"God, we pray power and holiness down from heaven upon pastors and their churches. We speak that the treacherous plague of divorce and illegal marriages is stopped by your holy men, right now, in the Mighty Name of Jesus!"

Covenant marriages
The good news is that your covenant marriage will stand forever. It will stand against bolts of lightning hurled, and against every fiery dart. I knew a man who divorced His wife and told her to return to her first (covenant) husband. As dreadful as that sounds, he was hearing from God correctly. He said the Lord dealt with him about marrying her and told him, she is not your wife, but she needed to wait for reconciliation to occur with her covenant husband. She and her first husband are working on reconciliation. We shall see what the Lord does. Nevertheless, If God has not joined you together; don't try to bond what He has not connected. Recognizing the power of truth will keep you free from meaningless acts of defeat. Putting together two unstable compounds will only explode in the fire is idiotic.

<u>*"What God has joined together let no man put it under!"*</u> *(Matthew 19:6)*

The right one
Holy relationships attract the favor and breathe of God. They honor the Lord and have the concrete necessary to hold together. God-ordained relationships produce life-long, durable marriages and happy, emotionally healthy children.

Alignment and Investigation …

A quiz about your mate
- We have a great and respectful friendship
- _____ loves the Lord passionately
- I know _____ is sincere and has a deep relationship with Jesus
- We communicate well. I have no intuition that there are secrets or dishonesty
- Are you fighting about significant issues/values
- _____ deeply honors and respects me
- There is mutual submission in goals
- _____ trust you, or do you see paranoia, fear, and jealousy
- _____ has older, stable friendships
- We can shut down the works of the flesh
- _____ is teachable
- I feel deep joy, peace and righteousness with _____
- What are _____ struggles
- Are all _____ life and business issues resolved
- If divorced, does _____ take responsibility or blame a former mate
- What was his/her part? How do you really feel about that
- _____ feels _____ about my children
- Will this be a problem for _____
- Is _____ legally divorced or has _____ disobediently left a covenant mate
- Is _____ absolutely sure that he/she is not supposed to reconcile with a former mate
- Is _____ forgiving or do they hold grudges
- Is _____ healed completely?
- Does _____ have weird or unusual ways
- Am I using _____ to gain life, money, prestige or approval
- I have a feeling _____ will hurt me in the future
- _____ can hold their own emotionally, or _____ is always zapping me for love, vision and energy
- _____ tends to set him/herself up for self-punishment/disappointment
- What are _____ most prevailing subconscious feelings
- _____ has a sense of destiny and inheritance without me
- _____ is listening to God's spiritual voice
- Does _____ absolutely know that God really said yes about me
- _____ has goals and plans to remain pure before God
- We are yielding to and endorsing a sexual relationship before marriage and know the consequences thereof

Just to be sure of your yes. Try their Spirit by the Spirit of God to see if they are from God or from another spiritual source. Read Christian marriage books together and get into lots of quizzing. Get to know each other from the inside, out. Remember God is never in a hurry.

About you

- I am completely committed to Jesus Christ
- I have deep passion for the Lord
- I have heard God speak for myself
- I absolutely know that _____ is the right person for me
- I am feeling peace, joy and righteousness
- I feel no uneasiness, fear or uncertainty
- I have no other warnings in visions, dreams or unction's
- Our situation is righteous
- I feel the pleasure and presence of God on this relationship
- This is a holy-spiritual connection
- We have holiness, stability and self-control
- I know I have God's approval (And, I don't know is still a NO)!
- I have educated myself about _____
- I have deep feelings of love and worthiness for myself
- I am honest about my feelings and communicate what God says
- What are my struggles
- Are all my past issues resolved
- Am I showing _____ my real self
- What am I hiding
- If divorced, I take responsibility for my part, or do I blame my former mate
- What was your part
- I feel _____ about his/her children
- Will these feelings be a problem later
- I am legally divorced or have obediently left a former mate
- I am sure my former marriage was not my covenant mate from God
- Are _____ and I suppose to reconcile
- I truly have forgiven _____ and I hold no grudges
- I am healed completely
- Is _____ using me as a mini-god to gain prestige, money or approval
- I hold my own emotionally
- My life is happy or desperate
- I tend to set myself up for self-punishment
- I falsely take responsibility
- These are my most prevailing, subconscious feelings
- I have a sense of destiny and inheritance without _____
- I am listening to my spirit man
- Did God really say "yes?"
- I have goals to remain pure before God or I will yield to lust.
- I am yielding to and endorsing a sexual relationship before marriage, and understand I will have to pay the devil back for it.
- I am getting **who I am.** How is _____ answering the need within you
- Is it time to reevaluate the relationship
- Is it time to cut your losses and realign with God

If you are not sure: I have deeply considered the consequences of making my own decision outside of God's peace?
- Will we end up hating each other later? ... You know all things.
- You understand the consequences of your insubordination will possibly last a lifetime
- If they are not God's choice, are they worth the penalties and unspeakable outcomes that come with the package
- If they are not from God, is losing valuable time, substance and focus alright with you
- If they are not from God, are you prepared for your walk through a personal abyss
- You understand that sin/disobedience is pleasurable only for a season and then the payback comes
- Are you ignoring the warning signs in your heart
- You listen again and always get an absolute "yes" from God
- You will not empower the enemy of my soul
- You understand God only wants to bless and protect us

God is never in a hurry, so allow more time for greater wisdom to work. Let every emotion settle down. God will give you strength you didn't know you had. Discuss each component with your mate. Look beneath your desire and listen to what the Holy Spirit is saying.

"Do not awaken love, until it is time. (Song of Solomon 8:4)

GOD'S LOVE CONQUERS ALL　　　　　　　　　　　　Chapter 16

"Your steadfast love is higher than the heavens and Your faithfulness reaches to the clouds. (Psalm 108:4)

"For as the heavens are high above the earth, so great is His steadfast love toward those who fear and honor Him." (Psalm 103:11)

Listen to the loving voice of Jesus that declares, "You are pleasing in My sight. The next time your inner critic points a merciless finger of judgment at your past, rebuke it. Tell the voice of the enemy, "I am beautiful and wanted. I am a winner! You, devil are the failure!" Remember … You are deeply loved and have ravished God's heart! You are honored, important and needed!" Stop, feel and believe the affirming words of your Beloved. Accept that you are worthy and beautiful in His sight. Do not protest or accept the enemy's words any longer. Believe God's Words. Hear; feel and know the scriptures. God's words really are true.

Receiving, glorious life from God is a gift that one must breathe and accept. Your righteousness is from God and triumphs over human characteristics and past failures. He lives within you, so past misconceptions can be changed into wisdom and strength. You are successful, because God loves you; therefore, you must love you too. Loving you is in harmony with God's will. A balancing virtue occurs when you take your rightful position, by allowing His love and acceptance to permeate your being daily. You must release pain, anger and disappointment again and again, until they are gone. You have asked for forgiveness and God has forgiven you; you must accept his forgiveness and redemption now, because Jesus can make you "New" again." Wow! Just imagine you can walk in "newness of life" today! What a God we serve!

Believing in the love that God has for you will generate peace and security. Let His adoration and goodness help you love yourself and others more. Through His sacrifice, receive a consciousness of success, instead of self-condemnation and failure. The sacredness of Jesus helps you detach from pain and the five-sense realm. A sphere that keeps you looking at what you don't have, instead of what you do have. A realm that contradicts that you are the abundance and life of Jesus, your greatest reality! God's awesome spiritual world supersedes more than you can imagine. Let Jesus show Himself strong to you again today.

"Let the beloved of the Lord rest secure in Him, for He shields us all day long. The one the lord loves rests between His shoulders. (Deuteronomy 33:13)

Accept and give forgiveness
Realizing that Jesus took your place on the cross to absorb all your sins, you must forgive those that hurt you too. We must do what Jesus did on the cross. He said, Lord forgive them for they don't know what they are doing.

> *If you don't forgive people, your Father will not forgive your wrongdoing. (Matthew 6:15) "Faith, hope and love abide, but the greatest of these is love." (1 Corinthians 13:13)*

Fear removes love
Buried in our minds is the world we knew as children. Childlike hopes can hold deep levels of kindness and good feelings. What are some of the thoughts you can recall? Thoughts that made you *feel* loved or unloved? What message is playing on your subconscious recorder? We can feel afraid, because there is a spirit of fear in the earth. We can be afraid that God will not help us; that we are in a wrong or right relationship. We can be afraid of dying young, of getting too old; sometimes we can be more afraid of life than of death. We can be afraid that we should be better people and too often we are disgusted with ourselves.

We are afraid that we will fail and can hold ourselves back from success. We can despise ourselves and fall short of understanding. We learn the hard way that we cannot control others. We can live in denial by endorsing disorderly acts and harmful behavior. The child within can be afraid that people won't like or approve of us. We can believe we are not important. We can worry that we are missing a chromosome (something within us that is significant). Too often we refuse to focus on the perfect love of Jesus. We forget that He has cast out all fear and dread. We can take on personality disorders like those of the narcissist, codependent or worse.

Fear is the absence of love or is love-less-ness. The spirit of fear endeavors to press in on us from within and without. Fear gives constant false testimony of the absence of God's love. Expressing fear, we recognize it as: anger, abuse, disease, pain, greed, addictions, selfishness, obsessions, corruption or pride. Jealousy, un-forgiveness, control, sedition, violence or war can also steal our peace. In the perfect Kingdom of God's love, there is no place for fear, because fear generates punishment and hate. Fear keeps us from coming into the fullness and perfection of life in Jesus!

Real love never goes away
Do you, or can you remember feeling spiritually connected to God's softness and innocence as a child? As Christians, we can experience a world of true reality and wonder-filled vision! True love is a symbol of a world beyond our physical eyes; a world of completion, love and light. When submersed in Jesus, we can see it with our spirits. Yes, it is there and God loves to bring us back into His original state of peace and confidence. When we fail to understand God's

wonder and purity, His true love is muddied and surrounded by mental mist. We then lean on our own understanding, instead of truth.

If you are going through a terrible trial, continue to fall into God's love, innocence and beauty; and know that with worship you will see God turn it all around, before you know it. He's going to make everything beautiful just in time. Nothing is impossible with God. If you have come through an awful time of distraction, allow that time to be over right now. The experience is safely put away in the hands of God. He will continue to make every part of your past; gold, joy and bread. He already has. He owns the pain, shame and disappointment. It is not yours anymore. Thank God, He is using the ashes from your fiery experience to bless and promote you. If you let Him, God will work to prevent future transgression and self-betrayal from misleading you again. He is bringing you through and out of every damaging place; so, hold your torch high! You are more than doing just fine.

You are victorious and blessed! Focusing on God's magnificent love and splendor is your necessary peace. Your only task is to lean on the prosperity of His truth. Enjoy His softness and innocence again, or for the first time. Have you looked at yourself in the Lord lately? If you belong to Jesus; aren't you a beautiful sight! You were born to make a difference. How can you fail with God on your side? You cannot.

Mighty soldier and benefactor of the King, you are taking ground and making up for lost time. You will fight boldly and win for the Sake of the Cause of Christ. God has already given you territories you have not thought about; because you must possess what belongs to you. God is love, God is faithful, and God will keep you.

Today is the time to increase the gift of you.
The King needs you to make a difference in the world.

"There is no fear in love, but perfect love (God) drives out fear. (1 John 4:18)

A natural tendency to love
We are created with a natural tendency to want love. According to God, love makes you a victorious world overcomer. If you fail to depend on the love that God has for you, you don't know the real Jesus. Love is God and God is perfect love. Love sent His only begotten Son into the world because He loved you. Love consists of this: God loved us and sent Jesus to take our sins away. He sacrificed His Son to help us know and participate in His love. Love came down to us, to give itself away! Clearly, God loved us enough to give. Our capacity to love is possible only because God loved us. We can love Him back, only because He first loved us. He gives us love to love Him back with. What an awesome God we serve!

Love comes to perfection through God's work within us. -- His love helps you face the Day of Judgment, (trouble) fearlessly. If Jesus lives in you, you have become love in the world through Him. God's love remains in you and comes to perfection through love and trust. Love is proof that Jesus lives within you. God has given you a share of His spirit and love through the Blood that Jesus shed. You can put total faith in the love of God. His love is perfected through you.

"Beloved, let us love one another, for love is from God and whoever loves has been born of God and knows God. Anyone who does not love; does not know God, because God is love." (1 John 4:7-8)

Love is power; not weakness
Although we were born in a fallen and sinful world, God programed you perfectly with His very own DNA. Trust His work in you. His ways and commandments are not burdensome. When you are quiet, you can sense the miraculous Jesus within. You can feel His Image coalesce and merge with your essence and being. You understand, it is no longer you that lives, but Jesus Christ who lives within you. His blueprint transcends your thinking and imagination. When we live our lives linked to our Savior, we flourish and do exploits.

<u>We become a part of His fascination and connection. God's world is a much richer world of love that you are a part of -- You are not of another source.</u> We are not anonymous to God or disconnected from Him. He is not a drowsy detached grandfather, but God knows you and see's you. He delights in empowering your soul and life. His incredible love gives you the presence and power you long for.

"We love Him because He first loved us." (1 John 4:19)

Through Jesus, I have attained reconciliation with God. No sin is against me (Romans 5:13)

I have been crucified with Christ. It is no longer I who lives, but Christ who lives in me. And the life I now live in the flesh, I live by faith in the Son of God; who loved me and gave himself for me. (Galatians 2:20)

Fascination
When we follow the real Jesus, we are stirred with fascination. Nothing is more important to a newborn baby, as we hold them close to our hearts; than feelings of warmth and love. The touch of loving hands and strong arms on baby's tiny body makes pleasant the warmth of feeding and touching. A child's definition of love begins in the womb. Though he or she cannot speak, they can feel warmth and love or rejection. The early formative months are important to our ability to receive love and warmth. Although God loves as the Mighty Breasted One, the influence of criticism, rejection and disowning has stolen the wonder and expectation we had in our hearts as children. God's love affirms us, but Satan's

deceptions work to destroy our purest understanding of adoration and confirmation.

God's love and affection is much more advanced than the love we have known from earthly parents. It is pure, protective and holy. We are accepted in our beloved, without conditions. He loves us with faithful, fierce and passionate love - Love that fights and wins! It is essential that you accept and know your Father's perfect love this way. Knowing that God loves you eternally; will be the reason you succeed or fail. The power of love accomplishes every task and conquers every devil.

If we fail to walk in the deep enthrallment of love and acceptance, we give away pieces of our true selves to enemies. We lose the knowledge of God's mesmerizing and captivating love. At heart, we long for His grand adventure of love, trying to find it in relationships, drugs, food or work. Ask your father to give revelations of His personal love for you. When it is all said and done, it's all about love. Be fascinated by Jesus and let his love drive out fear and trepidation. His perfect love will nullify the sound of every enemy. When God controls your destiny – Who can defeat you? What else really matters?

> *The LORD your God is in your midst, a mighty one who will save you; he will rejoice over you with gladness; he will quiet you with his love; he will exult over you with loud singing. (Zephaniah 3:17)*

> *I love those who love me, and those who seek me diligently find me. (Proverbs 8:17)*

Jesus' contribution

God is not angry with you. He desires to prosper you, by giving you the desire of His heart. Because of His Holiness, Abba (Father's) anger and judgment were applied to His Only Son, Jesus on the cross. Jesus came to take the power of sin and judgment away from us. What a wonderful sacrifice! If we accept His gift of love, mercy and compassion, Abba can fully dwell with and within us. Jesus' death and resurrection prevents sin's assertion against us. Jesus' last prayer was indeed invasive and penetrating. It was about His love for us. His passion and travail deeply touch my heart. He desired that we see Him in His glory and become one with each other within His love. Precisely, He wanted His life, triumph and magnificence to live in us.

Why wouldn't anyone want to be separated from His love and wonder? Jesus is our wonderful Savior. Is there anything more than love like this?

> *"I have given them the glory that you have given me. Lord that they may know you sent Me and have loved them even as You have loved Me. Father; I want those you have given me to be with me where I am. I want them to see my glory - the glory you have given Me. You have loved me before the*

creation of the world. Righteous Father, the world does not know You as I know you, but they know that You have sent me. I have made You known to them and will continue to make You known. Lord let the love You have for Me, be in them, and let Me personally be in them."
Let them be one as you and I are one (John 17:22-26)

(Declare) "The law of Life in Christ Jesus has set me free from the law of sin and death. Sin will never have dominion over me. For the law of the <u>Spirit of life in Christ Jesus has made me free</u> from the law of sin and death." (Romans 6:18 and 8:2)

There are no limits

We can imagine the unimaginable with Jesus, because of His love. His vibrant world of love and preordained destiny eliminates reluctance and limits that are self-imposed. His love unveils ability to be one and unique in God. His romanticism gives us irreplaceable comfort and positive expectation. We can release self-reclusiveness, doubts and walls that have hindered love – We can know and feel His protection. We can understand that He is our source of supply. There is no scarcity in Jesus. When God awakens our love, our dreams come true. We can rest assured that we are accepted, valued and approved of; in Christ Jesus.

Knowing we are endorsed by God makes us power houses who defy deficiency, sickness or disease. We become stout hearted, fearless and unafraid to fail.

But God shows his love for us in that while we were still sinners, Christ died for us. (Romans 5:8)

Loneliness

Being confident in His love, we can see His glory above insurmountable odds. We know that His love will never allow us to be alone. He is always there, you can never be alone! His love fills your life and home with joyful expectation. When nothing else can heal you, His love lifts you up! There is no aloneness in Christ. We are accompanied by all of Heaven; Father, Jesus, Holy Ghost, and a host of angels and praying saints. We can trust in His full attendance and faithfulness. God is love, truth and honor. <u>His love is His power</u>. Our dynamic Father is our true source of identity. Through Him you can see yourself inhabited in a magnitude of ability; enough to scale tall walls and to walk on mighty waters. Your Father is unconditional Love.

Jehovah God's love is our shield, fortune and confidence. "Neither death or life, nor angels or rulers, nor things present or things to come, nor powers, nor heights or depths, nor anything else in all creation will be able to separate us from the love of God in Christ Jesus our Lord." (Romans 8:37-39)

"For God so loved the world that he gave his only Begotten Son, that whoever believes in him should not perish, but have eternal life. (John 3:16)

"God showed how much He loved us by sending His Only Son into this wicked world. He came to bring to us eternal life through His death." (1 John 4:9)

But God, being rich in mercy, because of the great love with which he loved us, even when we were dead in our trespasses, made us alive together with Christ; by grace you have been saved. (Ephesians 2:4-5)

Synchronization
Heaven is open to those who trust and relinquish themselves to Father's love. Heaven is a place of enrapture, ecstasy and delight. God is completely whole, balanced, synchronized and in harmony with Himself and Heaven. There can be no disharmony or imbalance in Him. As Christians, we live inside God's righteousness, pleasure and wholeness. There is only agreement within God. There can be no conflict or indifference to cause separation or disconnection. Therefore, we must also live in harmony; resisting all disobedience, resentment, conflict, devaluing and unworthiness.

"Being one" in "God's oneness," is daily aligning with truth, light and accord. We make parallel and equivalent His peace, value, oneness and exuberance. Depression, lack, fear, doubt, disorder or low self-esteem has no part within the ambiance of God; neither can they be *in* us. If we exist inside of God's perfection, we are joy-filled individuals having great ability to live worthy lives.

Speak this out loud: "I am worthy *in* Christ Jesus. Therefore I walk in harmony with God's exuberant life!"

If you have lived beneath your essence and potential, you will have to work to become the "godly supernatural you." The "You" that is found in Christ Jesus. This new life has to be received and honored daily. The reality of true Christianity illustrates confidence, prosperity, faith, power and a sound mind. You are not of another; you were created in Christ Jesus! You are precisely the very life of Jesus Christ. The true you, are designed to be His very character. Like Jesus, you must forcefully resist all that is against the truth and Word of God.

"Anyone joined to the Lord is one spirit." (1 Corinthians 6:17)

"Be perfect (mature, whole, complete, finished) as your Father in Heaven is perfect." (Matthew 5:48)

"Greater love has no man than this; that a man gives up His life for His friends!" (John 15:3)

"There is one body and one spirit. You were called to one hope." (Ephesians 4)

The great price paid to love you
Because God is holy, in biblical times, an animal blood-offering was required and necessary to wash away sin. A young bullock was the highest suitable offering. Blood offerings were an intricate part of Old Testament worship, because a sacrifice was needed to remove the sin of man. The matter of sin was and still is a serious one; but the Blood that Jesus shed for you took care of sin. <u>Jesus finished the job of abolishing confessed sin</u>, and it cost Him everything to do it! We must never take His awesome sacrifice lightly. He is God, but still allowed His Only Son to be killed by the very men He created. The world was not worthy of Him, but He gave His all to deliver you; so that He could be your Father. You are not your own, but you have been bought with a price. You are the image and life of Jesus Christ and have been set free to serve and know Him.

"For the worshipers would have been cleansed once for all, and would no longer have felt guilty for their sins, but those sacrifices are an annual reminder of sins. Because it is impossible for the blood of bulls and goats to take away sins, but we have been made holy through the sacrifice of the body of Jesus Christ once and for all. By one sacrifice He has made perfect forever those who are being made holy." (Hebrews 10:3-10, 14)

The precious Blood of Jesus
When, we accept the Blood sacrifice of Jesus, we declare, He is the Son of the living God. Then, we have the power to cast down demonic-thought systems, based in fear and judgment. The same power that raised Jesus Christ from the dead is available to live, as "power" inside you. Through Him, the wisdom of the ages and the might of many armies belong to you. He loves to fight for you, His precious one. What a wonderful Savior we have! God's has made His perfect love available to share with you, His creation.

When you know God, you will allow the light of His love, oneness and harmony to flow through you. You are *one spirit* within His love and dynamic light. In Christ, you reign in true identity and rule by His authority. He creates the vision you need and the words to speak scriptures that declare positive results. God will give you what you give yourself. He will OVERRULE what you overrule and disallow what you disallow. The Blood of Jesus accomplished everything, already for you!

"God, for whom and through everything was made, chose to bring many children into glory. And it was only right that he should make Jesus, through his suffering, a perfect leader, fit to bring them into their salvation."
(Hebrew 2:10)

In this the love of God was made manifest among us. God sent his only Son into the world so we might live through him. In this is love, not that we have loved

God but that he loved us and sent his Son to be the propitiation (appeasement and replacement) for our sins. Beloved, if God so loved us, we also ought to love one another. (1 John 4:9-11)

Loving God back
We have a wonderful privilege to build an intimate relationship with life and love itself. What an honor it is to enter the presence of the King, which dissolves every care, concern or need. The deep longings of our heart are rewarded through loving God, the dimensional changer. His wonderful mystery of love lifts us up; and gives us the ability to love him back. Here our perception of life and existence are sweet. Think about it, you can exuberantly love and enjoy the "King of Kings" for yourself. Lose yourself; forget about you and just enjoy the lover of your soul. Your time in His presence will bestow transcendent, surpassing love that touches the heart of God! There is nothing under the sun to be gained, but Jesus. Know Him by loving Him for yourself. Apprehend your Most Beloved!

My determined purpose is to know Him in the power of His resurrection and in the fellowship of His suffering, (resisting of evil and submission to obey God). Conforming to His death, I follow Jesus that I may apprehend Him." (Philippians 3:10-12)

Everything to gain
The "Day of Lord" will come as a thief in the night. Heaven and earth will pass away with a great noise and the elements will melt with fervent heat. The earth and works of your hands will burn and dissolve too. Only what you do for Christ will last. If you have never asked Your Creator, the Famous Jesus Christ to come into your heart; do it right now. This is the right time to partake of His goodness, love and glory. There is no saving power and love like Jesus' love. He died to prove it to you.

Jesus shed His Precious Blood; on an old rugged cross to wash away your sins, mistakes, unhappiness, sickness and disobedience. He dissolved your sins through His work on the cross. Jesus was the only way possible for us to absolutely experience relationship with God. He wants to be your Savior. Now is the time to be of eternal conversation. Your confession of faith and repentance will bring Jesus to you and His wondrous plan of love and power.

"For it is God's light that makes everything visible. "Wake up, O sleeper, rise from the dead and Christ will shine on you." (Ephesians 5:13)

"God exercises His workings within us; He is able to do infinitely more than all our highest prayers or thoughts. To God be the glory in the Church and in Christ Jesus to all generations, world without end." (Ephesians 3:20)

For all have sinned and fall short of the glory of God

God wants all men saved from sin, self, pain, hell, and death; and to come into the knowledge of the truth." (1 Timothy 2:4)

Heaven
If you haven't received the best gift that will ever come your way; receive Jesus now. Receive His Wonderful Presence and Essence and give your life to Him. He will willingly forgive and restore you; just ask. Your Heavenly Father longs for your companionship. He wants you …You are His precious creation. What else shall we live and die for?

You have a real heaven to gain, and a real hell to reject. Hell is a place of unfathomable darkness, separation and death. There is no hope or light there. Screaming and torment engulfs those who chose not to honor and awesomely respect the love that Jesus offered. Nevertheless, today you can receive the Redeemer and His great life! Throughout the rest of your eternity, you can consume the treasurable advocacy of Jesus Christ and His Precious Blood. Use your faith to receive Him now!

If we confess our sins, he is faithful and just to forgive us our sins and to cleanse us from all unrighteousness

"For everyone who calls on the name of the Lord will be saved."

And there is salvation in no one else but Jesus; for there is no other Name under heaven given among men by which we must be saved."

*"If we say we have no sin, we deceive ourselves and the truth is not in us."
(1 John 1:8)*

"Brothers and sisters, I want you to know, through Jesus the forgiveness of sin is proclaimed to you." (Acts 13:38)

*"God so loved the world that He gave His Only Begotten Son that whoever believes in Him will not perish. You will have everlasting Life. (John 3:16)
Jesus said to him, "I am the way, and the truth, and the life. No one comes to the Father except through me.*

Ask God in faith
You must come to Him while He is calling you. According to the Word, the Holy Spirit does not always tarry with mankind.

No one can come to me unless the Father who sent me draws him, and I will raise him up on the last day. (John 6:44)

Say these words in faith and sincerity

"Lord, I want you. Forgive me for my sins and transgressions. I am sorry I have hurt you. I believe in You Jesus ... I receive You in my heart and life right now. Lord, make Yourself real to me! Help me love you, as you love me. Lord, I receive your life by faith right now. Amen."

Responding
You may or may not have felt anything, but by faith, you have received Jesus, the Lord of Glory. Amen! Welcome to the Kingdom! Celebration and Congratulations are in order! You are now part of the family of Jesus Christ - The best family on earth! Praise the Lord! Proudly tell someone about your grand acknowledgment and event! Be proud you have received Jesus in your life. Begin to read the New Testament and meet the authentic Jesus for yourself. Your eyes have never been opened like this before.

Find sincere people in a genuine Bible believing, spirit filled church. Develop friendships with those who will guide and teach you the ways of the Savior. His love and protection will become a solid wall of virtue for you. Don't walk alone, but build strong spiritual relationships. Be renewed one day at a time. Jesus is always with you. He will help you prepare for blessings, trials, tribulations and end-time events.

Jesus really is coming back. Read a good commentary on Revelations and see how the power of your Jesus' Light and Brightness alone, consumes our enemy. The devil never had a chance! Your God is loving, awesome, brightness and powerful! *(Email me. I want to know that you received my Savior)!*

"The Lord shall consume with the spirit of His mouth and shall destroy with the brightness of His coming." (2 Thessalonians 3:8)

"You are part of the light. You are not in darkness that this Day should overtake you as a thief; therefore, let us watch." (1 Thessalonians 5: 1-6)

Surrender
The moment you surrender, you receive God's leadership. He will tenderly move you into your glorious purpose that begins with worshipping your God for his goodness and sacrifice. Your surrender brings power, not weakness into existence. Surrender is not passive. Retreating into God's love will get you what your intellect or will power could never attain. The confidence of Jesus flowing through you is providing temperance, balance and blessings. Stay connected to eliminate fear and apprehension. Getting yourself out of the way will give you much more than you know.

You are setting aside the ordinary and typical to enjoy God's awesome vision and supernatural power. Enjoy Jesus! He is a safe life connection! You will now supersede the frictional, to enjoy a gentler, but more powerful mode of progression.

"And know the love that surpasses knowledge that you may be filled to the measure with all of the fullness of God." (Ephesians 3:19)

For I know the plans I have for you, declares the LORD, plans for welfare and not for evil -- to give you a future and a hope. (Jeremiah 29:11)

Don't reject His sacrifice

If you separate from God, you separate from love

"If we deliberately keep on sinning after we have received the knowledge of the truth, no sacrifice for sins is left. There is only a fearful expectation of judgment and of raging fire that consumes the enemies of God. Anyone who rejected the Law of Moses died without mercy on the testimony of two or three witnesses.

How much more severely do you think a man deserves punishment after trampling the Son of God under foot - who has treated as an unholy thing, the Blood of the covenant that sanctified him - who has insulted the Spirit of grace? For we know him who said, "It is mine to avenge; I will repay," and again, "The Lord will judge his people." It is a dreadful misery to fall into the hands of the living God." (Hebrews 10:26-31)

"All sin is rebellion against God." (Psalm 51:4)

"He who rebels against His authority is rebelling against what God has instituted. Those who do so bring judgment on themselves. There is no terror for those who do right, but for those who do wrong. Do what is right and He will commend you. He is God's servant to do you good, but if you do wrong be afraid; Jesus does not bear the sword for nothing. He is God's servant, an agent of wrath to bring punishment on the wrongdoer." (Romans 13:2-4)

Live remarkably

Belonging to Christ, can you comprehend the vastness of who you are in Jesus? Becoming one with God solves every past, present and future struggle. The Kingdom of God is a marvelous, expanding and revolutionary habitation. It moves with action, might, and power like an airplane ejecting itself from the earth. We too are supernatural and magnificent Spirits in the Lord, single or married.

Belonging to Christ, we are God's re-presenters and ambassadors in the earth. The sufferings and resisting of this present world will fade when the glory of Jesus is seen! Therefore, we can live remarkable, worthy and righteous lives. Otherwise, how can we keep up with God?

"God, how do you do what you do; so well?

You do turn ashes into beauty and joy!"

Belonging to Christ
He is greater than the sea and more than enough for you. Jesus is the question and the answer? He is the voice at the beginning, middle and at the end. We have a true anchor for our soul in Jesus. We are continually amazed to see how the Kingdom of God comes with power, love and security. Be conscious of your true redeeming glorious-purpose. You are the very life of Jesus Christ and part of His celebrated revolution! Belonging to Christ, Your world is a mirror of another world - a world that consists of God, triumph, life and eternity.

"That He might present to Himself a glorious church not having spot or wrinkle or any such thing. As God's Church, we are holy and without blemish. We, who trust in Christ, first should be to the praise of His glory." (Ephesians 6:27)

"Do you not know that God's people will sit in judgment upon the world and angels? We are of those that belong to Life." (1 Corinthians 6:2-6)

"Surely there is a reward for the righteous. Surely, He is God and judges in the earth." (Psalms 58:11)

Life affirming choices
The seasons are moving faster than ever before. The ages as we know them are ending. Each day we see more of the Apocalypse unfolding. It speaks; telling us to make eternal life affirming choices. A time is coming when people, places or things will not matter to you. Nothing will matter, but the light and love of Jesus Christ. Your personal relationship with the Lord of Glory will be your most important, "one thing" that day. What you've done for Jesus will be your most valuable asset and accomplishment. Your relationship with God will be the only life-empowering factor that will make a difference.

He is your ultimate reason for living today, tomorrow, or in a million years. Are you ready to hear your master say, "Well done, my good and faithful servant?"

Righteousness and inheritance are credited to me, through His Precious Blood. I believe in God who raised Jesus from the dead. God raised Jesus to life for my acquittal. He was slain for my sins. (Romans 4:24)

Eternity
We know the times and seasons are winding down. The world is in trouble and is passing away. Eternity must be considered for those around us too. No one knows the day or hour that Jesus will return or when our days will end. There are thousands of beings on their way to heaven or hell. Precious souls are enjoying heaven's glories or burning and tortured in a very real hell, under our feet, at this very moment. People are in hell, because they choose not to receive God's love, grace or truth. They didn't want Him to be part of their lives; although He so badly desired to be their Savior. Jesus wants no one to be

separate from His love or protection. He sends no one to hell or pushes Himself on no one; but people choose not to accept Him.

Time is crucial. There is an earthy end for each of us; therefore, it matters that you speak to as many people as possible in your realm of influence. Help others see and accept the beauty of Jesus. Share the goodness of the Lord with them by faith. Ask God to give you a heart to share with those in your world. Share your testimony and help strangers, friends and family accept Jesus' love and forgiveness. Be uncompromising in helping them prepare for eternity present and future. Our job is to advance the Kingdom of God in every way. The Lord is depending on us to have oil in our lamps and to win souls with Him. Night is coming when no one can work.

"But of that day and hour no one knows, not even the angels of heaven, but My Father only. As in the days of Noah, the coming of the Son of Man also comes. For as in the days before the flood, they were eating, drinking and marrying, until the day that Noah entered the ark. He did not know until the flood came and took them all away; so, will the coming of the Son of Man be. Watch! You do not know what hour your Lord is coming." (Matthew 24:36-42)

"Noah, divinely warned moved by faith with godly fear and prepared an ark for the saving of his household. He became an heir of God's righteousness." (Hebrews 11:7)

God will judge the earth
But the day of the Lord will come as unexpectedly as a thief. Then the heavens will pass away with a terrible noise, and the very elements themselves will disappear in fire, and the earth and everything on it will be found to deserve judgment. Since all these things are to be destroyed in this way, what sort of people ought you to be in holy conduct and godliness (2 Peter 3:10)

Encounter
There is an indescribable dimension of heaven for you right here on earth. You can move and dwell in this unique and exceptional place of light with God, at all times. True life is exploring the wonder filled, glorious paths of God to come, as well. He gives us hints of Heaven and how enamored saints feel when they take their first steps there. They cannot fathom how brilliantly bright and extraordinary Heaven is! There is no comprehension or comparison of this exuberant, luminous realm, called the God demesne! In the future, we will commemorate the Magnificent Life of Jesus Christ, and drink the marriage wine of Heaven face to face! Yes, God has prepared a wonderful marriage supper for us. It will be the best Dinner Party we ever attended. In the days to come; we can look forward to this grand celebration, and we'll have crowns from our obedience to throw at His feet. We won't miss this date for any reason. No day has ever been like this one will be! We will see Jesus, our Father and Holy Ghost face to face! How amazing! How indescribable!

"Now to the king immortal, invisible, the only Wise God be honor and glory for ever and ever. Amen." (1 Timothy 1:17)

Your walk
Your walk will be an exceptional one. You can and will hit the mark this time. You are a mighty and disciplined warrior, who is an obedient lover of God! You are committed to trusting your Lord. You are devoted to His cause. Let Him be your truest continual desire of heart; and keep your relationship intimate enough with Jesus? Let your fruitfulness with God be more fulfilling than any goal, career or unwarranted man or woman. God's astounding plan for you, is what you desire, not a self-contrived, unnecessary and miserable struggle. What else shall we live or die for, but Jesus? What is more valuable than a deep personal relationship with the King of the world?

"Since you have been raised up to be with Christ, you must look for the things that are above where Christ is sitting at God's right hand. Let your thoughts be on things above, not on the things in the earth. You have died to self and now you are hidden with Christ, in God. When Christ is revealed, if He is your life, you will also be revealed with Him in His glory." (Colossians 3:1)

"Then He said to them all, 'If anyone wants to come with Me, he must deny himself - take up his cross daily and follow Me.'" (Luke 9:23)

"It was fitting for Him, for Whom all things were made and by Whom all things were made to bring many sons (daughters) to glory; to make the Captain of our Salvation perfect through suffering (and resisting unrighteousness)." (Hebrew 2:10)

Prayer
Lord, I appreciate You and every awesome day that you give me life and richness. No matter what it looks like or feels like, I will trust in You. Thank You God that You cause me to take truthful paths, prepared ahead of time for me. I know that You will perform what you have said. Your Life and Light absorb and nullify my self-existence. My life is Yours. I die to all self-sufficiency to find myself in You Lord. I belong in your presence, gazing upon your beauty. I am in You and live abundantly in Your oneness! I walk in Your Kingdom love, covenant, principles and fullness. I commit to experiencing You by faith.

Lord, thank You for going ahead of me to make crooked places straight. Thank you that I am living the good life You prearranged and made ready for me to live! I am fully persuaded of your goodness. Your rich plans are unfolding for me and I love them. I am always blessed and secure in You. I appreciate Your excellence and trust in your leadership and illuminating love for me. You continue to teach me how to live the superior life. I trust in Your times and seasons. I give You my emotional pain, trouble and feelings. In exchange, I receive Your gifts of truth, encouragement, support and life. I feel wonderful when I am beholding You!

Thank You that I have no life of my own, but I am fully connected and hidden in You! Your Spirit Life is better and far above the fivefold, sense realm. I love to do Your will! I am bonded with You. I have no cares or needs. You satisfy my soul and take tremendous care of me. Thank You that Your Presence and grace are sufficient for me. I lose my life is the fullness of Your eternal significance. I won't be moved by what others say or think; good or bad. I belong to You and You belong to me, my love.

I am safe, inside Your love. I submit to Your order and control. I am veiled under Your wings, where the Fowler cannot come. Thank You for fighting for me, lover of my soul. I dare to be as glorious and dynamic as you made me. I won't be afraid of my strengths. Your perfect love for me has cast out all fear and causes me to win. You know me and I accept Your best for me. I lean into Your wisdom, provision and desire. I love You and give you my love.

My heart is ready to pray; Lord, I give You What You want. Thank you for saving my soul and making me a conqueror over darkness. Thank you that I am special and famous in your eyes and that changes everything. Thank You for fascinating me! You alone have the Words of life. I trust you with my future and for the mate you have for me. I trust you for a strong and righteous marriage. My foundation is built on you, my Rock and Truth. Thank You Father, Jesus and Holy Ghost! Amen."

"Those whom God loves, He has called according to His purposes. God turns everything to our good and decided beforehand to call, predestine and justify us. Those whom God justified, He has brought into glory.

God has called many sons to glory." (Romans 8:28-30)

*"Neither will terror make me afraid.
Neither will your hand be heavy upon me." (Job 33:7)*

God speaks softly
The wisdom of listening at the gates should be employed in every area of life. Listen ... Hear and obey, and you will know the answer. In the days to come you must hear precisely. You must love and wait upon the Lord. You will be patient and listen. Let there be no offence in your heart towards God for any reason. Trust in His love for you.

God speaks in a still small voice, but has never lost his voice. He has prepared you for the difficulties of life through His own particular sound. Throughout history God spoke to Adam, Eve, Moses, Samuel, Abraham, Jacob, Joseph and Mary; He also speaks to you. Your God constantly communicates with all His magnificent creation. He offers Himself to you and desires to enter every happening of your life. The light and power of the resurrection is available during every moment of your life.

Listening is a genuine attitude of the heart

God's whispers help you plant good seeds for the present and eternal life. His whispers speak and show you matters to come. God's words, dreams and visions are His audio-visual department; designed for your discretion, discernment and foresight. Let Him articulate His love, defense and purpose clearly ... Let the presence of His life speak freely through peace, righteousness and joy. Listen for His holy directives ... Listen for His words of comfort and courage. Listen well ... His whispers are giving you wisdom and shedding light on your path of purpose. Relish the voice of your King. Let every harvest fill you with the goodness that comes from listening entirely to every "Whisper From God."

"Be still and know that I am God. I will be exalted among the nations, I will be exalted in the earth." (Psalm 46:10)

He stilled the storm to a whisper. He hushed the waves of the sea. (Psalm 107:29)
He got up, rebuked the wind and said to the waves, "Quiet! Be still!" The wind then died down and was completely calm. (Mark 4:39)

'The LORD said, "Go out and stand on the mountain in the presence of the LORD, for the LORD is about to pass by. Then a great and powerful wind tore the mountains apart and shattered the rocks before the LORD, but the LORD was not in the wind.

After the wind, there was an earthquake, but the LORD was not in the earthquake - After the earthquake came a fire, but the LORD was not in the fire, after the fire came a gentle whisper." (1 Kings 19:11-12)

Jesus and I love you so very much!

I know you will Listen to Your Father's Whispers of Love

DOROTHY MURRAY ELDER

WHISPERS FROM GOD

And ...

IMPACT

Transforming Lives and Relationships! Stirring Vision!

Helping Individuals and Families break barriers and cycles of defeat.

Dorothy Murray Elder revolutionizes lives and relationships, empowering and enriching those who want to fulfill their purpose and destiny!

Since 1980, Dorothy serves as a minister, speaker, author, life-coach and relationship consultant. Her passion comes from Jesus and seeing the many untold stories of depression, rejection, lack of vision, faith and finance.

Readers and participants reach new levels of wisdom and strength to walk in God's truth and vision.

Dorothy has worked with CBS Television, morning news, universities, businesses, churches and schools; to impact lives.

Dorothy brings anointed Bible-based teaching, ministry and prayer to transform lives, futures and relationships! More than anything, Dorothy counts her relationship with Jesus Christ as her most precious possession.

"Therefore, endure hardness, as a good soldier of Jesus Christ."
(2nd Timothy 2:3)

Obey God!

**Enjoy pertinent teaching and ministry for today
… because destinies are at stake!**

Conference, Church, Groups or Event:

Books include …

"Whispers From God"

"Marriages that Endure the Fire"

Or "Your Innermost Truth"

ARISE CONFERENECES!

impact-dorothymurrayelder.com

whispersfromgodbook.com

dorothyelder@aol.com   *face book/whispers from God

*You are loved, valuable
and weighed down with glorious purpose!*

We are here to pray and believe God for and with you!

Made in the USA
Lexington, KY
11 June 2017